ROWED TRIP

FROM SCOTLAND TO SYRIA BY OAR

ROWED TRIP

COLIN ANGUS AND JULIE ANGUS

MENASHA RIDGE PRESS

Published by arrangement with Doubleday Canada,
a division of Random House of Canada Limited.

U.S. publication by Menasha Ridge Press
Distributed by Publishers Group West
First U.S. edition November 2009
Printed in the United States of America

Front cover photos courtesy of Colin Angus and Christoph
Boeckheler

Library of Congress Publication Data:
  Angus, Colin.
    From Scotland to Syria by oar / by Colin Angus and Julie
    Angus. – 1st U.S. ed.
      p. cm.
    ISBN-13: 978-0-89732-711-4
    ISBN-10: 0-89732-711-X
    1. Angus, Colin–Travel. 2. Angus, Julie–Travel 3.Rowers–
    Scotland–Biography. 4. Boats and boating. 5. Rowing.
    I.Angus, Julie. II. Title.
    GV790.9.A65 2009
    797.1230922–dc22
    [B]
                         2009032691

Menasha Ridge Press
P.O. Box 43673
Birmingham, AL 35243
www.menasharidge.com

10 9 8 7 6 5 4 3 2 1

To our families

CONTENTS

ROWED TRIP

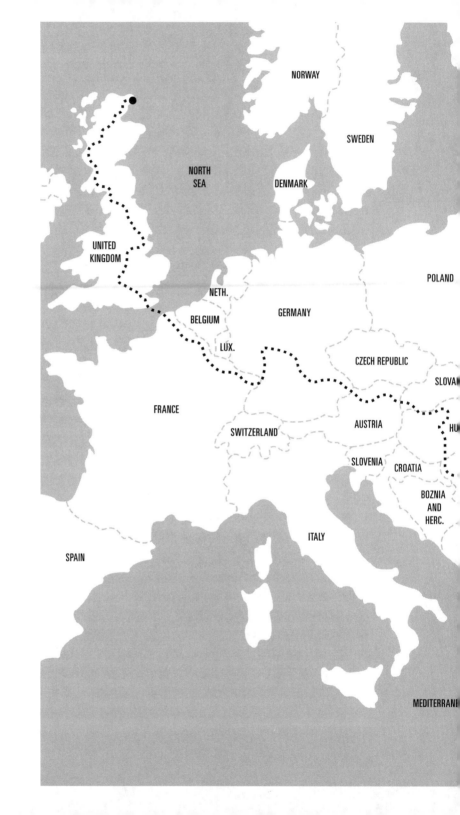

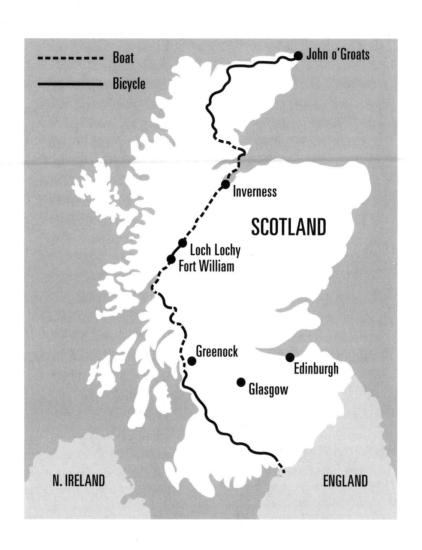

Boat

Bicycle

John o'Groats

Inverness

SCOTLAND

Loch Lochy
Fort William

Greenock

Edinburgh

Glasgow

N. IRELAND

ENGLAND

THE RIGOURS AHEAD

SCOTLAND (*Colin*)

Y FAMILY TREE IS NOT LUSH AND BOUNTIFUL. Instead, its branches have been savagely pruned; sometimes entire limbs were sheared off by the Darwinian forces at play in Scotland's far north. Traditionally, whisky production and fishing were the main livelihoods, meaning that those who didn't succumb to the sea were liable to drink themselves to death. When I was a young boy, my mother would tell me stories about her homeland. My eyes opened wide as she regaled me with tales of hairy cows, vast moors of mist-drenched heather and men who wore skirts yet had the fortitude to stare down the Romans.

I was intrigued by this distant nation, awed by my mother's stories, and I knew that, through my heritage, I was indelibly connected to Scotland. Along with the tales of Robert Louis Stevenson told to me as I drifted to sleep, my mother's Scotland was filed in the part of my memory reserved for fiction, fantasy and folklore. And like the children in *The Lion, the Witch and the Wardrobe*, I felt I had a secret connection to another world. I was sure that one day I would make that journey.

That day arrived in early March 2008. My wife, Julie, and I slipped over the border from England in a rental Dodge Caravan with two homemade rowboats strapped to the roof. The interior of the vehicle was in shambles, jammed to the ceiling with camping gear, bicycles, cameras, oars and a miscellany of other equipment. As we ventured farther north, following single-track lanes through unpopulated moors, horizontal rain and gale-force winds buffeted our top-heavy vehicle. Dark clouds scudded towards the elongated black hole of a horizon, and sodden sheep stood with their rumps to the wind.

"It was a really gay day, wasn't it?" Julie said, breaking an extended period of silence.

"What was a gay day?"

"The day we decided to do this trip."

I wasn't sure if she meant it was a happy day, which it was, or if the decision we made that day, which led to committing ourselves to a desolate, freezing world with only a tent for shelter and 7,000 kilometres to travel using only our arms and legs, was a dumb idea. A *South Park* kind of gay.

I slowed the vehicle to allow a mass of soggy wool to cross the road. The trailing shepherd nodded to us, his face lost in the shadowy folds of a black poncho.

"I suppose so," I said. "I'm sure this weather will clear up shortly."

We'd come up with the idea for this journey two years earlier on a sunny day in Germany. At that time, Julie and I were engaged and were inadvertently testing the bonds of our relationship by travelling together from Moscow to Vancouver solely by human power. The crux of the expedition was a 10,000-kilometre row (yes, row, as in propelling a tippy little boat on a pond) across the Atlantic Ocean. As we cycled across Europe, most of our thoughts were focused on the maritime challenge ahead, instead of the rich cultures, landscapes and architecture around us. And because of the urgency of reaching the Atlantic Ocean ahead of the stormy season, our route was mainly confined to busy highways.

On occasion, these vast ribbons of fumy asphalt traversed rivers or canals, and we paused on the bridges to observe the scene below. River barges, rowboats and sailing dinghies plied murky waters bordered by orchards, farm fields and stone villages. Paths often flanked these waterways, and we watched enviously as cyclists followed meandering courses to nowhere.

We noticed the road atlas we were using to navigate across Europe also outlined the waterways, and closer examination revealed Europe's labyrinth of water corridors. Julie traced a route of interconnected canals, rivers and coastlines that led from my parents' homeland of Scotland past her mother's home in Germany and on to Syria, where her father comes from. We could paddle all the way from Scotland to Syria and visit our relatives, she said half-seriously.

Whether this comment was made in jest or not, a seed was planted. Over the following months, we researched the possibility of paddling or rowing from Britain to the Middle East. My family comes from Caithness in Scotland's most northeastern corner, so this was where we would start. From there, we could follow a network of canals, lakes, rivers and shorelines all the way through Britain to Dover. We'd row across the English Channel, then journey into Europe's interior by paddling up the Rhine River or navigating France's extensive network of canals. The European continental divide would be crossed on the manmade Rhine-Main-Danube Canal, which connects the Rhine River and the Danube. And once the headwaters of the Danube were reached, it would be possible to voyage downstream to the Black Sea, through the Bosporus and finally on the Mediterranean to Syria.

The plan appealed to our sense of adventure, but more importantly it promised to be a journey that would allow us to explore our roots in a more compelling fashion than a quick online genealogy search followed by a two-week tour package being bused to tourist shops selling stuffed Loch Ness monsters, Middle Eastern rugs and the made-in-China

American Indian knick-knacks. No, this would be a seat-of-your-pants adventure that would immerse Julie and me into the cultural and physical forces that had shaped our families and made us who we are. It would give us greater perspective not only on our heritage but also on the distances and lands separating the regions we come from.

The more we researched, though, the more we unearthed questions we could not answer. Would we be able to make our way against the swift current of the Rhine River? Would a human-powered craft be allowed to navigate the canal locks that are normally used by power boats? How difficult would voyaging the British coast be in late winter?

There was too much uncertainty, and although it was theoretically possible to travel on water for every inch of the journey, we felt an efficient portage system was required. Julie and I pondered the various possibilities, from lightweight canoes with padded yokes to sea kayaks and rugged dollies. We came to the conclusion that nothing on the market met our needs.

"Maybe we could tow our boats behind bicycles," Julie said, thinking of the trailer she uses for cycling home with a heavy load of groceries.

It seemed like a practical idea except for one thing: what would we do with the bikes and trailers while on the water? A sea kayak doesn't have the cargo capacity to carry such a load. While a canoe could easily carry a bicycle, it lacks the seaworthiness to cope with some of the rougher coastlines we planned on paddling. We considered using a dory, which is seaworthy and has sufficient cargo capacity, but decided the weight would be prohibitive. Eventually, we realized the ideal boats had yet to be made. We would have to make them ourselves.

We designed the boats and built them in the backyard with plywood and fibreglass. They looked like large sea kayaks, but had sufficient cargo space to carry our bicycles, trailers and all our camping gear within sealed compartments. The boats were shaped so that in the event they capsized, all the water would drain from the cockpit when they were righted. They were also decked with watertight hatches, ensuring the equipment would stay dry in big waves or in the event of a capsize. As a finishing touch, we created a system that would allow them to be joined together as a catamaran with a platform large enough to erect the tent on. This arrangement would allow us to camp in urban areas where conventional tenting was not an option.

We chose a sliding-seat rowing set-up because it provides much more power than paddling and would allow us to propel our burdened boats easily and quickly through the water. It also offers a full-body workout, exercising not just the arms and shoulders but also the back, stomach, buttocks and legs. If we were going to spend six months in a boat, we reasoned, we might as well get fit in the process.

The trailers were custom made by Tony Hoar, a Vancouver Islander who specializes in making unique bicycle trailers. They were designed to disassemble and fit in the boats' centre compartment along with the bicycle. But despite our best efforts to build quality vessels, we worried that our amateur-built craft might not be up to a 7,000-kilometre journey.

Now, as Julie and I drove in inky darkness with the boats on the roof of the van shifting dangerously in the heavy winds, I prayed our homemade contraptions would be able to withstand the rigours ahead. The vulnerability of their thin plywood bodies was accentuated in a world where stone seemed to offer the only true defence against the North Atlantic's wrath. As if to further emphasize the point, the crosswinds intensified, and we were forced to stop the van in the middle of nowhere to avoid losing our rooftop cargo. We had no choice but to wait for the weather to improve, and so we spread our sleeping bags in the back and fell asleep in the violently shaking vehicle.

The following morning, we reached our destination, Castletown, a village of about three thousand located six kilometres from mainland Britain's northernmost point. The surrounding landscape was a rocky moor with occasional stunted trees and pastureland. Swollen steel-grey waves collapsed onto a jagged shoreline next to the town, and wind snaked through the streets, lifting dust and rattling windows. The flagstone buildings were indifferent to gusts that almost bowled us over.

Although my mother and father were born in Edinburgh and Glasgow respectively, their roots lie here. Castletown was where my paternal grandfather lived, descended from a line of shipbuilders and fishermen, while my maternal grandfather came from Wick, a coastal town 20 kilometres away. Between these two communities in the tiny oceanside hamlet of Keiss reside the last of my known relatives in this region.

We checked into the town's sole hotel, a Victorian-era stone building.

"Sinclair?" the proprietor said, noting my middle name in my passport. "I have a good friend, Peter Sinclair, in Keiss."

Of course. That's how it is in these tight-knit communities. Peter Sinclair is my second cousin, the son of my mother's aunt. Coincidentally, the name Sinclair is my paternal grandmother's maiden name, but there is no known blood connection from my father's side. I would soon be meeting this branch of my family for the first time. As well, my half-sister Betti Angus would be joining us, making her way up from her home outside Glasgow. Betti and I are linked through paternal blood, but I had met her only once, when I was twenty-five. She was still an enigma. It has always seemed odd to me that I have a sister who speaks with a broad Scottish accent, and I was pleased that she had offered to join us as we sleuthed to understand our origins.

Our hotel, the St. Clair Arms, was surprisingly comfortable considering its modest price and remote location. Decorative wallpaper and colourful bedding created a welcome contrast to the cold world outside. As Julie and I sorted our equipment, a knock on the door announced Betti's arrival.

Betti was born two years before me, also in Victoria, British Columbia. Her parents divorced when she was an infant, and her mother had not been able bring up a child on her own. Our father, being a sea captain, could not look after Betti, so she was adopted by his childless sister and brother-in-law. Betti was raised an only child on the tiny Isle of Islay in the Inner Hebrides, a world away from her birthplace on Vancouver Island.

Julie opened the door and Betti welcomed us with bear hugs. As with the last time I saw her, I was struck by her resemblance to the man who sired us. She had his elfin features and sandy hair, but it was the shape of her sea-blue eyes that was most strikingly similar.

That evening my mother's cousin Helen, her son, Peter, and his wife and children made the short trip from Keiss to meet us in the cozy hotel pub. I'd never before met this branch of my family, and I wondered if they were the tougher ones—those who didn't flee the gales, rain and midges of Caithness.

Helen was rotund and kindly, while her son, Peter, in his mid-forties, had the robust build that comes from years of lobster-fishing in open boats. Over glasses of whisky, the stories began to flow.

"You've probably noticed there's a disproportionate number of Sinclairs in the ground to the ones alive today," Peter said, gesturing south towards the cemetery. "Aye, there were many scrapping clans around here, and we didn't always fare so well in battle. The last clan war involving our family took place over a hundred years ago with the Campbells."

The waiter paused by the table, eager to hear the story he probably already knew.

"They had a cunning plan to subdue us Sinclairs. A cask of whisky was dropped in the burn above our village. Of course, the Sinclairs fished it out, thinking it was a gift from the gods. The party began, the whisky was drunk, and . . . Well, that's when the Campbells came with swords raised.

"Only those already dropped by the drink were spared. Saved by the whisky!" Peter laughed, holding his glass high.

Only a Scotsman could draw this moral from a story where heavy drinking precipitated a family massacre. It seemed the natural laws of evolution here had been rewritten by the folks at the local distillery.

"Saved by the whisky," I said, toasting with another shot of its good self.

Before my grandparents' era, migration was limited, and so it can be assumed that my family was partially descended from tribes that settled this region around 3500–4000 BC. These Stone Age hunters, gatherers and rudimentary farmers migrated from Continental Europe following the retreat of the last Ice Age. Lower sea levels exposed a land bridge that connected what are now Britain and France, and which humans began crossing around 9500 BC.

On the nearby Orkney Islands, just 25 kilometres from where our family sat enjoying a meal of haggis, mashed turnips and roast beef, lay Europe's best-preserved neolithic village. Ten houses still stood in the settlement of Skara Brae, which was occupied from 3100 until 2500 BC. The homes were constructed of flagstone, driftwood, whalebone and turf-thatched roofs, and were partially built into the ground with mounds of dirt piled on top for protection from the gales. The islands are also home to four-thousand-year-old stone circles, which are thought to have been used for astrological observations and pagan ceremonies. The best-known in the region, the Ring of Brodgar, contains sixty stones in a 104-metre-diameter circle.

Eventually, the tribes of northern Britain formed a loose confederation and were known by the Romans as Picts, meaning tattooed or painted people. The Picts were fierce fighters and were successful in fending off many invading cultures, including the heavily disciplined Romans.

The next major wave of immigration wasn't until 500 AD, when the Celtic people came over from Ireland and settled in western Scotland. The Celts originated from Continental Europe in the lands north of the Alps (as portrayed in the famous *Asterix* cartoons), and two groups migrated to lower Britain and Ireland, but only those from Ireland made their way into Scotland. There, they intermarried with the local people, and Scotland became a mix of the original indigenous population and Celts.

The Vikings were next on the scene, and these seafaring ruffians were a significant cultural influence in Caithness and the Orkney Islands. Beginning in 793 AD, Norwegian warriors launched a wave of invasions against Scotland and England. Amid their pillaging, they also established settlements, taking local women as their wives and farming the land. Caithness was the area most heavily populated by Vikings, and my family's names speak of these and other ethnic influences.

Swanson, my great-great-grandmother's name, is Norwegian in origin (originally Svensson) and was introduced during the Viking conquests. Angus is an ancient Celtic name (originally Aonghus), meaning one choice. It is prevalent as a surname across Scotland, but most abundantly in Caithness. My mother's family name, Bremner, is Flemish (meaning weaver) and was possibly introduced when a group of Dutch settlers were invited to the region in the 1490s to operate the ferry service to the Orkney Islands. These settlers included the founder of the ferry system, Jan de Groot, after whom John o' Groats is named.

As I looked at my family members seated around our table, I pondered the complex chain of events that had brought us all here. I was snapped out of my historical reverie by a rather startling question from Peter.

"Do you know anything about our rampant cock?" he asked.

Helen frowned at her son.

"No, tell us about him," Julie said, her interest in my family history suddenly piqued.

"It's not a he, it's an it," Peter said. "An animal."

I groaned inwardly. This was it; Julie was going to start hearing sordid tales of what goes on in this remote region during the dark days of winter.

"It's part of our family crest, the rampant cock. The Sinclairs possess the same strength and grit as a tough old rooster. And the clan motto is Commit thy work to God."

The family profession of lobster-fishing certainly spoke of this fortitude. Peter's deceased father had been a full-time lobster fisherman, but dwindling stocks meant his son needed to augment the family trade with work on the North Sea oil rigs. Currently, the crustaceans were in reasonable supply, and early the next morning Peter would drop traps in the Pentland Firth, the body of water between the mainland and the Orkney Islands.

I asked him if he was concerned about the forecasted 70 kilometre an hour winds and 12-metre swells.

"Nay," he said casually. "It's always like that. You get used to it after a while. Besides, we look after each other. The biggest danger is blowing a motor and getting raked over the rocks, but most likely you'd get a tow from another boat before that'd happen."

In the past three days, the swell hadn't dropped below eight metres. Julie and I had watched in awe as liquid mountains exploded against rocky headlands, sending plumes of aerated water 30 metres into the sky. I was relieved our trailers and bicycles gave us the option of travelling overland on our own journey.

The following morning, while Peter braved the Pentland Firth, Betti, Julie and I went to visit the cemetery, just south of the village. The disused burial ground could have been a set from a Bela Lugosi movie. Crows eyed us from perches in skeletal branches of wind-sculpted trees as we walked between eroded tombstones. An abandoned church, its roof caved inwards, lay at one end of the property, and a disintegrating wall lined the premises. Dates on the legible stones ranged from the 1700s to the 1920s.

Betti pointed out the graves of distant relatives. I was struck by the prevalence of our family names; it seemed half the stones had Sinclair, Angus or Bremner etched into their pitted surfaces. I tiptoed gently over my long-decomposed family.

"What kind of stone are these made from?" I asked Betti, pointing to the roughly cut marker stones.

"Flagstone. The same as what the entire town is made of. It protects us in life and guards us when we fall."

"For a while," said Julie, eying a toppled stone with a weather-obliterated inscription.

Flagstone from this region wasn't used just for building around Castletown. During the 1800s, local quarries created a huge boost for the economy when the layered sedimentary rock became a popular building material in southern Britain. It is said that all the roads of London were paved with Castletown flagstone in the mid-1800s. Eventually, demand ceased, and now the quarries are silent, surrounded by rusting machinery and mounds of flat, cracked stone.

The local library contained a compilation of census and wedding records for the region. Through these statistics, and Betti's earlier sleuthing, we traced my father's side of the family back to the 1700s. The records showed many marriages between the Sinclair and Angus families through the generations. "Da, na, na na na na . . ." As she studied the names, Julie hummed the banjo tune played by the inbred kid in *Deliverance*. "Look, I think they made a mistake here," she said. She was pointing to the marriage of William Angus to Margaret Angus in 1741. "They put her married name instead of her maiden name."

"I don't think it's a mistake," I said. "But that's how it worked with the clans. They all married each other. Otherwise they wouldn't be clans, would they? It doesn't mean they were brother and sister. There were probably more than a thousand Anguses in the clan."

"Da, na, na na na na na . . ." hummed Julie. "Can you play that tune on the bagpipes? Or were your clan members too busy playing with each other's rampant roosters to learn any instruments?"

~~~

A CHILL WIND OFF THE NORTH SEA trumped the sun's rays, which reached the earth through a tear in the clouds. We were at Duncansby Head, a promontory of rock jutting defiantly into troubled grey waters. Around us, on sheep-manicured grass, lay a disarray of equipment—bicycles, disassembled boat trailers, clothing, sleeping bags, camping gear, cameras and two brightly coloured rowboats. In a few hours, we would begin our 7,000-kilometre, entirely human-powered journey to Syria.

Julie and I worked quickly, organizing our gear and packing it into the watertight compartments in our boats. The forecast called for storm-force winds and rain, so we opted to begin our voyage overland. We quickly assembled the boat trailers, slotting the tubes together and tightening the quick-release mechanisms. We placed the heavily loaded boats onto the trailers and secured them to our bikes. Each bike, trailer, boat and share of equipment and food weighed almost 135 kilograms and was eight metres in length.

In this world of stone and no-nonsense fishermen, our contraptions looked flimsy, bordering on ridiculous. Nobody had ever done a long-distance journey with a set-up like ours, and I was beginning to wonder if we would be able to haul our 270 kilograms of gear all the way to Asia. Nonetheless, we were now committed and had no choice but to continue.

A small group had gathered to watch us depart, including Helen, Betti, Peter's wife and kids (Peter was out fishing) and Martina Cross, a local photographer. After bidding our last farewells, Julie and I clambered to the small beach below, touched the water with our Helly Hansen sailor boots and returned to our bicycles.

After more than a year of preparations, we were finally on our way. I was overjoyed that the wind was in our favour, and firm pressure on the pedals coaxed the bikes and laden vessels into motion along the single-lane asphalt track leading to John o' Groats. Shortly after we started, a modest incline necessitated a quick drop into the lowest gear. I pumped my legs furiously, trying to maintain cycling speed, while Martina snapped photos and the rest shouted encouragements.

Our pride-propelled propulsion fizzled, and we both dismounted, gasping as we pushed our bikes to the top of the rise. Our act had done little to assure our cheerleaders (or myself) that we would charge proudly through Scotland, England and a dozen other countries to our destination, or that our boats would deftly navigate great rivers and seas, taking us to our homelands and the lands between. At the top of the hill, we remounted our bikes and resumed pedalling, helped forward by strong tailwinds and a flat stretch.

The quiet road cut through rolling hills of heather and grass. Three hundred metres to our right stretched the ocean, a deceiving Caribbean blue illuminated by sunshine that was as cold as a fluorescent bulb. We sped through the community of John o' Groats, a scattering of about ten buildings that prides itself on being Britain's northernmost community. Occasional stone farmhouses appeared amid flagstone-fenced fields of sheep and shaggy Highland cattle. An old water mill, its paddlewheel now rotted and silent, was perched at the edge of a tannin-stained burn burbling towards the sea.

I imagined my ancestors working this stony, acidic land and braving the waters below in order to survive. Our family's quirks, strengths and weaknesses are tied to this land that slipped beneath the wheels of my bicycle.

In the last hundred years, globalization and easy migration have brought an end to the tightly knit community system that developed over many millennia. My family is now spread over the world, each member focused on individual pursuits. Now, when we build a home, it is no longer a neighbour or nephew who helps place the cornerstones, but the bank. Part of me regretted this loss of our traditional family system, the shared struggles to maintain a simpler way of life. But I knew it was gone forever. Even the adventure Julie and I had just embarked on seemed incongruous with the uncomplicated values we were discovering in our not-so-distant past. Nonetheless, I was excited to move forward and explore all that was ahead of us— and to do that with my best friend and wife, my family.

We had planned our route carefully, choosing to avoid busy roads. Our course would head west along the north coast, before turning south through the remote Highlands, where we expected little traffic.

Two hours after departing Duncansby Head, we clattered into Castletown. It was already getting late, so we decided to stay one last night in the St. Clair Arms Hotel. After a hearty breakfast the next morning, we waved goodbye to our new friends and continued west. I was pleased that we had made it this far with the equipment still functioning smoothly.

Next was Thurso, a city of about nine thousand. We approached this community cautiously, worried about navigating our contraptions, each longer than a mid-sized U-Haul truck, through the congested narrow roads of a bustling town.

Fortunately, the absurdity of our set-up worked in our favour. As a long queue of cars trailed behind our boats, few drivers expressed any signs of impatience. Instead, they smiled broadly and occasionally waved. In the typical nonchalant fashion of the British, passersby clutching Sainsbury or Marks and Spencer's bags offered their two bits: "Expecting rain?" or, "Don't think our tides come this high," or, my personal favourite, "You two look a couple of boats shy of a fleet."

Thurso, a Norse name meaning bull's water, is Britain's northernmost town. Between 1955 and 1958, its population rapidly expanded from 2,500 to 12,000 with the opening of the Dounreay nuclear power plant 14 kilometres west of the town. The power station was shut down in 1994, but the facility is still the largest employer in the region with a decommissioning process that will extend beyond 2025.

We were relieved to reach the outskirts of town. From here on, we would encounter only small villages until the city of Inverness, some 200 kilometres distant. The weather quickly deteriorated as the predicted frontal system moved in, and we were blasted from behind with gale-force winds. Steep hills confronted us as we followed the convoluted coastline, but Mother Nature's intimidating power helped us overcome these obstacles.

After travelling 25 kilometres in five hours, I realized that cycle-touring with rowboats requires a deviation from mainstream cycling philosophy. Cycling magazines, retail outlets and how-to books place an emphasis on lightweight and high-quality equipment to maximize performance. This advice all goes out the window when you attach a boat to the back of your bicycle. Two years earlier, when I had cycled on a fully loaded bike through Europe, I averaged 120 kilometres a day; now it looked as if we'd be lucky to manage 30 kilometres. We were ascending gentle rises at the pace of a slow walk, which to someone used to normal cycling speeds is somewhat humbling. Nonetheless, when looking at it from a portage perspective, the efficiency is unparalleled, since lugging a loaded canoe just a few hundred metres without wheels is an unwieldy and exhausting experience.

Bloated black clouds sped across the sky, but the rain held off. Most of the time we could see the ocean, and occasionally the road came close enough for us to hear the thunder of waves battling rock. It was a remote landscape, making the sudden appearance of a nuclear power plant surreal. First, we spotted a large golf-ball-shaped dome, then a collection of peripheral buildings.

The power plant was strategically placed in this remote location so that if it did pull a Chernobyl, the rest of Britain would be unaffected. Judging by the prevailing weather patterns, it seemed the radioactive cloud would be carried across the sea towards Norway—perhaps justified as retribution for past inconveniences suffered at the hands of horned invaders.

Although meltdowns aren't a part of its history, the facility has a less than ideal safety record, and nuclear contamination in the region is a problem. Spent waste was dumped in a shaft not designed for disposal, and radioactive material has leached into the ocean. As a consequence, the beach fronting the facility has been closed since 1983.

We learned from our guidebook that the power plant was built on the site of a military airfield, which had been relocated to a place in the Orkney Islands called Twatt. We would soon learn that Britain is fraught with peculiar place names. Over the following months, as Julie and I studied our road atlas and corresponding street maps, I began to wonder if domestic geography is an X-rated subject. Names we encountered included Sandy Balls, Cockshoot Close, Minge Lane, Fingringhoe, Back Passage, Hole of Horcum, Cocknmouth Close, Butt Hole Road, Fine Bush Lane and Lickfold.

For now, however, seven weeks from reaching Cockshoot Close in Oxfordshire, I was more concerned with the steep hills and decaying weather than Britain's sordid naming practices. On one particularly steep rise, we stopped halfway up gasping for breath and leaning over our handlebars. We were beside a small rectangular building, not much larger than a double garage, with coal smoke streaming from a stovepipe. The door opened and a man in his fifties with wild long hair, an enormous beard and a top hat approached us.

"Hello," Julie said.

He didn't reply. Instead, he pointed a crooked finger to a prominent headland surrounded by a mane of exploding water and without a word of introduction began reciting a poem:

> "Oh, the Lion, so proud she sits
> Watching, watching those pesky ships.
> She is the king who needs no crowning
> For sailors will bow when they are drowning."

The man slowly turned his attention from the headland and fixed his watery eyes on Julie and me. "I am the watcher of the Lion."

I wasn't quite sure what to say. Had living in a shack at the top of the world done this to him or did this place attract the eccentric sort? Was this a hidden Scottish trait that would surface in me if I spent too much time alone?

We squeaked out our introductions as a younger man emerged from the building wearing a conductor's hat. His name was Popeye.

I felt like Alice in Wonderland.

"Cuppa tea?" offered Popeye.

Driven by a curiosity about our new acquaintances and a desire to escape the cold winds, Julie and I entered the small building. The interior was rustic and colourful. A small coal stove smoked in the corner. Rich yellow walls were crowded with knick-knacks. A painted jester with a missing tooth and a giant nose peered out from the kitchen wall, and the larder door was detailed with flowers painted in oil.

Our eccentric poet introduced himself as Murray Croft and pulled out two heavy wooden chairs for us. A Jack Russell terrier positioned himself near our feet, ready to vacuum up cookie crumbs. Murray told us about himself. He had moved here from England in 1981 after a motorcycling accident. He used the funds from his settlement to acquire this remote property (formerly a post office) and had lived there ever since.

"I'm a much richer man now," Murray said, gesturing at the wild landscape beyond the window.

He spent his days fishing and watching over the Lion. Murray took us to a small cabinet in the back and showed us the skulls of various large trout that he had caught.

"See this one?" he said, handing Julie a large wide skull. "It's a bass I caught from the sea. In the past, they never lived this far north, but now the water is warmer."

We said goodbye to Murray and Popeye and continued up the hill and into a desolate brown landscape of heather and bog. We cycled half an hour without seeing a sign of humans, before deciding to retire for the evening. A slight rise 50 metres from the road offered firm ground to place our two-person tent. After locking the boats and bikes together we retreated from the wind.

In Thurso, we had bought six days' worth of food, enough to last until Inverness. Our "larder," situated in the rear hatch of Julie's boat, consisted of oatmeal, powdered milk, dried fruit, coffee and tea for breakfast, bread, cured meats, cheese, tomatoes, mayonnaise, miscellaneous fruits for lunch, cookies and sweets for snacks, and an assortment of thawed but fresh freezer meals for dinners. The average temperature wasn't much above zero degrees Celsius, ensuring our goods stayed fresh.

After a meal of madras curry and rice, I fell asleep quickly, revelling in the warmth of my sleeping bag while the tent flapped in the gale. At daybreak, we had a quick breakfast and broke camp. The winds had intensified to what I guessed to be about 90 kilometres an hour. Unbeknownst to us, the storm was wreaking havoc across Britain, with trucks toppling and trees falling. My mother watched the chaos unfolding on the six o'clock news in Canada, hoping we were holed up in a snug hotel.

Instead, we wrestled our violently flapping tent into its bag, packed our gear and began our second day of pedalling. At noon, we reached the village of Bettyhill, a small coastal community that marked the end of our westward journey along the north coast. From here, we would turn due south, heading inland through the Highlands on a single-lane track.

A rare burst of sunshine illuminated Bettyhill into a postcard-perfect scene. Vast sandy beaches, serrated rocky headlands and a small cozy community of whitewashed buildings and slate roofs offered a final farewell to the north coast. We stopped at the Bettyhill Hotel for a lunch of roast beef and vegetables while enjoying the view from beside the fireplace.

Beyond Bettyhill, we entered a world of solitude. Here, we turned inland on the B871, a road barely wide enough for a single vehicle. We encountered only two to four vehicles an hour, and habitation was virtually non-existent. The ruins of crofters' homes and toppled walls were everywhere, but the people were gone.

It wasn't always like this. Before the 1700s, this land was populated by Highlanders, Gaelic people who lived a sub-sistent lifestyle according to the rules of the clan system. Unfortunately, they didn't own the land they lived on; instead, they paid rent or taxes to distant landowners in places such as Edinburgh. During the eighteenth century, the landowners real-ized they could make more money from intensive farming than by taxing the meagre earnings of the Highlanders. They began evicting their tenants en masse and turned the Highlands into large-scale sheep-farming operations.

This period is known as the Highland Clearances, and it was a major blow to a culture that had inhabited this region from prehistoric times. The decision of the ruling class, spawned by greed, was the cause of famine, dislocation and the end to a traditional way of life. This forced migration resulted in large numbers of Scots moving to Canada, Australia and other parts of the Commonwealth and Britain.

The sheep that replaced the people eventually became less lucrative, and their numbers have dropped precipitously. Now the Highlands are one of the most sparsely populated places in Europe, a land of snow-capped mountains, heather and chat-tering streams.

The peaceful solitude with its tragic cause did at least provide ideal conditions for cycling. The narrow road, absent of traffic, seemed a bike lane purpose-built for touring this inspiring landscape. The road followed the banks of a river, its waters stained brown from the peat, that ran between hills of grass and heather. Interpretive signs marked areas of interest, such as the locations of old villages or of clan battles. Despite the relentless wind, I was glad we were travelling outside tourist season and had the place to ourselves.

The mountains in this region have been somewhat subdued by the scouring forces of the great glaciers that once covered them. To the south, the Great Glen valley, running along the border of two tectonic plates, marks the southern border of this geographical region. After the retreat of the last Ice Age, vast forests of pine, birch, rowan, aspen, juniper and oak carpeted the region. Humans decimated these vast boreal forests and now only one percent of the original 1.5 million hectares remain. In recent decades, an effort has been made to replant, and the total area of forest is gradually increasing.

Six days after leaving Dunnet Head, we had travelled a modest 120 kilometres. We camped near the terminus of the River Tain and were surprised to awake to perfectly calm conditions. A radiant sun blazed through a cloudless sky, warming our tent, the earth and the dozens of shits surrounding it.

"These turds are pretty disgusting," Julie said, as she carefully examined the cooking area for excrement before lighting the stove.

Only after setting up the tent had we noticed that we had chosen the roadside *au naturel* toilet for our camping spot. Finding a camping site the previous night had been particularly difficult, as we were in a more developed region. We were thus initially pleased to see this widening in the road with wild scrub fronting the river offering the privacy we sought.

I tried to ignore the smell permeating the tent and focused instead on the fine weather. "We can go in the boats today! This river leads into the Dornoch Firth, and we can travel along the coast down to Inverness where the Caledonian Canal starts."

We were both excited to finally launch our vessels and

explore Scotland from the water. Hurriedly, we broke camp and manhandled our boats through willows and brambles to the water's edge ten metres away. As we carried our gear, an oozing slipperiness beneath my right shoe reminded me of the hazards afoot. Streams of white paper fluttered on a branch, an empty symbol of defeat from the adversary crushed beneath my weight.

In what would eventually be a well-oiled routine. Julie and I began the task of removing the seat, wheels and pedals from the bicycles, disassembling the trailers into an armful of pipes and packing it all into the centre compartments. The various components fit together like a jigsaw puzzle, but it took several attempts to pack everything compactly enough to secure the hatches. Lastly, using stainless steel bolts, we installed the rowing riggers (arms that distanced the oarlocks from the boat) and inserted the oars. In total, it took over an hour to make our rig ready for the water, a time we hoped to halve with practice.

With the boats seaworthy and our safety gear at the ready, we struggled into dry suits and clambered into the cockpits. A gentle prod at roots and mud with oar tips propelled us into deeper water and we were free. After almost a week of hauling our boats up and down endless hills, drifting on the seemingly frictionless water was a joy. The current created by the out-going tide, combined with gentle oar strokes, sent us on our way at 12 kilometres an hour. The water itself was gentle and smooth, and we drifted past stands of pine and willow, farmers' fields and the occasional riverside cottage.

Although it was only mid-March, the weather was nice, perhaps a blessing from the gods, I joked to Julie. For those who believe in mythology, it's not such a far-fetched notion. My boat, after all, is named after a son of Zeus, the god of sky and thunder. Its name, *Tantalum*, is derived from Zeus's son Tantalus, and Julie's boat, *Niobium*, is named after Tantalus's daughter, Niobe.

The names tantalum and niobium are also shared by two elements produced by our main sponsor, Commerce Resources. They are sister elements (always found together), although their applications differ. Tantalum is used extensively in capacitors, and niobium in high-grade steel alloys. Commerce Resources' mandate is to extract these minerals in an environmentally and socially sensitive manner, offering a clean source for essential building blocks in cellphones, computers and MRI scanners. Since their goal to promote sustainability in exploration parallels our goal to encourage environmental stewardship through exploration, we decided to work together.

Within half an hour, Julie and I reached the mouth of the river and sluiced through a labyrinth of diverging channels exiting into the firth. The dropping water exposed large expanses of mud, and as we navigated towards the sea, we were careful not to ground our boats on the expanding banks. A variety of birds, including scaup, red-breasted mergansers and oyster catchers, plied the nearby shallows of this estuarine environment.

Along the shores of the kilometre-wide inlet was a mixture of forests, farms and the newly built cinder-block retirement/holiday homes that proliferate on Britain's coasts. Our boats easily cut through a rapidly forming chop as the sun disappeared behind thick black clouds, its balmy caress replaced by forceful icy winds. We slipped under the giant Dornoch Bridge, a steel and concrete structure spanning the firth.

A collection of stone buildings, giant vats, puffing steam and a faint malty aroma indicated we had reached the famed Glenmorangie distillery, where whisky has been made for 270 years. Unfortunately, 300 metres of exposed mud separated us from the distillery and quashed our ambitions of dropping in for a tour and a sampling. Instead, we continued through breaking waves to the nearby town of Tain. This charming

community of skilfully crafted limestone and sandstone buildings is Scotland's oldest royal burgh, having been granted its
first imperial charter in 1066.

We had expected this coastal town to have a marina, or
at least a dredged harbour, but were disappointed to see it,
too, was fronted by an expanse of impassable mud devoid of
channels. The wind had intensified and now gusted up to
60 kilometres an hour with waves that thundered onto the
mud. To continue would be dangerous, especially with an
exposed headland coming up. I scrutinized the muddy shoreline
for options and finally noticed a tiny stream carving a passage
through the mire. We rowed into this narrow opening, leaving
the turbulent waters behind, and poled/pushed/paddled our
boats through the shallows until reaching a solid bank near a
playground. We hauled our boats from the water, assembled
our bicycles, and pedalled into the countryside. We found an
ideal camping spot behind an abandoned farm workers' camp.

By the following morning, the adverse weather had abated,
and we returned to the water, rowing past rocky headlands and
tiny beaches of finely ground shale. Bedrock sculpted by the
North Sea's wrath formed sea arches, caves and precipitous
cliffs—the domain of thousands of screeching gulls. Seals occasionally surfaced and watched our red and blue boats ghost past.

We sped through the glassy swell and by mid-afternoon
reached the dual sand spits jutting out from both sides of
the Moray Firth. Beyond these natural breakwaters was the
Highland capital of Inverness. To the south, the popcorn report
of artillery fire echoed from Fort George, arguably Europe's
mightiest artillery garrison. This impressive multi-walled structure was completed in 1769, built to replace a nearby fort
destroyed in the Jabobite uprising of 1715. Nobody has dared
attack this heavily guarded fortress, and to this day it has been
used continuously as a garrison and training facility.

We arrived in Inverness elated to reach such an important milestone. Here we would enter the 100-kilometre-long Caledonian Canal, a system of canals and lakes leading diagonally southwest across Scotland to the west coast. A third of the route is manmade, and the remainder comprises three chain lakes, including Loch Ness. This waterway follows the Great Glen Fault, a rift valley that traverses Scotland and is part of a 400-million-year-old fault line that extends across the Atlantic (although somewhat broken up by the Mid-Atlantic Ridge) to Newfoundland, where it is known as the Cabot Fault.

The canal, completed in 1822, allows ships to traverse northern Britain without having to endure the treacherous route around the north capes. It was rebuilt in 1847 to allow passage for larger ships. Now it is primarily used for recreational boaters, who chug through in sleek canal boats, admiring the dramatic Scottish Highland scenery and drinking whisky in pubs along the way.

To those tut-tutting my use of the word "lake" to describe the lochs of Scotland (I received a flood of reprimanding emails for similar usage in a web update), let me say that it is entirely correct to do so. Just as I don't necessarily call lakes "*lacs*" while chronicling travels in France (apart from proper nouns), I often describe inland bodies of water with their common English name.

Inverness is a busy city of about fifty thousand located at the mouth of the River Ness. It is the Highlands' administrative capital and a hub for tourism in Scotland's north. We planned to stay there for a day to prepare for our upcoming leg along the Caledonian Canal.

After a stressful ride through the city centre, we checked into a bed and breakfast. It was a dowdy residence with floral wallpaper and carpeted bathrooms, but the owner was friendly and didn't mind when we trudged through his flower garden to store our boats in his side yard. With the boats and gear safely stored, we set about running errands. As we milled through the busy shopping district looking for a supermarket, I couldn't help but notice that physical beauty is not an inherent trait in this region. Overall, the people aren't sinewy and rugged like the stereotypical Highlander portrayed in movies like Mel Gibson's *Braveheart*. Instead, most are pasty and flabby, with freckled loose skin enveloping knobby knees and protruding paunches. Even slim young women lack the curvaceous physique of their Eastern European counterparts, instead sporting flat bottoms and poorly toned forms. Scotland boasts the highest rate of cardiovascular disease in Western Europe, a condition attributed to poor lifestyle choices. I can only assume that there is a correlation between maintaining a healthy heart and preserving pulchritude.

Despite not being the fittest people, the Scots are efficient, and we were able to finish our chores quickly and easily. Most important, we obtained our free canoeing permit from British Waterways, allowing us to travel on the canals. The friendly lass working behind the desk informed us of the abundant amenities on the route (showers, washrooms, laundry facilities and free camping sites), and I felt I was about to embark on a pleasant summer camping trip. Since pubs were strung along the length of the canal system, a pint and hot meal would never be far away.

"Geez, how are we going to convince the people at home we're on a hard-core adventure?" I said.

"Somehow I don't think easy street is going to lead the entire seven thousand kilometres to Aleppo," Julie said. "Enjoy it while it lasts."

Given that it was still mid-March I expected the weather might pose a few challenges, especially when we reached Loch Ness, which is known for its cantankerous conditions.

Fortunately, we had the choice of rowing across Loch Ness or pedalling on the adjacent road. Both had advantages and disadvantages, and we had decided to pose this question to the students involved in our adventure learning initiative.

We were partnered with two organizations dedicated to fostering healthy lifestyles in youth, Healthy Heart and Active Communities, and had developed an interactive online school program that ran in conjunction with our expedition. On our website the project included resources, multimedia updates, and most importantly a program we developed called "Choose Your Own Adventure." Each week we posed a logistical or navigational question along with relevant information. Kids were encouraged to vote on the choices, and we would follow the consensus. The students could actually change the course of the expedition through their input and this garnered a lot of enthusiasm. When we returned to our bed and breakfast, Julie checked the results online.

"Row with the monster," Julie said with a laugh.

Despite Loch Ness's cold waters and frequent storms, the students had overwhelmingly voted for us to stay on the water and avoid the busy adjacent road. And so we would.

We launched our boats in the early morning just above the Muirtown Locks, a series of four locks within Inverness. We had packed a week's groceries into the boats and intended to enjoy this serene leg of our expedition to the fullest.

Our boats slipped quickly across the water's mirrored surface, and we navigated between canal-side walkways. The water was devoid of traffic, but the banks were lively with people walking dogs, jogging and cycling. Occasionally, we encountered low drawbridges, but we slipped underneath by leaning back and allowing our momentum to carry the boats through. Eventually, urban parks and wealthy estates gave way to a more rural landscape of Lowland farms.

Beside us the spirited Ness River ran from Loch Ness to Inverness, but our waters were absent of current. We rowed for two hours, had a relaxing lunch on an empty pontoon next to a rowing club, and in the early afternoon reached our first barrier, Dochgarroch Locks.

I strolled up to the lockkeeper's small office, where a college-aged woman and a slightly older man greeted me.

"Is it possible to go through the locks in our rowboats?" I inquired.

I assumed the answer would be a straightforward yes. The official ruling with British Waterways is that human-powered craft should be portaged if possible, but for heavily loaded or difficult-to-carry boats, it is permissible to go through the locks. Ultimately, the lockkeeper makes the final ruling and can deny a boat passage if he or she feels there is a safety issue. Since our boats would take two hours to portage (the trailers would have to be unpacked, assembled, disassembled and repacked), a ten-minute ride through the locks would be the preferred route. With twenty-nine locks to negotiate in this canal, portaging would be virtually impossible.

"Uh, I'm not sure," the girl said. "The head lockkeeper isn't here."

"Aye, he makes the calls, and I don't know when he'll be back," her companion added.

The girl looked nervously towards the parking lot and finally said, "Let's just go for it. Drag your boats forward and we'll open the locks."

Hydraulic gates opened ahead of us, and using ropes, we pulled our boats into the lock compound. The steel gates closed, and the surface bubbled and roiled as water flooded through submerged sluice gates and raised the level by three metres. The gates on the far end of the compound opened, and we towed our boats out.

"Hmm, they sure seemed to fear the head lockkeeper," I said to Julie. "I hope these guys aren't the grumpy sort."

"I'm sure they'll be fine," Julie reassured me. "Besides, the girl at the office said there's no reason why they wouldn't let us through."

Fortunately, we had no more locks to contend with for over 40 kilometres. The canal widened, taking on a lakelike appearance. Tangled forest merged with tall reeds along the shore. The water, still and deep, seemed the perfect domain for a monster. We were entering Loch Ness.

There's something about voyaging Loch Ness in a rowboat that makes you feel you're getting the full Scottish experience. At 37 kilometres in length, Loch Ness is Scotland's largest lake by volume and second largest by area (following Loch Lomond). It contains more water than all the lakes and rivers in England combined, and its incredible depth, 230 metres, is much greater than the nearby North Sea. It's no wonder the mysterious reaches of Loch Ness have given rise to the world's best-known mythical lake monster.

The Loch Ness monster first garnered world attention in 1934, when the *Daily Mail* printed a photograph of Nessie taken by a vacationing London gynecologist. It was later revealed as a hoax; however, the photo has remained one of the most celebrated representations of the monster. Since that time, there have been dozens of sightings along with accompanying blurry images and shaky video. This shy creature has created a robust tourist economy for the region.

"See anything big down there?" Julie asked.

I was peering into the water looking for submerged logs, but Julie obviously had monsters in mind.

"Yeah—he's heading straight for your boat."

Loch Ness harbours a far more serious threat than the monster. The volatile weather of this region, combined with the lake's great length, means the water can be whipped into a foaming maelstrom in a very short period. The woman at the British Waterways office warned us that two-metre waves were not uncommon, but this afternoon there was barely a ripple. The weather was unusually calm, and we savoured the last rays of sunshine. The lake was now a couple of kilometres across, but we hugged the northern shore to avoid being caught in a sudden squall.

Mountains rose up on both sides of the loch, and the A82 road carved a sinuous route along the steep northern flank. The shores were mostly rocky, although occasional patches of sand beckoned invitingly.

As the sun slipped behind the mountains, we reached the remains of Urquhart Castle. The eight-hundred-year-old sawtooth ruins perch on a rocky promontory surrounded by low bushes and manicured lawns. Evening light erased the interpretive signs and tourist paths, and I had little difficulty imagining what it was like in medieval times when this castle was one of the largest strongholds in Scotland. By now, archers would be firing upon our vessels, and Sir Robert Lauder, the proprietor, would be scratching his head in puzzlement as our unusual boats approached.

The shoreline had become rocky and steep, but a few hundred metres beyond Urquhart Castle, we found a relatively level section of loose rocks on which to beach our boats. We shifted the ochre boulders, creating a flat platform, erected the tent and enjoyed our dinner of ravioli and red wine. Stars reflected off the smooth water, and soft splashing noises sounded in the distance—most likely muskrats or other small animals, but possibly something larger and more serpentine.

The following morning we reached the head of the lake, where the mountains funnel together and form the mouth of the River Oich, an outflow from Loch Oich. Here, the pretty village of Fort Augustus, a collection of whitewashed stone buildings, encircles the five locks leading out of Loch Ness. We pulled up to a wooden dock fronting the canal entrance, and Julie went to look for the washrooms.

A group of four or five men who had been leaning against a wall idly chatting sauntered over.

"I see you've got the right idea," an older man with a cane said.

"Yeah, it sure is a great way to explore Scotland," I said.

"No, I mean bringing your wife along to do the cooking and cleaning. You're lucky you could convince her to go on a canoeing trip in March."

The skinny man beside him began complaining about the upcoming Easter weekend, when the canal would come alive with traffic. They took turns grumbling about the city folk who made them open and close locks all day. That's when I realized these layabouts were the lockkeepers. During the busier season, they would be posted at the various locks along the canal. Now they simply congregated in the pub-rich community of Fort Augustus complaining about the tourists who kept them employed.

Fortunately, when Julie returned, they obligingly pushed the necessary buttons to open and close the lock gates, allowing us to guide our boats up the five-level aquatic staircase. When we rowed away from Fort Augustus, we were 12 metres higher. On the town outskirts, we found a grassy knoll next to pine forest and set up camp.

The following morning at eight-thirty, we encountered our next lock. The lockkeeper grumbled a moderate amount but eventually acquiesced and said that we could go through the lock with the next boat. When he realized there would be no other boat for a long while, he relented and opened the lock for us.

It wasn't long before we reached Cullochy Lock, the final barrier between us and Loch Oich, which at 32 metres above sea level is the highest point on the Caledonian Canal. No lockkeeper was present, but a number was posted for boaters to call.

I punched the number into our cellphone.

"There's a fishing boat coming through in an hour," the lockkeeper informed me. "You can go through with them."

An hour later, the lockkeeper, a grizzled overweight man, arrived. "Where are you going?" he asked.

"Syria," I replied.

"You wouldnae catch me going to visit those dodgy ragheads. It's tae dangerous." He punctuated this remark by clearing his throat and discharging the phlegm near our boats.

The fishing boat, a trawler from Mallaig, arrived, and we chatted with the friendly crew while our boats were lifted in unison to the next level. They expected to take twenty-six hours to cross from Inverness to the west coast. The canal route was a little shorter than going around the top of Scotland and much safer. Theirs was only the second boat we had encountered on the canal since leaving Inverness, and after its rumbling engines faded, we were again alone on a swath of water cutting through forests of cedar. I felt almost as if I was home in British Columbia, travelling on a slow-moving river. The tree plantation gave the area a wild, untouched look. Even the stone edge lining the canal was overgrown with moss, enhancing the natural appearance.

We crossed Loch Oich and, in mid-afternoon, reached Laggan Locks on the far side of the lake. Once again, the lock was deserted and I called the posted number.

A gruff voice answered, "Yes?"

"We're a couple of boaters at Laggan Locks," I told him. "Would it be possible for us to go through, please?"

"You're the canoers, aren't you. I'm afraid we can't let you through."

"Why not?" I asked.

There was a pause. "Safety."

"I don't understand. You let us through all the earlier locks, and there were no safety concerns. Why is it suddenly an issue?"

"I don't think your boats are safe."

I argued that our boats were unsinkable and had every piece of required safety equipment and more, and that we were seasoned boaters. The lockkeeper was unrelenting. I could hear the sound of a televised sports game in the background.

I was getting annoyed. "This isn't anything to do with the fact you guys are too lazy to get off your bottoms to do what the British government is paying you for, is it? Better to watch the footy game on public coin than assist a couple of pesky canoeists, eh?"

He snorted and the conversation was finished. I knew my remarks would guarantee refusal of lock service for the remainder of the canal, but I was aghast at the people employed to run this system. I wondered how British Waterways had succeeded in acquiring such a collection of louts for what must be highly sought-after jobs. The pay was reasonable, beautiful homes were provided, and the locks were in some of Britain's most stunning regions.

In the presence of such beauty, it was hard to stay angry for long. The locks themselves were impeccably maintained (not by the lockkeepers), and we dragged our boats up onto the grass. Loch Lochy shimmered on the other side of the lock barrier, and a light snow dusted the landscape like icing sugar. We ended our day early and set up camp on the grass.

The next morning, snow, gales and rain besieged us. Winds, gusting at tree-snapping speeds, pushed our boats in erratic directions and waves pounded us. By the time we had rowed eight kilometres, halfway across Loch Lochy, conditions were too treacherous to continue. We pulled ashore and huddled in our tent, surrounded by towering trees creaking under the force of the wind.

Beyond Loch Lochy we would face thirteen locks, and the following day, when we reached the far side of the lake, we decided that rather than portaging each lock individually, it would be easier to tow our boats behind our bicycles for the remaining distance. We followed the B8004, a quiet country road leading from Loch Lochy to Fort William on the west coast. Farms, bed and breakfasts, and retirement homes lined the edge of the road, and the canal paralleled us at the base of the valley.

As we entered the outskirts of Fort William, a string of police cars, cameramen and television reporters crowded the edge of the canal. We had reached Neptune's Staircase, Britain's longest staircase lock, where a string of eight locks steps the canal down nearly 20 metres to sea level. But a line of yellow police tape prevented us from photographing the locks.

"What's going on?" Julie asked a photographer.

"Murder-suicide. They've got divers in the water hauling the bodies out," the man replied.

We later learned that the deaths had resulted from a disastrous love triangle. A local woman had dumped her lover, who then arrived inebriated at her door, threatening suicide. He persuaded her to get into his van, which the police later found parked at the edge of the canal. As the officer approached, the man stomped on the accelerator and plunged the van into the canal. The canal ahead was closed indefinitely, so it was a good thing we had decided to pedal this leg.

We left the growing number of rubberneckers and cycled to the end of the canal, where it exited into Loch Linnhe, a convoluted inlet leading into the Atlantic Ocean. A placard marked the terminus of the canal. It was a commemoration of the Caledonian Canal's twin, the Rideau Canal, which links Ottawa and Kingston. The sign celebrated the canals' shared historical function and purpose. The Rideau Canal was completed a decade after the Caledonian, was overseen by an English engineer and involved Scottish stonemasons in the construction.

Two kilometres away, the city of Fort William stretched from the water's edge up the lower bare flanks of Ben Nevis, Britain's highest mountain. Despite the dramatic scenery of this region and Fort William's position as a tourist hub, there was a strong flavour of discontent and decay in the outskirts. Gangs of youths eyed us stonily, cigarettes hanging from their mouths, and small, partially vacant shopping districts were rundown and adorned with graffiti. We were anxious to get away from the city before nightfall so that we could find a secure camping spot.

Loch Linnhe is renowned for treacherous waters attributed to a strong tidal influence and powerful winds. The world's third largest whirlpool, Corryvreckan, is situated partway down the inlet. When strong winds combine with an opposing current to form standing waves, the whirlpool becomes so violent its thundering slurping waters can be heard 18 kilometres away.

We had planned to voyage the length of Loch Linnhe to the Crinan Canal, a 16-kilometre shortcut slicing south through the 130-kilometre-long peninsula of Argyll and Bute. Our experience on the Caledonian Canal, however, motivated us to avoid Scottish lockkeepers, and we planned an alternative route.

The sun was close to setting by the time we had our boats ready to depart from a wooden dock at the mouth of the Caledonian Canal. A group of teenagers above tossed rocks, dislodged from a nearby wall, into the adjacent waters. A brisk outgoing tide helped speed us on our way, and we soon found a remote beach on the far side of the inlet on which to camp.

We were cheered to finally be on the west coast, and as we set up the tent, Julie practised imitating the thick brogue of the Glaswegians farther south.

"Did you hear about the naive young Canadian woman who came out to Scotland?" she asked.

"No. Was that you?"

Julie ignored my comment and continued with her joke. "She met a Scotsman on the shores of Loch Lomond and he was wearing a kilt. 'What do you wear under your kilt?' the woman asked. 'Why dunna ye look for yerself?' the Scotsman replied. The woman proceeded to lift up his kilt. 'It's gruesome!' she shrieked. 'Och aye. And if ye give it a wee stroking, it'll grew some more.'"

~~~

IT WAS EASTER WEEKEND, and Loch Linnhe provided us with a fitting experience for this spring holiday. The snow we'd been experiencing for the last section of our Caledonian Canal traverse abated, and we were treated to rare sunshine. We rowed leisurely past Castle Stalker, one of the most enchanting bastions yet encountered. The seven-hundred-year-old structure is remarkably intact and situated on a tiny rocky islet a few hundred metres from shore. Snow-coated mountains rising all around completed the calendar-perfect scene. We stopped for lunch on an uninhabited sandy island and watched hundreds of Canada geese grazing on the nearby grass.

In order to avoid the Crinan Canal, we opted to follow a different route through the labyrinth of lakes and inlets down the west coast to Glasgow. These waterways were not all connected, and we would have to negotiate the land in between on our bikes. We turned off the main channel into Loch Etive. This long, thin inlet boasts the Falls of Lora, one of Britain's most dramatic tidal features. During outgoing tides, the water is channelled through a narrow entrance over a submerged reef, creating a powerful recirculating hole and a series of standing waves. The resulting maelstrom can be surfed by kayakers, making for an exhilarating ride.

As we rounded the corner into Loch Etive, we rowed hard into the boils, upwellings and mini-whirlpools created by the strong outgoing current. Eventually, the flow became too powerful, and we stopped below the turbulent Falls of Lora in the village of Connel. Once the tide slackened, we paddled through glassy waters to Airds Bay, where we camped and prepared our bicycles for the next overland leg.

I was pleased with how the boats were holding up after almost three weeks of travel. They had been dragged over rocks, bumped into piers and repeatedly knocked and banged while on the road, but still performed flawlessly.

After Airds Bay, our journey embraced the definition of amphibious, and we continually altered our set-up for land or water. We cycled along the B845, a quiet mountain road leading to Loch Awe. The road ended in the tiny lakeside village of Annat, where we launched our vessels and crossed to the far shore. Here, we connected with another minor road and pedalled our way over the mountains to the town of Inveraray on the edge of a long inlet leading out to the sea.

It still seemed surreal, pedalling to the seashore and then departing in our own boats. The road we followed led to the main wharf, where fishing boats were readying for sea. We coasted down a ramp leading to a gravelly beach, chatted with the fishermen as we packed our bikes, and then slipped into the black-blue waters. Our maps indicated a tiny road leading up from the other side and over the mountains to the village of Lochgoilhead.

At last, we spotted the one-lane road curving up a steep hillside. There was no public land adjacent to the water here, so we landed our boats at the base of a beautifully landscaped estate. Although Britain is mostly privately owned, unlike Canada it has a wonderful law regarding public rights-of-way. Any stretch of land that has been continuously used by the public as a byway is declared a right-of-way, and landowners must allow people to traverse their private property. This means that trails criss-cross the nation, passing through farms, estates and even people's backyards. These direct routes are not only convenient; they also provide an intimate perspective of the region being walked.

We took the footpath that crossed the estate, but we were a little concerned when we reached a locked gate. Nonetheless, we couldn't see any alternative, and so we hauled our bikes and boats over the fence. As we were securing the vessels back into their trailers, a middle-aged man in tweeds approached. I still was not used to the right-of-way system and expected to be scolded for trespassing. Instead, the man warned us of thorns on the trail ahead. He explained that he was the butler of the Victorian mansion on the hillside, and that he lived a lonely life because of absentee owners.

"It doesn't get much nicer than this for a place to live," I said, gesturing at the panoramic view.

The gentleman shrugged. "I suppose so. This sunshine is pretty rare. Most of the time it's pouring with rain. And in the summer it's godawful with the midges."

The day before, we had struggled through two inches of snow, and this brief spell of sunshine transformed our world into a Garden of Eden. Around us, fruit trees bloomed and daffodils radiated colour. Redwoods, cedars and pines, planted several generations ago, graced the estate. We pushed our bikes and trailers up the extremely steep drive to the road above and began ascending a series of corkscrew switchbacks.

The course we were following from Inveraray traced the traditional public transportation route connecting Inveraray to Glasgow. In the past, passengers were transported from Glasgow to Lochgoilhead by steamer and travelled through the treacherous mountain pass in a four-horse coach. Not far from the estate where we had beached was a pier where a connecting boat would take passengers the final leg across the inlet to Inveraray. Today, the A82 connects the two centres on a longer, but much faster, route, which meant Julie and I found ourselves alone as we travelled through Hell's Glen, a dramatic wilderness of cliffs, snow-capped mountains, burbling springs and pine forests.

The sinuous road ended in the sleepy village of Lochgoilhead, which, as indicated by its name, is situated at the head of Loch Goil, an arm of the Firth of Clyde, the inlet that Glasgow is on. Near the entrance of the Firth of Clyde is the small waterfront community of Largs, a major milestone for Julie and me. My aunt and uncle lived in this town, and we looked forward to taking a few days off soon and escaping the miserable weather.

We camped in a small park beside a spirited stream just outside the village and lit the stove. Until now, we had been very sparing with our fuel because white gas was virtually impossible to find in Scotland. Fortunately, however, we had outlined this problem on the student page of our website, and the kids at Margaret Avenue Elementary School in Waterloo, Ontario, had done some sleuthing on our behalf. They informed us our stove could actually run on gasoline, a fuel source easily obtainable. We luxuriated with cups of hot tea and soon the rain lulled us to sleep. In the morning, the deluge continued, and I could tell Julie wasn't looking forward to breaking camp.

"Just a few more hours of rowing, and soon we'll be enjoying hot showers at my aunt and uncle's," I said, trying to cheer her up.

Julie was silent, munching her oatmeal, eyes fixed on an open map.

"And the weather forecast is for decreasing rain in the afternoon." I omitted the fact they also called for increasing westerly winds.

Julie remained quiet.

Maybe her sullen attitude had nothing to do with the weather or fatigue. I wondered whether it was something I had done—or not done. Perhaps she hadn't been able to go back to sleep after I had peed out the door at four in the morning. Or maybe she was still harbouring a grudge from when I snapped two days ago during a disagreement over camping spots. Was it my optimism that was grating?

It was time to bring out the big ammo. I rustled around in the dry bag and found what I was looking for.

"Look what's in here—the last Lindt chocolate bar. And look, it's dark chocolate." I unwrapped the bar and offered Julie a piece.

"No, thanks. It doesn't go with porridge."

This was really dire. We packed our sleeping bags and began clearing the vestibule. Torrents of water flowed down both sides of the tent.

I cleared my throat, willed myself to become Johnny Cash and began singing in as gravelly a voice as I could muster, "You are my sunshine, my only sunshine. You make me happy when skies are grey . . ."

A small smile cracked the corners of Julie's mouth. We finished packing and rolled down to the water.

Our journey through the Firth of Clyde was difficult as gale-force winds whipped up two-metre waves. The area, close to Glasgow, is heavily populated, and we manoeuvred carefully so as to avoid the numerous ferries criss-crossing the harbour.

After a ten-hour day of miserably cold rowing, we pulled to shore a few miles short of Largs. We were too tired to assemble the bicycles, so instead set up the tent on a patch of grass a few feet above the breaking waves and out of sight of a collection of ramshackle buildings.

The following morning, we finally reached our destination and were treated to hot showers, delicious food and a panoramic view of the frenzied ocean from the comfort of my aunt and uncle's home. Avril served us a dinner of roast beef, haggis, vegetables and Yorkshire pudding, with trifle and whisky for dessert. It was a fitting meal to celebrate the near completion of our journey through Scotland.

"So tell me," Tom asked as we settled in the sitting room, cradling glasses of Glenmorangie single malt. "What was your favourite thing about Scotland?"

I struggled with this question. Apart from the lockkeepers, the entire trip had been enchanting. The miserable weather was expected and in a way was a part of the Scottish charm. I thought back to the precipice-lined shores, heather-cloaked hills and warm, jovial people. It was a gorgeous country, and I loved its rugged beauty, but perhaps what resonated with me the most was that this was my home, too, and much of my family still lived here.

But that all sounded rather cheesy, so instead I replied, "The haggis, of course."

2

"YOU WON'T STAND A CHANCE IN THOSE BOATS"

ENGLAND (*Julie*)

I WAS READY TO LEAVE SCOTLAND. We had travelled through the country slowly, like children struggling to school through snowdrifts, and although the north won my heart with its undulating hills of heather and charging rivers, the last four days—since we'd left Colin's aunt and uncle—were dominated by music-blaring cars using country lanes as race tracks. We rode mostly on bike routes, or so the little green signs suggested, but heavy traffic combined with limited width seemed to contradict this designation.

A few days earlier, we had almost launched our boats and escaped the traffic. A school bus laden with seven-year-olds had stopped so that its young driver could tell us in his thick brogue that we were approaching his favourite paddling route. He pointed out the River Nith on our road atlas and said we could follow it all the way to the Solway Firth, a long tendril of the Irish Sea that carves into the western coast of Britain separating much of England from Scotland. We stopped at the river, just past the last dam, and packed our bicycles and trailers inside the boats. But then we wavered.

What if there were weirs on the river we couldn't portage? Or worse, what if we became stuck in the mud of the firth miles from shore? Where the river reaches the sea, it is too wide to cross directly to England, and we would have had to head deeper into the shallow inlet renowned for its vast expanses of exposed mud at low tide. Swayed by prudence, we reversed our decision, unpacked the bikes and trailers, and continued cycling.

The countryside rolled with sheep farms and pregnant fields awaiting spring's warmth. Small towns that were once quaint and charming, but now heaved with commuter traffic and satellite subdivisions, appeared often enough to allow us to buy the occasional coffee or bag of chips and to fill our water bottles before each night of camping. We tented on the edge of side roads, nestled against farm fences. In the night, cars thundered past, sneaking into my dreams and jolting me awake with threats of pending collisions.

On April 4, we reached our final destination in Scotland: Newbie. Stretching the definition of "community," Newbie is a collection of row houses scattered around several large factories guarded by chain-link fencing. The place wasn't marked in our road atlas, and I could understand why: no one would come here if they could help it. The only reason we were here was that a tiny river flowed nearby, offering passage to the Solway Firth and bypassing the marshes and thick mud that make direct access unfeasible. Signs pointed us to a small forested park with a grassy meadow sloping down to the river.

It was the perfect launch spot. Our boats could slide down the grass, off a short bank of mud and into the river, which flowed to the firth. England beckoned from across the water, low hills bathed in sunlight during a momentary parting of clouds.

"It'll be high tide in an hour," I said, looking at my watch.

"Great," Colin said. "We should be able to reach England at slack tide."

Voyaging at high water meant we wouldn't encounter any of the quicksand I had read about in numerous descriptions of the Solway Firth.

As we pushed our bikes over the grass, Colin asked, "Do you want to eat lunch now?"

It was only eleven, and I knew Colin was asking for my sake, as he's usually pretty nonplussed about a delayed meal, even when it's haggis, which it wasn't. I smiled at his thoughtfulness.

"No, that's okay, honey," I said, doing my best not to let my growling stomach get the best of me. "It's probably better to get the boats ready first."

We slipped into our well-established routine. Colin sang the Transformers theme song, "Transformers, more than meets the eye," as we set about modifying our boat/bike arrangement for the water. I took apart the bikes, Colin the trailers, and we packed this equipment carefully into the middle compartments. In just over half an hour, the boats were ready, with no trace of a bicycle or trailer. It looked as if we had rowed up the river and stopped for a picnic.

We sat on the grass eating peanut butter and jam sandwiches and drinking tea from our Thermos. Two middle-aged men in jeans and oversized jackets strolled past, each with a fierce-looking dog at the end of a leash. They took no interest in us as we stepped into our dry suits, shoved hands and heads through tight neoprene openings, and waddled around in our bright-orange spacesuits. I pushed my boat down the bank and stepped into it.

It was a joy to be afloat again. My oars sliced effortlessly through the water, and the enormous weight of the boat disappeared. After a few hundred metres, the river ended and we were in the firth, where steep waves replaced placid waters. I glanced nervously behind me at the stretch of water we needed to cross. The low hills of England were now a hazy blur in the distance, fronted by rolling waves and sporadic whitecaps.

Though my boat moved smoothly through the turbulent waters, I felt uneasy. A stiffening breeze and dark clouds hinted at change. It was a couple of kilometres across the firth, and I knew that in the middle, a strong current would be ripping out to sea. The waves grew to almost a metre in height, occasionally sending spray over the side of my boat.

We had planned for any emergency. If the weather deteriorated too much before we reached the halfway point, we would turn back. If either boat capsized, we would right it and continue. If a vessel took on water and was foundering, we would abandon it and continue together in one boat. In the worst-case scenario, where both boats sank, we would swim to shore in our dry suits while alerting the authorities on our VHF radio.

Having backup plans was reassuring, but it didn't put me entirely at ease. The water was now very rough and just a few degrees above zero Celsius. Something as simple as a small tear in a dry suit, combined with a capsize, could spell disaster in minutes. And when was it too rough to continue? We had never discussed that all-important detail. We were now in the midst of the current. The opposing wind created 1.5-metre standing waves that sent water crashing over our boats. And yet we both continued forward towards England. Should we turn back? I troubled over this decision for a long time before suddenly realizing we were halfway there. Turning back now would be a fruitless exercise.

I concentrated on my technique in the big waves, timing my strokes to get maximum purchase. Despite the turbulence, we were still moving at 9 kilometres an hour according to the GPS. Scotland faded, hidden behind a grey wall of rain, while the details of the English shoreline became distinct. As the current subsided, the waves diminished and I began to relax.

Two millennia ago, this narrow body of water marked the northern boundary of the Roman Empire. This natural barrier was augmented by a 117-kilometre stone and turf barricade,

Hadrian's Wall, which stretched to the North Sea and was erected to keep Colin's ancestors from attacking the Roman garrisons. Nonetheless, attacks were commonplace, and invaders would have navigated these very waters to perpetrate acts of vengeance and heroism, to risk their lives for their beliefs or for their leaders. They would have searched this shoreline looking for a place to pull their boats ashore, just as we now did.

The tide was dropping, but the mud was still several feet underwater, allaying our fears of getting stuck in quicksand. Instead, the higher exposed shoreline, a few hundred metres away, was sculpted bedrock, eroded into deep rivulets and potholes and blanketed in a thick mat of dense, marshy grass. Above the high-tide line lay small boulders and patches of sand. A quiet country road, leading between the occasional stone and brick homes, paralleled the beach.

I nosed my boat against a grass-covered green boulder, careful to avoid thumping against the bare rocks, and stepped ashore. The long blades of grass and algae were slippery against the rubber soles of my dry suit, and I staggered like a drunk from boulder to boulder. We slid our boats out of the water and high-fived. We had reached England! For someone travelling by car, this might not seem much of an achievement, but Colin and I had struggled for almost a month to get here. This had been the shakedown leg of the journey, and our equipment had proven it was up for the job.

Besides, we were tired of the snow, hail, rain and gales of Scotland. Now we would be rowing and cycling beneath blossoming fruit trees and enjoying the mild April days England is renowned for.

And that's when the hail and snow started.

We hurriedly reassembled our bicycles and trailers and began pedalling through the white sludge that was beginning to stick to the road.

I was struck by the contrast to the opposite shore. The Scottish side had been industrial and extremely busy. Here, traffic was almost non-existent. When cars did pass, it was at the unhurried pace of someone with a relaxed schedule. The region was dead flat, part of a large delta with an abundance of agriculture testifying to the rich soil. Farmers' fields and the occasional well-tended home lined the road, and cows, not sheep, were now the dominant livestock.

Our road followed the shoreline, and we watched the retreating tide expose a muddy expanse stretching far out to sea. This area is a wildlife sanctuary and is the third largest intertidal habitat in the United Kingdom. It is a winter getaway for millions of birds from Iceland, Norway and other northern regions. Even though Colin and I shivered, it was already too balmy for many of the geese and swans who had returned to their thawing breeding grounds.

Colin stopped to photograph a sign warning of the swift currents, tides and treacherous sands, while I took off my rain jacket and pants; the snow had stopped and the sun was now shining.

"It doesn't say anything about the quicksand," Colin said, disappointment ringing in his voice.

"What about radioactive contamination?" I asked.

The military has shot some six thousand depleted uranium shells into the Solway Firth for training practice, which by some estimates totals 20 million tonnes of nuclear waste. The actions were highly controversial, sparking public protests amid growing concerns over radioactive contamination, and the practice was stopped for several years. But then the previous month, it had resumed, and the military spent five days discharging depleted uranium.

"Nope," Colin said.

We turned away from the shore, following the road as it curved upwards towards the small village of Bowness-on-Solway.

This community marked the northwesternmost outpost of the Roman Empire and was where Hadrian's Wall terminated. The barricade was no longer visible here, but farther east, sections of it remained and can still be seen. Bowness-on-Solway's stone homes were ornate but unpretentious, built in an era when labour was cheap. Cattle guards had been installed at the foot of driveways to prevent livestock from grazing in the gardens. The road led us to the Kings Arms, a large white-stone building with red trim that was the town pub. A line of cars out front hinted that we had reached an important edifice.

I looked at Colin and smiled. It was too early for dinner but we couldn't pass up this fitting opportunity to celebrate our arrival in England.

The pub was typically British, with ornate wood trim and carpeted floors, and we sat down at a corner table with two pints of Jennings.

"Are you hiking the trail?" the bartender asked. Eric was a jovial man in his mid-thirties, with a quick smile and a penchant for talking. "Last year we had over seven thousand hikers stop here. Lots of people walk the full length of Hadrian's Trail, but some come for only a section or two. It's a great way to see the countryside."

"No," Colin said and explained we were en route to Syria and only intersecting the trail. This pleased Eric, as it did a handful of eavesdropping afternoon drinkers. Stories of other unusual visitors began to emerge.

"You'll have to join the wall of fame," Eric said, pointing to the stuffed hog's head mounted over the fireplace.

We all laughed. He brought out the heavy, leather-bound guest book, which contained a disproportionately high number of Dutch and German entries, and we wrote the details of our journey. Just as the conversation finally swung away from us and onto the Roman bath found by a neighbour excavating for a swimming pool, a portly man walked through the front door.

"Some bugger's run aground out here," he said.

His exclamation cleared the room like a fire alarm, and cozy seats were abandoned in favour of kicking the tires and prodding the hulls of our vehicles.

"Blimey, you wouldn't catch me out on the firth in these bathtubs," a tattooed bald man said.

His drinking companion peered under the boats at the trailers. "Me missus is pissed off that I blew our 'oliday savings on my sixteen-foot runabout, especially now our car is knackered. Maybe she'd be impressed if I towed it behind me bike to the firth."

His buddies roared, and one interjected, "You can't fit your big arse on a bar stool, never mind a bicycle seat."

Colin and I returned to our seats by the fireplace, and Eric joined us.

"Have you ever seen a Cumbrian terrier?" he asked. Cumbria was the county we were in.

"No, I don't think so," I said, looking quizzically at Colin. "Are they used for sheep-herding like the border collies in Scotland?"

"Not quite," Eric said and led us to through the pub to a back door that opened into a small yard. He called out and two dogs rushed over, one stretching its paws high on the screen door.

"That one's a German shepherd and this is the Cumbrian terrier."

The terrier was smaller and stouter with long grey and black hair that hid its eyes and a broad, flat, upturned nose. There was something peculiar about the dog, yet there was a familiarity I couldn't put my finger on.

Colin suddenly burst out laughing. "It's a pig!" he said, between guffaws.

Eric grinned, pleased with our response. He tossed a handful of chips, cannibalistically bacon-and-sour-cream flavoured, to the eager swine, and explained the troubles this treat had caused. The pig used to have free run of the bar, but that privilege was revoked after it went on one too many ransacking sprees in search of potato chips; it got behind the bar and destroyed bottles, glasses and countless other items. It still went wild at the sound of a chip bag opening, requiring a warning for anyone drinking (and snacking) on the patio. Eric locked the patio door—the pig knew how to open doors—and we went back inside, feeling slightly guilty about our fondness for full English breakfasts. We finished our second round of beer, poured free despite our feeble protests, and made excuses about needing to find a campsite and groceries before the sunlight faded.

We cycled on quiet roads to the neighbouring town of Kirkbride, which had the only store in the area. The small shop was sufficient if you were looking for a bottle of whisky or a pack of Marlboros, but little else. People here have to drive 20 kilometres to Carlisle for their groceries, and those who can't, like us, have to settle for freezer-burned microwave dinners retrieved from the bottom of an aging freezer.

The countryside was checkered with hedgerow-lined fields that contained young crops, cows and the occasional stone house. It was tidy and neat, every piece of land privately owned and well cared for, which was pleasant unless you were looking for a place to pitch your tent. As we searched for a thicket of trees or vacant field, we suddenly realized that we had forgotten to fill our water bottles in Kirkbride. This meant we couldn't camp even if we found a field that wasn't full of crops, cattle or large, steaming mounds of manure. We knocked on a farmhouse door, where an ample woman with deep creases in her face filled our water bottles and gave us advice.

"I wouldn't camp in the empty fields," she said. "That's where they bring the cows after milking. You might find it hard to sleep with cows tromping around your tent."

I nodded in agreement: sleeping amid a herd of half-ton animals didn't sound particularly inviting. Mind you, we seemed to be in a predicament. If we couldn't camp in the empty fields, where could we go? We found a sliver of grass between a gorse hedgerow and the single-lane road. It wasn't ideal, but we were tired and it was getting dark.

In the morning, we made our usual breakfast of oatmeal and coffee and resumed cycling through the English country-side. We travelled on the quietest roads we could find, thin yellow lines on our road atlas that took us through villages with names like Wiggonby and Whinnow. Cars and tractors occasionally passed us at a leisurely pace; benches appeared in every town (and sometimes in between); and divergences in the road were clearly signposted on striped poles that looked as if they had been taken from a barber shop.

A group of two dozen spandex-clad cyclists sped past us, followed shortly after by a man on a single-speed bike en route to a ploughing competition. He stopped to chat, explaining that the competition was restricted exclusively to animal-drawn ploughs, and delved into the nuances of the dying skill.

"Some of the best ploughmen in the world come from Cumbria," he said. "This competition helps keep pride and community interest in an art that would otherwise be lost, ploughed over by the tractor."

He told us about the team he was betting on: a Clydesdale-drawn cast-iron plough guided by a "young buck" who could run a ruler-straight line blindfolded. I found myself wishing we could attend the event, but it was too far off our route. I couldn't imagine English farmers giving up their modern machinery en masse to return to the horse and plough, but there was something heartwarming in the fact that skills that had been a fundamental part of the development of Britain were still recognized and appreciated.

It was our seventh day of camping, and we planned to spend the night in a hotel so that we could update our website, submit our newspaper articles and research the route ahead. I was also looking forward to a hot shower, and maybe, if I was lucky, a bath. But in Raughton Head, a tidy farm village with about eight houses and a bench, the sole bed and breakfast had closed. And in Blencow, an even more charming village composed of peach sandstone buildings, the farm B & B we stopped at did not have wireless Internet. This was disappointing, as it promised to offer the freshest full English breakfast yet and was run by a sweet couple. They were so kind that they went to great efforts to find another place for us to stay. They searched the B & B guide, looking for Internet availability, which, unfortunately, wasn't a popular feature in this region, and eventually concluded that we'd need to go into the city of Penrith. The hotels there would be at least £110 ($220) a night, they surmised, except for the Travelodge, to which they drew us a map. We didn't like the thought of negotiating our 5.5-metre boats through busy narrow city streets, not to mention paying an extra £60 ($120) for that privilege (their B & B was £50 a night with breakfast), but we had no choice.

The Travelodge was a characterless motel on the side of the highway next to a fast-food restaurant. Unfortunately, the wireless Internet was £5 an hour, which, with the extensive work we needed to do, would end up costing a small fortune. The staff had no suggestions for an alternative, so we cycled back a hundred metres to the Limes Country Guest House, a classic three-storey 1800s home surrounded by lovely gardens, which cost the same as the motel and included breakfast, but unfortunately was without Internet.

The next day, we rode our bikes into town, leaving our boats with the proprietor, Jonathan, a tall, balding man with the polite and reserved manner of an English butler. Penrith is a modest city of grey and red townhouses, the typical assortment of franchises (Morrisons and McDonald's), an attractive pedestrian-zoned downtown, and a sixth-century castle ruin adorned with placards. It is the gateway to the Lake District and boasts a healthy tourist population in the spring and summer.

We checked into the Internet-equipped Station Hotel, priced at only £27 ($54) for one person or £55 ($110) for a couple. This typical British system of pricing was rather amusing, if not slightly annoying. Why was it more than twice as expensive for two people to share the same room? If we checked in individually, we would save a pound, despite collectively using more square footage and requiring two beds and bathrooms to be cleaned instead of one. It seemed all too obvious that this nation of "no sex, please, we're British" was expressing its disapproval of twosome-togetherness through pricing policies.

Another British hotel quirk, which straddles the line between quaint and sickening, is the penchant for laying carpet in bathrooms. The aroma of urine and mould emanating from these rugs necessitates the use of footwear when venturing to the loo.

This hotel was nicer than I expected, despite the carpeted bathrooms. Although the brick building was a little rundown, like an aging aristocrat, it had maintained its elegance. It was decorated with deep-blue carpet, heavy wallpaper and original oil paintings. It had a restaurant on the main floor with the rooms above. It was our first hotel room with a bathtub, and immediately it became my favourite. Our last week had been a struggle, and I enjoyed finally resting my muscles while spending the day writing, updating our website, answering emails and relaxing in the bath.

It had started to snow again, and from the comfort of our room, we watched heavy flakes blanket the city. It was now early April, but the scene outside seemed anything but. Cars inched forward, tires spinning in the snow. Men with snow shovels worked below our window trying to free a stuck bus, while children attacked each other with snowballs. The narrow streets, stone buildings and fresh snow reminded me of a Christmas scene from a storybook. We later read in the *Daily Telegraph* that it was the worst April snowstorm in twenty years.

By morning, the snow had almost completely melted, and Colin and I rolled out of town towards the Lake District. This region is one of Britain's premier domestic holiday destinations, and it is filled with hundreds of glimmering lakes squeezed between miniature mountains and rolling fields of sheep and stone fences. Yesterday's snowstorm had covered the peaks with snow, like dusted confectioner's sugar. In the summer, the area is overrun with tourists, but the unpredictable spring weather kept most away, making it the perfect time to visit.

Eleven years earlier, when I was an exchange student at the University of Leeds, I took the bus here and trekked over the hills and countryside on an all-too-short vacation. I told myself that one day I would return, but I had envisioned it would be with a backpack and hiking boots, not a rowboat-toting bicycle. Any region known for its mountains is generally not the best place to cycle—especially when towing a god-heavy load.

Nonetheless, crisp sunshine and splendid views were a balm that eased the pain of struggling up hills. By noon, we had reached Ullswater Lake, and we paused at the tiny ferry terminal to sip a coffee and relax in the sunshine. A small ferry was the only vessel on the lake. Farms and forests lined the lake's perimeter, a rumpled green duvet cloaking the flanks of snow-capped mountains. We continued through this serene countryside with burning thighs while gradually veering southwards.

A man on a well-worn road bike pulled alongside while eying my boat.

"Expecting rain?" he asked, a refrain we had heard with some frequency.

He introduced himself as Dave. He was in his early forties, tall, lanky and athletic. He was a drystone mason with a wife and two kids and lived a few kilometres down the road. Dave was also a keen cyclist and told us that he and his wife had pedalled throughout much of Europe, South America and the Middle East.

"Have you been to Syria?" I asked.

"Yes, it's a beautiful country with some of the friendliest people in the world—always inviting us in for tea."

I was eager to hear more. Until now, when people commented on our destination, they always spoke of the dangers we would face: robbery, swindling, kidnapping, dangerous driving. But none of these armchair speculators had ever actually been to Syria, and I was pleased to hear a first-hand account from someone who had—and on a bike, too. We stopped on the roadside to snack on a chocolate bar and an apple.

"Did you go through Aleppo?"

Dave was quiet for a bit before answering. "That's the only place we had problems. My wife and I went to a coffee house. We spent the evening playing backgammon and talking to two men we met there. When closing time came, they invited us to their place."

A cow leaning over a nearby wall interrupted the story with an almighty moo. Dave smiled at the cantankerous bovine and continued.

"We got in the back of their jeep and they started driving. But they took us out of the city and soon we were in the country, in the middle of nowhere. We asked them to turn around, but they didn't. We didn't know where we were going or what they were going to do with us. Nobody at home knew where we were, and it would be months before anybody came looking for us. They were driving fast, but our only chance to get out was to jump."

"Wouldn't they just come back for you?" Colin asked.

"Exactly, so we had to wait for the right moment. A brightly lit building materialized. We leaped out and ran towards it as fast as we could. The jeep turned around, and we could hear it screaming towards us. The building turned out to be a twenty-four-hour ice-cream-cone factory, and the staff hid us inside and kept our kidnappers out."

It was a worrying story.

We reached Dave's large limestone house, and he invited us in to meet his family. Parts of the exterior wall had been rebuilt, while other areas were cracked and awaiting repair. A slate roof was supported by giant wooden beams. Dave had bought the 150-year-old house ten years earlier, before prices in this popular region skyrocketed. We followed him up thick wooden steps into a living area with exposed stone walls. He introduced us to his wife, Jane, an attractive woman dressed in a flowing skirt, and his kids, a young boy and girl who played quietly in the corner of the room.

While we munched toasted muffins with honey and drank tea, Dave asked about our upcoming route. I pulled out our road atlas and he began laughing.

"You're navigating with *that*?" he said.

Incredulity was a common English response to our means of navigation, and I found it somewhat puzzling. So far, our road atlas had been very accurate, and sufficient for route-finding through the maze of country lanes we had encountered. What the natives expected us to use were Ordinance Survey maps—highly detailed physical relief representations. The problem, however, is each Ordinance Survey map covers only a tiny area of Britain, and we would have needed dozens or even hundreds to allow for route options. At $20 a map, the price alone would make this option prohibitive, never mind their weight.

Dave pulled out his own Ordinance Survey map, and I traced our planned route into York, through the Pennine Mountains and to the headwaters of the River Ouse.

"Blimey, you think you'll be able to haul your boats over this pass?" said Dave, pointing to a spot in the Pennine Mountains. "The reward, though, is that you'll be able to enjoy a pint in the highest pub in all of Britain—Tan Hill Pub."

This was a worry. I didn't want to drag my boat up the side of the English Himalayas. Even sipping a pint while gasping for air in the razor-thin air seemed unappealing.

"How high are these mountains anyway?" Colin asked.

"The pass is 528 metres and the highest peak in the range is 893 metres."

I almost burst out laughing. Still, I didn't want to pedal up any extended hills if I could help it.

"Are there any lower passes we can go through?"

"Yes, this route here is equally picturesque, and it's much less steep." Dave ran a finger along a road just to the south of where we had planned on going.

We were sold. For perhaps the fifth time, we altered our planned route. I loved the infinite possibilities that came with following a course that included both land and water.

It was wonderful meeting Dave, Jane and their kids. It felt homey, as if we were visiting old friends, and I was sorely tempted to take up their offer of staying for tea (as some

English people call supper) and spending the night on their spare couch, but we needed to keep to our schedule. As a parting gift, Dave presented us with a book, *The Unlikely Voyage of Jack de Crow*, written by A. J. Mackinnon, an Australian who had sailed and rowed a Mirror dinghy from England to the Black Sea—paralleling much of our own planned route. We waved goodbye, promised to stay in touch and set off towards the River Ouse.

We were crossing England from the western side of the water divide into North Yorkshire through the Pennine Mountains. The Pennines are considered the spine of northern England, and a national park runs along their length. I was struck by their grandeur, which seemed disproportionate to their diminutive size. Rugged peaks jutted out from hillsides of heather, and valley bottoms were mostly peat bogs. The bedrock is mainly limestone, and the area is renowned for having extensive cave systems. We followed a quiet, narrow lane that meandered from village to village. The writer Bill Bryson was so enraptured by this wild part of England that he bought a house and moved his family to a village only a few kilometres from where we pedalled.

At the top of a rise, Colin paused. All the way up, he'd been staring at the land intently.

"This is a karst landscape—made from porous limestone. Have you noticed how few streams there are?"

"No." It was getting late, and we needed to find a camping spot.

"That's because all the water flows underground, through caves. Pretty neat, eh?" He pointed to a small pond about 300 metres away. "See how that pond is surrounded by a bowl-like landscape. Where does the water escape when it overflows? Let's go check it out."

"Yeah, let's," I said without enthusiasm.

I was hungry and tired, but I trudged after him. We trekked down a slope through boggy peat and heather. At the edge of the 200-metre-wide pond, we heard a slight burbling sound. Colin honed in on the noise. A small stream of water flowed about five metres from the pond and disappeared into a boulder-choked hole in the ground.

"See? This water flows into a cave," Colin said.

He tried moving an armchair-sized rock blocking the entrance.

"Maybe we should move on and find a camping spot," I suggested.

Colin was disappointed I didn't share his enthusiasm.

I continued, "It's late and I'm hungry, and the last thing I want to do is to crawl into a wet hole in the ground. We can go spelunking some other day when we find a hole at a reasonable hour."

"Cave," Colin corrected me. "And I'm holding you to it."

Three days after leaving Dave and Jane's, we reached the River Swale, a tributary of the Ouse. We stared at the river from an arched wrought-iron bridge near Myton-on-Swale, a modest town surrounded by imposing estates. I had been looking forward to this moment for a long time. It was the start of the interconnected system of rivers and canals that (with the exception of the English Channel) would take us all the way to the Black Sea. There was something magical about travelling through a continent on its waterways, rowing along transportation corridors that once were vital to movement and commerce. Now, railways and freeways dominate, and these ancient water courses have become sleepy backwaters, all but forgotten. I was excited to explore the villages, towns and countryside from the lanes of yesterday.

We lifted our boats, bikes and trailers over a barbed-wire fence and began readying our equipment for the water. Grazing sheep retreated to a safe distance, but slippery brown pellets littered the ground around us. The rain intensified, and I skidded on the mud/shit medley. I didn't mind the rain, but I was nervous about rowing on the river. The brown water was swirling and fast moving with spring runoff. Branches and trees extending out from the shore narrowed the river's width to two or three metres in places. I had never rowed on a fast-moving river before, and I was anxious about my ability to manoeuvre in such a restricted space.

"Be careful of sweepers," Colin said, pointing to the branches that reached into the water. "That's how people get killed. You'd never guess the power of the current until you're pressed helplessly into a sieve of branches."

He tossed out these bits of advice casually, as if he was talking about the weather. To Colin, this was child's play, but I hung on every word. I stepped into my boat and pushed into the flow. The current immediately caught my boat and pinned it against the bank. With great difficulty, I freed myself and was underway.

After that, things got better. I concentrated on staying in the middle of the river and began to enjoy the passing scenery. Willows, birch and brambles clawed at my boat from the shore, and grazing sheep watched us from fields at the top of the bank. Birds scattered as we approached, and panicked swans rocketed down the river ahead of us. Occasionally, fatalities from spring lambing season bobbed in the eddies.

It wasn't long before we reached the confluence of the River Ouse, and the flow widened and slowed. I was now completely at ease and realized just how much I loved river voyaging. It is one of the most peaceful ways to travel.

We had the river to ourselves on the upper Ouse and drifted slowly past fields of newly planted canola, wheat and sunflowers. In the evening, when we nosed ashore to camp in an empty field, the river lived up to its namesake. The foreshore was thick mud, and almost impossible to traverse. The ooze sucked at our boots and trickled over the tops.

Eventually we pulled our boats from the water and moved our gear to firmer ground. We pitched our tent and ate noodles with beef stew while cows mooed in the distance. The sun set just before eight, and shortly after we were cocooned in our sleeping bags, falling asleep to the sound of rain pattering on our nylon roof.

Sliding back into the river the next morning was a little easier with the aid of gravity. Upon nearing the city of York, we began to encounter boats moored against the bank. As we passed a rusting hulk—an old cargo barge with a gaff rig and leeboards—converted into a live-aboard, the owner appeared through a hatch to watch us. He was wearing a headlamp, and a black cat circled around his feet.

"I saw you two yesterday stuck in the middle of the A1 trying to cross traffic," he said as we came within earshot.

For one silly second, I wondered how he recognized us.

"Where are your bikes and trailers now?" he asked.

"They're packed inside the boats," I replied.

"Good god, that's a trick. Where are you going anyway?"

"Syria," I replied.

"Good god."

We had almost drifted beyond earshot, and I could barely hear his parting words: "Watch out for the bore downstream."

"What's that?" I said, rowing in reverse.

"The bore!" the man replied. "I've only seen it once, and that was enough. It's unlike any wave I've ever seen, just a flat-faced wall of water roaring up the river. You'd better make sure you're off the water before it hits."

This wasn't the first we'd heard of the bore. Several others had warned us with vague descriptions of its destructive powers, but no one had any concise information. A bore is the true definition of a tidal wave (often used incorrectly to describe tsunamis, which are waves created by seismic activity). These solo waves are created when a strong tidal current is funnelled up an intertidal river, creating a powerful breaking wave that can come as a shock to anyone enjoying otherwise placid waters. In some places, like England's Severn River, the tidal bore is big enough to surf. In fact, the record for the world's longest surfboard ride is held by Englishman Steve King, who in 2006 rode the Severn bore wave for 12.2 kilometres. He surfed the wave for an hour and sixteen minutes!

We didn't harbour any foolish plans to test our rowboat's surfing prowess. Besides, it was more probable that our encounter with the bore would result in a capsize and destruction as the surge smashed us against rocks and trees. But we didn't need to worry about that for now; we still had locks and weirs protecting us from the tide.

Our first set of English locks were a far cry from those on the Caledonian Canal. Linton Locks were small and without a cantankerous lockkeeper. It was a do-it-yourself affair, but the two sets of heavy wooden doors had to be opened with a crank handle we had yet to obtain from British Waterways. Instead, we portaged and continued down the river past weeping willows and startled bleating sheep. Aside from the vocal sheep, cows and ducks, we had the river completely to ourselves.

Distant buildings were silhouetted on the horizon, and the city of York gradually appeared. We slipped under a large concrete bridge and suddenly the river came to life. Four sleek rowing shells powered by university teams plied the river, while tour ships passed with loudspeakers blaring. We wove through the traffic and continued towards the heart of the city.

A number of ornate bridges spanned the water, and brick and stone buildings, converted into pubs, homes and other businesses, bordered the shore. A towering wall lined the river's edge to keep its waters from flooding the city. (In 2000, the wall proved not quite tall enough when the Ouse reached its highest level in 375 years; water spilled over and flooded hundreds of homes and businesses.) Red ferry boats zipped past us, while we leisurely admired the old architecture and crowds from our relaxing vantage.

Downstream of York, the river was busier. Small, unkempt cabin cruisers and live-aboard barges bobbed against rickety wooden piers and pontoons made from rusting oil barrels. Derelict wooden shacks, often missing roofs or walls, were perched adjacent to the cluttered moorings below. Scattered along the bramble-overgrown foreshore were decomposing picnic benches, chairs, life preservers and several waterlogged mattresses. A rotten-egg aroma alerted us to two sewage treatment plants, well before we spotted the discharge pipes.

The 6.5-kilometre-an-hour speed limit allowed us to keep ahead of the infrequent traffic. Human-powered craft were not restricted to this rule, and the university rowing teams of York often tripled the speed of motorized craft. A top-heavy fibreglass cruiser, which had been trailing us for an hour since York, finally chugged past as we stopped to munch granola bars.

Although the Ouse is a river, it has been canalized, making it navigable by larger boats. A series of weirs are placed along the river's length, raising its water level. Dikes have been built along the edge, preventing the higher waters from breaching the river's banks, and locks are situated at the weirs so that boats can traverse these small dams. Raising the river's depth also has the effect of decreasing the current, making it easier for boats to go upstream.

The thundering roar of heavily disturbed water indicated that we were approaching Naburn Lock and weir. Each second, more than 2,500 cubic metres of water poured over the lip of the weir and cascaded several metres through a jumble of boulders. A line of orange floats strung across the flow clearly marked the danger downstream. To go over the weir would offer a quick, and possibly tragic, passage to the waters below. A channel to the left led to the more orderly descent offered by locks. This was the final set of locks on the river, and the waters below were in the intertidal zone.

Naburn Lock has two adjacent lock chambers, allowing two-way flow of traffic. It was bigger than the previous locks, but we were still unable to find a lockkeeper. We assumed that it, too, was self-operated and prowled around the machinery trying to find a way to open the massive wood and iron gates. The hydraulic controls required a key to operate, but the system also had manual controls. I pushed the crank handle to open the sluice paddles but nothing budged. After a Herculean effort, water began seeping into the lock.

"We're doing it!" I said proudly.

"Self-manned locks are so much better than having to rely on idle lockkeepers who—" Colin began, his sentence interrupted by a man who had emerged from a nearby house and was now running towards us.

"Stop! Stop!" the man yelled angrily.

I hastily closed the paddles and tried to look nonchalant.

"You're not allowed through these locks," the man said furiously, his face red from exertion and anger. He was in his early forties with a stocky build. A black toque hid short-cropped hair, and a pouch of tobacco bulged from under his sleeve. He looked more like a barroom brawler than the local lockkeeper.

"Why not?" Colin asked, his voice tight. "The brochure from British Waterways states we're allowed to operate locks ourselves when no lockkeepers are present."

"You need a licence."

"We have one," I said, and pointed to the official sticker on our boat, which we had received from British Waterways in Inverness.

The man looked at it, dismayed. He lit a hand-rolled cigarette and said, "It's too dangerous."

"We've been through much bigger locks," I countered.

The lockkeeper paused. Surrounded by rusting cranks and cogs, I had little difficulty imagining a similar unit turning slowly beneath his toque.

"You need insurance."

"We have insurance," Colin said, referring more to our health insurance than anything covering our boats. We knew British Waterways does not require insurance for non-motorized craft, but there was no point debating this issue.

We were at an impasse. The lock was nearly impossible to portage, with steep banks and private land blocking the route. The lockkeeper was clearly torn; he had never allowed a paddle craft through his lock and was unwilling to make any concessions, but he couldn't see a way for us to get around it either. I was more than happy to stand there and hope the lockkeeper's eventual conclusions would match ours, but Colin was getting increasingly agitated.

"It's your job to let us through," Colin said. "What do they pay you for?"

"Canoes aren't allowed," the lockkeeper said, growing increasingly set in his opposition.

They bickered back and forth, regurgitating the same arguments. I felt our chances were dwindling. Colin's points were valid but his delivery could have used a bit of finessing, to say the least.

"Let's see what else we can do," I said, hoping to defuse the situation.

The lockkeeper walked away, and Colin loudly grumbled, "Lazy lockkeepers."

"That's not going to help us," I said. "Remember Scotland." After Colin told a Scottish lockkeeper off over the phone, we had to portage all the remaining locks on the Caledonian Canal.

"He's not going to let us through anyway," Colin said. "Besides, someone has to stand up to them."

Lockkeepers had become Colin's nemesis on this journey. He found a litany of negative traits in them and thought it deplorable that they treated with such disdain jobs that placed them in beautiful natural surroundings. I wondered if it had become a self-fulfilling prophecy, and if we were bringing out the worst in them. We milled about pondering alternatives, all of which involved a tremendous amount of work and a high likelihood of inflicting damages to our boat. Then, after twenty minutes, the lockkeeper returned.

"I'll let you through," he said. "But you shouldn't be travelling these locks."

"Thank you," I said quickly before Colin could say something acrimonious.

As the exit gates opened, the lockkeeper peered down from the controls 4.5 metres above us. "Hope you're not planning on going ashore tonight."

"Why?" I asked.

"The mud. When you step off your canoes, it'll come up to here." He held a hand to his waist. "And watch out for the bore. Make sure to get off the river quick if you hear it coming. You won't stand a chance in those boats."

Our biggest danger that evening wasn't the bore, the mud or the river freighters. It was a swan. She followed us through the lock, pecking at us and our boats in search of a handout. We tried to placate the belligerent creature with a few pieces of bread, but that only made her swim harder to keep pace with us. Eventually, she tired and disappeared behind a bend.

A lush pasture, illuminated jade-green in the evening sun, beckoned invitingly for camping. The steep, muddy shore was difficult, but not nearly as bad as the lockkeeper had led us to believe.

In the morning, we awoke to discover the swan, recognizable by her yellowed belly feathers and crooked beak, waiting patiently by the boats. When we emerged from the tent, she waddled up the muddy slope, her ample belly dragging on the ground. She joined us for breakfast—three packets of oatmeal for us and two for her.

With assistance from the ebbing tide, we zipped along at 12 kilometres an hour. The river was bordered with trees and bushes, and the adjacent area was all farmland. We were entering the vast lowland delta region created from the rich sedimentary deposits of the Trent and Ouse rivers. Dikes and drainage systems have considerably increased agricultural yield at the expense of estuarine habitat.

The mud and tidal influence were not conducive to pleasure boating, and we had left the endless clutter of decrepit vessels and moorings behind at Naburn Lock. Nonetheless, the semi-wild shoreline was still littered with plastic bags fluttering in low-hanging tree branches, deposited at high tide and left to hang like unsightly ornaments.

By lunch, we reached the outskirts of the agricultural town of Selby. This has-been community has a rich history in shipbuilding and as a port. The famous Greenpeace ship *Rainbow Warrior* was built there in 1957. Now, ship construction has ceased, and few cargo ships visited the port.

We had reached Selby just in time. We were out of drinking water, but more importantly we were sure the bore wave would hit us any second. Although we had received repeated warnings of the devastating tidal wave that frequently roars up the River Ouse, the stories were always vague and second- or third-hand, but invariably involved boats capsizing, picnicking families washed from the banks, and cattle swept to their demise. One old man, seated by his boat with spittle on his chin, mumbled something about their last Christmas party being ruined by the bore. I think he may have misunderstood my inquiry. What we *had* been able to ascertain was that the bore came thundering up the river fronting the incoming tide. At the moment, the outgoing flow had ceased, and the water was ominously slack. Any minute the tide would turn. With a heightened sense of alertness, we quickened our pace to find a sheltered marina in Selby.

Our visions of tying up to a dock and venturing onto solid ground for lunch were soon shattered. The oozing muddy shoreline before the town suddenly transformed to sheer concrete walls rising nine metres above the water. Hail poured from the sky, and Colin offered unencouraging phrases such as "I was worried it would be like this" and "Probably most of the towns downstream will be inaccessible."

We were almost at the end of Selby when we reached the lock entrance to a canal system entering the river. The giant iron gates were shut, but a metal ladder was bolted onto the wall. We tied our boats to the second-lowest exposed rung, aware that the tide would soon rise, and made our way up the slimy rungs.

There was a tidy lockkeeper's house nearby with a faucet on the wall. Careful not to draw attention to myself, I slipped over to the spigot and quickly filled our water bottles, worried that an irate lockkeeper would shoo us away. We lunched on a grassy patch out of sight from the house.

While we ate, a woman walking a dog approached. She introduced herself as the lockkeeper's wife and chatted warmly.

"Do you know anything about the tidal bore?" Colin asked.

"Ah yes," she said. "Nothing to worry about, love. It only

comes twice a year during the highest tides, and even then it's not that big—maybe a foot or so high."

We felt sheepish but relieved and continued down the river. The hail had stopped but the headwinds intensified, whipping the water into choppy waves. The rising tide creating an opposing current, and our progress was grindingly slow. We rowed past monotonous flat countryside dominated by the conical towers of the Drax Power Station, Britain's largest coalfired electrical generation facility. Its giant belching smokestacks were prominent throughout the afternoon given our slow speed, the flatness of the land and the meandering course of the river. In the late afternoon, we finally approached the city of Goole at the river's mouth. The scent of sewage combined with industrial chemicals signalled the city's presence before we could see it.

It was here that we planned on taking our weekly day off, but my longing for a warm, dry bed suddenly evaporated.

"Maybe we shouldn't stop here."

"We have to," Colin said. "It's been a week since we updated our website, and we probably won't find wireless Internet in any of the smaller towns farther on. Besides, it looks pretty rough and muddy out there in the bay."

Unfortunately, despite its size, Goole was as inaccessible as Selby. A great wall of corrugated iron devoid of ladders separated us from the town. We reached a set of lock gates that led into the sheltered waters of the city harbour, but the likelihood of being let through and into the industrial harbour was low. We elected not to waste the final hour of daylight arguing with a lockkeeper and continued looking for an escape.

At the edge of the city, a side channel appeared, and we rowed into it. The straight waterway led through the outskirts of the city and into farmland. Our only choice was to wrestle our boats up steep six-metre-high muddy banks. I nosed my boat against the shore and stepped onto a firm-looking patch. It held me. Then I took another step, leaving the safety of my boat, and sank up to my knees. The cold mud oozed over my boots and against my rain pants.

"I'm stuck."

Colin was a boat-length away, balancing one half-submerged foot on the mud and the other on the boat.

"We're going to have to unload these boats," he said, oblivious to my predicament. "There's no way we can carry them up fully loaded."

Since a rescue effort was apparently not forthcoming, I shifted my weight onto my right foot and pulled up my left. But all I managed was to further entrench one foot and lose the boot on the other. I shoved my foot back into its boot and sank a few inches deeper. It seemed weight distribution was my only choice, and so I sacrificed my last remnants of dignity, sat down in the mud, pulled my feet free and retrieved my boots by hand. I was coated in mud, but I didn't care any more.

We clawed our way to the top of the mud bank only to discover that we were penned in by a tall brick wall that ran along the length of the canal. I couldn't blame the residents of Goole for wanting to distance themselves from the goo and ooze of the Ouse, but I was devastated. It was almost dark and I was exhausted. All I wanted to do was crawl into bed, but we were in a buffer zone of tangled shrubs and grass, littered with broken bottles and empty potato chip packets. Somehow we needed to get all 270 kilograms of our equipment out of the mud, up the bank, over the wall and into a hotel room. At least finding accommodation wouldn't be difficult; crammed between two nearby factories were three bars whose signs also advertised hotels.

To say it was an ordeal is an understatement, but two hours later, long after the sun had set, we found ourselves on the right side of the two-metre-high wall with our boats secured to their trailers. Gangs of twelve-year-olds sauntered by—boys on BMX bikes smoking cigarettes and trying to look tough and girls giggling flirtatiously. We ignored their requests to "borrow" our bikes and set off to the hotel a hundred metres away.

While Colin stayed with the boats, I walked into the small smoky interior of a dingy pub.

"Kanna help ye, hen?" the tired barmaid asked.

About ten men braced against the bar's perimeter turned to see what was going on.

"Do you have any beds available in your hotel?"

Raucous laughter filled the room.

"'Otel?" a fat man chortled. "You don' wanna stay here unless you're rentin' by the hour."

The barmaid shrugged apologetically. "Nay, these are all jus' pubs round here. I dunno why they all have 'otel signs. Nobody's ever asked me for a room before. Ye might find somethin' downtown. I think the King's Head has rooms."

We rode our bikes and boats over a bridge in the direction the woman had gestured. An industrial warehouse greeted us emblazoned with "Welcome to Goole—The UK's Premier Inland Port." Fortunately a gas station materialized, and the clerk, a young girl with black and blond hair, told us that there were two hotels and directed us to the more respectable one. We found the Clifton Hotel five blocks away on top of a Chinese restaurant. It was rundown, but at £43 including breakfast, we couldn't complain. We carried our eight dry bags to our room, locked the bikes and boats, and collapsed on the bed. Finally our weekend had begun.

It was late but I was hungry and didn't feel like eating granola bars for dinner. So we changed out of our glistening, muddy slickers and into soiled, musty clothing we deemed clean and went to explore Goole. Nearby were three fast-food establishments, all serving kebabs, pizza and deep-fried chicken. We chose the cleanest-looking restaurant and devoured two flavourless kebabs.

Goole isn't a place for fine dining. It is a working town built around the shipping industry and agriculture. In the early 1800s, a navigation company constructed a canal from Leeds to Goole, making it an ideal hub for transferring goods from ocean vessels to river craft. The vast Humber estuary, a marshy region downstream, combining the Ouse and Trent rivers, places Goole 72 kilometres from the North Sea, making it Britain's farthest inland deep-sea port. The city also has a robust manufacturing industry producing glass and clothing. Despite having a sound economy and a large immigrant population, this region is not renowned for charm. Goole was voted the most boring (as in dull, not a wall of water rushing down the river) town in the country by the British newspaper the *Daily Express*, while Channel 4 ranked neighbouring Hull as the worst place in the U.K. to live as well as the fattest. I can't say I was surprised to discover the name Goole was derived from an Anglo-Saxon word meaning open sewer.

Back in our hotel room, we showered off the grime of the past week and slipped between threadbare sheets. Sleep came quickly and deeply, as it always does when I am that physically active. The dilapidated state of the hotel became meaningless—that is, until drunken shouting outside our room thundered through the paper-thin wall. Voices boomed in Polish, with a smattering of suggestive English phrases directed to the young Chinese woman working the front desk. I plugged my ears, hoping the proprietor would tell them to shut up, but she was shy and overwhelmed, as was her father, whose voice joined the conversation. The commotion moved closer, and our door thumped as it became a support for inebriated bodies. I realized I had forgotten to turn the key in the lock when the door yawned inward, spilling drunken men into our room. They weren't fazed by the mishap and went back to the hall to continue their salacious advances on the night staff. It was all I could take. I wrapped myself in a bed-sheet, tromped over to the open door, shouted stern words, and slammed—and locked—the door.

We found ourselves spending three days in Goole. It wasn't for the city's tourist appeal, but a pressing requirement to complete the final draft of my book *Rowboat in a Hurricane*, chronicling our previous expedition rowing across the Atlantic. With time, we began discovering the city's redeeming features: abundant bicycle lanes, cheap prices and pleasant people.

We found it strangely endearing that nobody in Goole ever thought we were tourists. Invariably, when shopkeepers heard our accents, they would ask when we had moved to town. "Tourism" was a word absent from the Goolish vocabulary, and foreigners were only here to work.

We abandoned our plan to continue downstream to the mouth of the Trent River and then row upstream. The mud was overwhelming, and it would only get worse, so instead we planned to cycle across the flat countryside towards the Oxford Canal.

The rich arable land adjacent to the Trent River included a vast network of quiet country roads servicing the farms, and we were able to choose a pleasant cycling route. Enormous swaths of brilliant yellow canola already bloomed, and other crops, too young to identify, unfurled from the damp earth. Fields were no longer hemmed in by quaint hedgerows, but were expansive, grown on an industrial scale like the Canadian prairies.

We passed through small austere communities of red-brick homes with names like Swinefleet, Reedness and East Butterwick, which bespoke of fertile origins. The first night we camped in a spruce plantation and the next in a farmer's field.

By the time we had pedalled 70 kilometres from Goole and bypassed the major city of Nottingham, the terrain became corrugated and hedgerows decorated the landscape again.

The villages were also more attractive. Ornate houses, some over 500 years old, were constructed of sandstone with slate roofs. Many even retained the high-maintenance thatched roofs, giving the communities a fairy-tale appearance. The names were equally fitting and rolled pleasurably off the tongue.

"Waltham on the Wolds," I said late one morning as we scanned our map looking for a place to stop for lunch.

"Nah, that's too far. How about Wiverton Hall?" Colin said.

"Wiverton Hall? We can make it all the way to Wymondham," I replied.

"Will you wuv me if I make it to Wymondham?" asked Colin. "I'm hungry for my wunch."

I giggled. No wonder everybody looked so happy out here. With names like that and equally beguiling pubs in each village, it was a pretty charming place.

It was now late April, and the weather had improved considerably. Rain was still frequent, but average highs were about 15 degrees Celsius. In the district of Daventry, Northamptonshire, we camped in a pasture at the base of a hill. It was only in the morning that I noticed a small statue on the far end of the field, and we walked up to investigate. The limestone obelisk was a tribute to a decisive battle in the first English Civil War. Three hundred and fifty years ago, Royalist and Parliamentarian armies clashed here in the Battle of Naseby.

An interpretive placard displayed an artist's seventeenth-century drawing of the battle scene, and I was amazed at how similar the land looked today. I traced my finger along hedgerows (which were still in the same location) and matched them to the scene in front of me. Snorting horses and bodies covered the ground exactly where our tent sat.

Hedgerows are as English as fish and chips. They've been around since 1000 BC when farmers cleared the fields around the parish and left thorny bushes, often gorse and bramble, at the boundaries. They served the same purpose as walls—keeping livestock in, wild animals out and creating visual boundaries—but required less labour and materials to create. The Romans used them, as did the Anglo-Saxons and subsequent generations, but it wasn't until the eighteenth and nineteenth centuries that hedgerows truly flourished. Britain passed the Inclosure Acts, which turned open fields and common areas into private land by enclosing them with hedgerows. This act was beneficial for nobility who acquired new tracts of land, but devastating for peasants who lost their animals' grazing grounds.

At one point, upwards of 650,000 kilometres of hedgerows criss-crossed England and Wales, enough to girdle the equator sixteen times. But their status went into free fall after World War II, when they were seen as an impediment to large-scale food production. Government incentives encouraged farmers to rip them out, offering payment per yard of hedgerow destroyed.

The tide has turned yet again, and the dividing bushes are now recognized not only for their aesthetic and tourist appeal but also for protecting wildlife and stabilizing the soil. Financial rewards are now offered to farmers who maintain and replant the hedgerows they'd earlier been paid to chop down. Thousands of kilometres of new hedgerows are planted yearly.

We passed hedgerows in various stages of growth and found the process intriguing. First, a row of gorse is planted, and the shrubby trees are allowed to grow to about 4.5 metres. The base is then cut about 90 percent of the way through so the tree falls over, remaining connected to the stump only by a strand. These fallen trees are aligned in the direction of the hedgerow, and the branches and trunk are woven through wooden stakes. Incredibly, the fallen trees do not die. The slender strand of cambium tissue connecting them to their roots is enough to sustain them, and allows the now-horizontal trees to resume growth. The damage at the base eventually mends, and thick impenetrable bushes form.

~~~

SINCE WE HAD STARTED OUR JOURNEY forty-five days earlier, we had travelled a respectable 1,400 kilometres, yet were only two-thirds of our way through Britain. Northamptonshire is not quite the geographical heart of England (that title belongs to neighbouring Warwickshire). Instead, because of its oblong shape and often overlooked status, it's been called the pancreas. Despite this rather unappealing description, it doesn't deserve to be bypassed. It's friendly and charming, and has an abundance of storybook towns with steeples, ringing church bells and homes from the Middle Ages.

The village of Althorp is one of those places. A 650-year-old free house, the Fox and Hounds, is its centrepiece, and we were drawn in by its thatched roof and immaculately maintained exterior. The interior had all the style of a quintessential British pub—expansive bar, wooden tables, ornate carpentry and historical pictures crowding the walls—and more, including relics from a different era: a massive stone fireplace and heavy wooden beams criss-crossing the plastered ceiling. We decided to forgo our six-day-old bagels and cheese for lunch, and instead we sat down at a thick wooden table next to the crackling blaze of hardwood and coal and ordered Northamptonshire beef sandwiches and a pint.

A middle-aged man, introducing himself as Harry, told us a little about the history of the village and the pub. According to him, Princess Diana came from here and her grandfather used to own this pub, which is now haunted with ghosts that like to "break glasses and the sort."

I asked him if he'd seen any. He had, and he regaled us with stories of shrouded shapes drifting past windows and eerie music emanating from nowhere. Harry was a tourist's dream, full of local lore, and we left the pub not only satiated but well informed.

Having accumulated another week's worth of grime and sweat, we decided it was again time to look for a hotel. This seemingly easy task was complicated by the fact that hotels in small villages usually lacked the Internet facilities we required, and we preferred to avoid the congested larger centres. We had learned to approximate a town's size by the pink smudges on our road atlas, and the nickel-sized aura surrounding the upcoming town of Brackley looked just right. The town was about 40 kilometres away, and we soon discovered that the hilly landscape and maze of country roads in between would require countless map breaks.

Perhaps not as well known as their penchant for discussing the weather is the passion the British have for giving road directions. Mention any destination in a pub and you'll learn there are as many ways of getting there as there are patrons. Our open road atlas and looks of confusion by the roadside attracted friendly locals like Scots to a bargain bin, but their advice wasn't always that helpful.

Colin and I stopped in heavy rain beside an unmarked crossroad and consulted our waterlogged atlas. An older man wearing a peaked cap and flanked by a border collie approached.

"Where are you going?" he asked.

"Brackley," I replied.

The man frowned thoughtfully before replying, "I'm afraid you've gone the wrong way."

Colin's jaw dropped. We'd just ascended a long, steep hill and this wasn't what we needed to hear.

"You needed to turn off eight kilometres back," the man continued. "It was the road with the gorse hedge on one side and rapeseed growing on the other. You then continue for three kilometres past Upper Weedon Farm and onto the south ramp for the A43."

"The A43?" I said. "You can't ride bikes on the A43."

"Hmm, I suppose you can't," the man said, eyeing our boats and bikes thoughtfully. "That's the way I normally go. Perhaps there might be another route."

"How about this road?" I said, pointing at the much more direct route in our atlas we'd planned on following.

"I don't know. I've never been on that one. Oh, but if you're going that way, you must visit Becksford Gardens," he said, pointing to a location about 60 kilometres from our track. "Why are you going to Brackley anyway? There's not much there. Northampton is the place to go."

We thanked him and continued on our way, quickly losing hope of reaching our destination by nightfall. At dusk, we resigned ourselves to another night camping and slipped through an open farm gate. We squeezed our bikes and boats onto muddy grass between a hedge and a field of bright yellow canola. The farmer's house sat at the far end of the field, but we were not in its line of sight. We'd long given up asking for permission to camp; invariably, we'd trek hundreds of metres to the wrong house and be told that the farmer lived two kilometres in the other direction. Instead, we just kept a low profile and hadn't yet been asked to move on.

Our position that night was a little more obvious, and I made Colin wait until it was completely dark to empty his bladder into the hedgerow. As the pot of pasta bubbled on the stove, I heard the deep grumble of a truck slowing and stopping.

I peered out and watched a middle-aged man in overalls and rubber boots walk towards us.

This was it. Our unbroken string of illegitimate camping was about to end. We'd be cast out into the cold, dark night, forced to repack our boats under the threatening gaze of an irate farmer. We hastily made up some compelling excuses, and I pushed Colin out the door to do the talking.

"Sorry to bother you," the farmer said, his voice surprisingly pleasant, "but I just thought I'd come by to say hello."

Maybe things wouldn't be so bad. Colin explained our intentions and apologized for our stealth-camping tactics.

The farmer laughed. "No need to apologize. You're not camping on the crops, and it does me no harm." He lowered his voice, looked left and right, and continued, "I'm only here bothering you on account of the Canadians."

"The Canadians?" Colin said.

"I just finished a long day's work and settled down to tea when the phone rang. It's roast beef tonight, my favourite, so I told my wife to let it ring. Then my mobile rang and I picked it up on the second try, thinking the barn must be ablaze. It was our Manitoban neighbours. Gypsies, they said. Gypsies were taking over my farm."

"So we're the gypsies?" Colin said.

"I suppose so. Just don't steal any livestock on your way out tomorrow."

I climbed out of the tent, joining Colin and the farmer.

"Usually it's the other way around," he said, still referring to his neighbours. "British farmers moving to Canada because of the cheaper land."

I nodded knowingly. With the price of food and hotels, I could only imagine what land here would cost. But beginning the year before, the price of food around the world had skyrocketed, and some crops, like grain, had doubled in price in a single year. I asked him about this potential windfall.

"It's not really a windfall," he said matter-of-factly. "Fertilizer and petrol are also more expensive, increasing my costs. But I'm not doing many food crops any more." He beckoned to the field of neon-yellow flowers next to our tent. "This is rapeseed—you call it canola in Canada—and it's all going into the fuel tanks of cars." He sighed. "And I'll tell you something, it costs more fuel to make than you'll get from it. The European Union doesn't understand this and they've structured things so we get paid more for growing air than food."

Five years earlier, the European Commission had decided that all gasoline and diesel fuel had to include 10 percent biofuel by 2020. In preparation for this law, Britain stipulated that automotive fuel had to contain 2.5 percent biofuel, a ratio that would be bumped up incrementally. The intentions were good. In theory, biofuels, which are created from materials such as corn, canola and other organic materials, create zero net greenhouse gas emissions. They take the same amount of carbon dioxide out of the atmosphere when they grow as they give off when they are burned. Lately, however, a barrage of reports has indicated that biofuels barely cut emissions, if at all. Nitrogen fertilizers, farm machinery, processing plants and other aspects of the industry emit the same amount of greenhouse gases as the process negates. In other words, if the biofuel industry was powered exclusively by its own product, it would likely have no yield.

The problem with this government-funded scheme was that fertile land and skilled labour around the world was diverted from the all-important task of creating food for humans. In a 2008 report, the World Bank found that biofuels were the main driver that saw food prices for staples such as rice, wheat and corn grow by 100 to 200 percent in two years, a price hike that devastated many developing countries. Instead of cutting greenhouse gas emissions, biofuel production created a global food crisis.

The farmer left us to finish our dinner, and I wondered if our meal could be considered a sort of biofuel. After all, we were consuming extra calories to propel our bikes forward, and we did seem to release a lot of exhaust fumes.

The next morning we reached Brackley, and I was happy to indulge in our well-earned break. We checked into the 750-year-old Crown Hotel and surrounded ourselves with great wooden beams and one-metre-thick stone walls constructed before Europeans knew North America existed. While I worked on website updates, Colin took the train to the British Waterways office in London to obtain our permit to voyage the Oxford Canal and Thames River.

We loaded a week's supply of groceries into the boats and pedalled the remaining 20 kilometres towards the Oxford Canal. We rolled through immaculate English countryside past the tiny hamlets of Hinton in the Hedges, Rowler, Newbottle and finally to Somerton, a collection of heritage stone buildings on the banks of the Oxford Canal.

Built in the late 1700s, the Oxford Canal was once one of the most profitable canals in England, transporting mostly coal, but it was soon superseded by a more direct canal, the Shropshire Union, and had thus never developed industrial communities along its banks. Unlike straighter canals, which cut through hills and use concrete walls to hold the water, the Oxford is more like a river following the land's contours and hemmed in by stone, grass and overhanging trees. It winds 130 kilometres from Hawkesbury Junction and joins with the Thames River at Oxford.

We crossed a one-lane arched stone bridge spanning the canal and coasted through a grassy pasture to the water's edge. The canal was placid, lined with willows, birch and brambles.

Across the water from us sat three berthed canal boats. These brightly painted steel live-aboard vessels were built on the lines of the original barges and, like the old stone buildings nearby, were a pleasure to regard.

Here, the waterway was relatively wide, but I could see it narrowing to about six metres just downstream of us. Under the stone bridge we had just crossed, the canal was only two metres wide—just wide enough to allow narrow-beam barges through. The banks were alive with colour as primroses, daisies and violets lavished in the late-April warmth.

As Colin and I packed our bikes into our boats beneath blue skies, I felt we were about to enter the pages of an old English storybook. This serene waterway might lead us to Toad Hall, or the back garden where Jemima Puddle-Duck lived. Or perhaps a gaff-rigged clinker-built dinghy under full sail might pass, with a crew from *Swallows and Amazons* nodding our way.

We slid the boats into the water, unshipped the oars and began gliding forward. The canal was just wide enough to accommodate the three-metre span of our oars, and the buildings of Somerton were soon replaced by bright yellow fields of canola and cattle-occupied pastures. The valley sloped up gently on both sides, displaying a checkerboard quilt of farmland.

Most of the time, we were alone on the canal, rowing through pastureland enclosed by stone fences and past stands of trees displaying delicate new leaves. The sky alternated between brilliant sunshine and black squalls. Frequent stone-arch bridges, their accompanying roads or tracks erased by time, offered temporary reprieves from the showers. It was peaceful and beautiful and I loved it, but the best was yet to come.

A thick wooden beam stretched across the canal ahead of us. We had reached our first lock. It was in the middle of a field. No road led to it and no buildings were nearby. There were no fancy hydraulic controls or cantankerous lockkeepers. These were self-operated manual systems.

We stepped out of our boats onto the stone landing, and I studied the system. While Colin readied the boats, I inserted our new crank handle, which Colin had purchased from British Waterways, and manually closed the lower sluice gate and opened the upstream side. Water gushed into the lock, filling it within minutes. I then pushed on a long wooden beam, which acted as a lever, to open the upstream gate. Colin guided the boats into the two-metre-wide lock. I closed the gate and opened the downstream sluice. Within minutes, our boats dropped 2.5 metres and we were again underway.

On our first day, we rowed 20 kilometres and passed through five locks, all of them self-operated. What was once a source of anguish was now a pleasant diversion. While we waited for the water levels to rise or lower, we relaxed on the benches, snacked on fruit or chocolate, and enjoyed the view. On average there was one lock for every three kilometres (forty-three locks in total on the Oxford Canal), and we looked forward to every one of them.

I could understand why the canal's function as an industrial highway was short-lived. It took up to two weeks for barges to make the return trip from the coal fields near Birmingham to London (a straight-line distance of about 150 kilometres). Even the more direct canals were slow, and they quickly fell into disuse with the advent of more efficient transportation. The nineteenth-century rise of the railway brought about the near death of the canals, and 7,000 kilometres of waterways fell into disrepair.

Since the 1970s, the canals have regained popularity for recreational use, and the British government has put vast resources into restoring and rebuilding them. The canal network is one of the jewels of Britain and is useful not just to boaters but also to sports fishermen and the millions who use the canal-side towpaths (built originally for horses to pull the barges) for cycling, hiking and jogging. In British cities, tour boats ply the canals offering visitors a water-based vista of the architecture and attractions.

Despite the popularity of British canals, we were travelling outside the tourist season, so traffic was almost nonexistent. After weeks of pedalling on the roads, I revelled in the meditative rhythm of rowing in almost complete silence past cows, trees and farms. In a few weeks, when the weather warmed, the canals would teem with vacationers sipping beers and chugging along in their rented boats at the limit of six kilometres an hour.

For others, inland nautical adventures are a regular pastime. Once a boat is purchased, it is a relatively cheap way to explore the nuances of Britain. An annual waterway permit for a twelve-metre canal boat is just over £600 ($1,200), which is quite reasonable, considering it allows unlimited use of the canals and locks as well as free mooring (usually up to fourteen days in one spot). From the comfort of your live-aboard boat, it is possible to visit the centre of London or the wild countryside of Wales. Like most things in Britain, the boats are pricey, but at least they hold their resale value.

Just before setting up camp in a meadow of nettles, we stopped at a red and blue canal boat named *Pan* that had been advertised at the last few locks as England's only floating farm shop. It was moored in front of a small farm and inside was an astonishingly large array of fruits, vegetables, homemade ice creams, wine, beer, jams and preserves. We mulled about indecisively, oohing and aahing at foods infinitely fresher than the stale bagels and bruised apples rolling in the bilges of our boats, before narrowing down our choice to homemade ice cream, bread and cookies. We dropped money into the self-checkout device (a tin can) and ate our ice cream at a picnic table on the shore.

If Gulf Islands hippies moved to Britain, this is where they'd want to be. An assortment of mismatched chairs accompanied rustic picnic tables, plastic flowers dotted the grass, and a cow wandered freely. The proprietor, a bubbly woman in her mid-fifties, poured us tea and lavished attention on the bovine, who, she proudly informed us, was the sole source of milk for all the dairy products on her boat.

For three days, we rowed on what may very well have been the most enchanting canal in England. Ivy-covered trees reached across the water, ducks fluttered out of our path, and male swans puffed out their feathers, belligerently guarding their nests. Even as we approached the city of Oxford, where houses and walking paths replaced farmland, the canal retained its charm.

Near the heart of Oxford, we slipped through a large lock and rowed onto the Thames River. The Thames was wider, with a strong current. One side of the river was lined with uninspiring row houses and the other with parkland and garden allotments. We passed under the busy Osney Bridge, an ornate cast-iron structure built in 1889, and arrived at the metal gate of an ultra-modern lock. The hydraulic controls were too cryptic for us to decipher, and we decided to turn back. Besides, we wanted to spend a night in Oxford, and the park we had just passed looked like too good a camping spot to pass up.

Some old friends, a Canadian couple living in the nearby town of Banbury, were coming to meet us in Oxford, and we arranged to convene at the canal-side pub just near the locks. We moored our boats below the old stone building and celebrated reaching the Thames River with a good dinner and a tasty English brew.

As the sun dipped near the horizon, we rowed back to the park. Our fears that camping in a city of 150,000 might be difficult were quickly allayed. We slipped under a chain that blocked an offshoot of the Thames and pushed against overgrown trees and weeds constricting the narrow channel. The trees parted, and we rowed into what looked like a grand swimming pool fallen into disrepair. The sides were concrete, and a partial staircase descended into the clear water. Beside it lay a meadow dominated by a sprawling chestnut tree.

In the morning, we awoke to the *tap tap* of flowers dropping onto our tent from the majestic tree above us. Sunshine streamed through the blue nylon. It was such a perfect camping spot that we decided to spend the day exploring Oxford and return to this same location for another night.

Despite Oxford's reputation as home to one of the world's leading scholastic institutions, it doesn't project the stuffy conservative atmosphere one might expect. It has the pulse of university towns worldwide. Students can be seen everywhere—riding bicycles, studying in coffee shops and walking on cobbled paths—and the streets are lined with centuries-old buildings adorned with crests, pillars and spires.

Oxford is the oldest university in the English-speaking world. When it first opened its doors in the early twelfth century, life in the ivory tower was not as peaceful and studious as it is now. As has been the case throughout history, students are often willing to risk their lives and work selflessly together to overcome social injustices. In 1355, a number of Oxford students disputed the quality of the beer at the local tavern. These insults escalated into armed riots between the townsfolk and students, with sixty-three scholars and about thirty locals killed. This tussle, known as the St. Scholastica's Day riots, fostered distrust between students and townsfolk for many years to follow. Judging by the popularity of Oxford pubs now, I assumed beer quality had improved over the past 650 years.

After exploring the college campuses, we visited the Pitt Rivers Museum. Tucked at the back of the Oxford University Museum of Natural History, it is a collection of often macabre objects collected during the early voyages of discovery. The room is dim and overflowing. Ancient wooden boats hang from the ceiling, and glass cabinets are filled with shrunken heads and voodoo dolls. There are mummies, ritual masks, ivory sculptures and even a totem pole from Canada. According to the museum, there are over half a million archaeological and ethnographic treasures, souvenirs collected during explorations like Captain Cook's second voyage to the South Pacific. Unlike those explorers, we didn't have the cargo capacity to be souvenir collectors, and when we began our journey down the Thames the following morning, our only extra baggage was groceries.

We carried enough food for the upcoming week, which weighed about 36 kilograms and included mostly dried goods along with a few cartons of UHT milk for breakfast. We had pondered adding more fresh fruits and vegetables to our diet, which would increase the weight of our baggage, and last week had posed that question to the students following the expedition. They voted 75 percent in favour of continuing to travel light and we abided by their decision. The question was intended to highlight nutritional requirements during elevated physical exertion and the limitations on resupplying due to carrying capacity, availability, etcetera, but it also had an inadvertent implication. It seemed people now thought we were constipated and one class wrote to suggest we "invest in some psyllium fibre cereal."

The Thames is the longest river entirely in England (the Severn is the largest in the U.K.) and is by far Britain's historically most significant waterway. It is used for transportation, provides fish and drinking water, dilutes sewage and

industrial waste and is becoming a popular recreational destination. Beginning in the Cotswold Hills, it flows 346 kilometres
to the North Sea, which was where we were going.

It was mid-morning when Colin and I reached the lock
below the Osney Bridge. A lockkeeper was now on duty, and
he watched us approach from his glass-fronted office. Potted
mint plants lined his door, advertised at £3 each. As the lean
middle-aged keeper approached us, I thought longingly of the
quaint self-operated locks along the Oxford.

"You want to go through?" he asked.

"Yes, please," Colin said tersely.

"All right, then," the lockkeeper said as he flipped a switch,
"Lovely weather today, isn't it?"

"Thank you so much," I gushed. "This is fantastic."

"Not at all," the lockkeeper said with a smile.

"Will we be able to go through all the locks downstream?"
Colin asked.

"Of course. How else would you get past them?"

"In Scotland they made us portage the locks."

The lockkeeper laughed. "My wife and I canoed the
Caledonian Canal, and the buggers wouldn't let us through
either. I tried bribing them with a bottle of whisky and still no
luck. I don't think those boys get enough sunshine."

We paddled our boats into the lock compound and waited
for the water to drop. The lockkeeper appeared at the lip and
handed down a series of pamphlets.

"I'm guessing you're probably camping. Here's a list of the
camping sites along the river and a map indicating the locks."

"I can't believe how friendly he is," Colin whispered to me.
"I've been dreading this voyage down the Thames because I
thought the lockkeepers would all be the same."

The giant steel gates opened, and we bade goodbye to our
lockkeeper and let the current carry us downstream.

In the Oxford suburbs, dozens of thin sculls darted across the water, whistles blew and megaphones filled the air with the sounds of early-morning rowing practice. It was the Oxford rowing team. We slunk along the river's side, keeping out of their way, until a coach hailed us from his platform on a motorized catamaran and invited us to join them for coffee. We stopped at their riverfront clubhouse and spent half an hour relaxing and chatting about rowing.

A few hundred metres downstream, we received another invitation from a different team. Sensing a developing trend that might keep us on the Thames until William was crowned king, we demurred and pressed forward.

The Thames River is much wider than the Oxford, but is still canal-like in nature. To make it navigable for larger boats, the current has been slowed and the depth raised through the use of dikes, weirs and locks. Unlike the locks on the Oxford, these were large and infrequent and staffed by unusually pleasant lockkeepers.

The chasm of dissimilarity in lockkeepers' attitudes puzzled us, and we whiled away a few hours discussing theories as to why the Scottish ones were so ornery.

"This is how it goes," Colin said, embarking on his daily calisthenics for the imagination. "The dying steel industry in Glasgow lays off most of its workers. The enterprising individuals retrain and find employment elsewhere. The layabouts collect the dole, drink profusely, get into fights and then stagger into the British Waterways office thinking it's the loo. They ask the hiring officer for some crack. He's Irish and thinks they said how's the crack, and next thing they're hired."

"No, you're giving them too much credit in thinking they would actually use a washroom," I said. "My theory is that they used to be pleasant, nature-loving lockkeepers with degrees in tourism and human relations. Their remote postings made them vulnerable to thugs who knocked them off, moved into their homes and assumed their identity."

The true answer, we discovered, was much simpler. The Thames River was run by the Thames Environment Agency, not British Waterways. The two organizations clearly had very different hiring policies as far as human relations, work ethics and manners were concerned. The British Waterways lock-keeper we had encountered near York was just as unpleasant as his Scottish counterparts, indicating these bitter attitudes weren't restricted to Scotland. Like that of U.S. customs and immigration agents, their unpleasant demeanour is not representative of the citizens of Scotland or England, who are perhaps two of the world's most polite populations.

The upper Thames was not at all industrial. Every bend revealed lavish country estates, villages dating back to Roman times, ornate cathedrals and the occasional castle. But as we approached London, the countryside became increasingly populated, making camping a challenge. Twice, we were forced to camp right beside a towpath busy with dog walkers and romantic couples. Once, we reached an organized campground, complete with washrooms and showers, on an island beside a lock; the rain poured down and we had the entire isle to ourselves. On another night, we camped discreetly in a park across the river from Windsor Castle, where our postcard-perfect view of the Queen's private residence inspired Colin to spend the evening imitating Her Majesty fussing over her corgis.

We paused at the River and Rowing Museum in the city of Henley-on-Thames, where we perused historic rowing shells and watched a video of rower Guin Batten dashing across the English Channel in three hours and fourteen minutes. Later, we rowed alongside boys from Eton College, the expensive school for boys that mass produces members of the British establishment, including eighteen prime ministers so far.

On the outskirts of London, in a commuter town called Sunbury-on-Thames, we pulled into a marina and dragged our boats into the secure dry-dock compound, which the affable owners let us use for free. We packed our essentials and took the train and subway into London, where we made a presentation to an inner-city school and spent a few nights with Colin's brother George. Compared to the water travel we were used to, the trip was surprisingly quick.

We had stayed with George and his wife, Randi, two months earlier while we prepared for our expedition, and we were excited to see them and their girls, Raine and Alexandra, again.

After a few blissful days of eating home-cooked meals, sleeping in a bed and indulging in comforts not possible when your world is packed into a rowboat, we returned to our boats refreshed. And we needed to be fresh, because we expected to encounter more challenging conditions after passing Teddington Lock (12 kilometres from where we left the boats), the final barrier to the tidal section of the Thames.

We knew this next section of the river would be made much more difficult by strong winds and currents, heavy commercial traffic and steep, erratic waves reflected off the sheer concrete and steel walls along the river's edge. The depth fluctuation is staggering, with a tidal range of 7.1 metres at London Bridge. As the tide drops, the massive exodus of water creates ripping currents that can be dangerous if there is an opposing wind. The gentle riverbanks we were used to would be replaced with six-metre wave-buffeted walls, preventing us from stopping on a whim or in an emergency. It would be critical to observe and plan for the changing water levels.

In *The Unlikely Voyage of Jack de Crow*, which we were eagerly reading in the tent every night, A. J. Mackinnon refers to the tide as a "kelp-handed robber" because it capsized his tethered boat (when the tide dropped and left it dangling in the air) and stole its contents not once but twice. He replaced his gear and spent a week fixing his boat, something we hoped to avoid.

Besides the tide, we had traffic to worry about. Roughly 7.5 million people lived in Greater London, more than the population of my home province, British Columbia, and its neighbour Alberta combined. Furthermore, the Thames River was the primary supply hub for not only London but much of Britain. Deep-sea freighters, oil tankers, river transport vessels, ferries, deep-hulled police boats, dredgers and pleasure boats (although relatively few for obvious reasons) plied these waters.

Our journey down the lower Thames began pleasantly with an unseasonable heat wave creating the feeling of a summer vacation. We reached the giant Teddington Lock and joined a handful of canal boats and pleasure craft also waiting to go through. The enormous weir lay on the left side of the river, cordoned off with protective buoys and rope to prevent incompetent boaters from slipping through and tumbling down a seething wall of water or through electric turbines. This weir is the largest on the Thames, with twenty electric turbines extracting energy from up to 54.5 billion litres of water a day.

We stayed far right and tied our boats to the retaining wall next to the barge lock. There was not one but three locks here. The largest was designed for multiple barges and was 7.5 metres wide and 198 metres long, about the same length as three hockey rinks placed end to end. Now picture filling that with enough water to raise a boat 2.1 metres. That is 8 million litres of water, enough to fill two and a half Olympic swimming pools or 160,000 baths.

The lock was in the midst of being filled when we arrived. A flotilla of boats travelling upstream crowded between the gates and slowly rose to our level. On the other side, dozens still waited their turn. We, on the other hand, were two of only five boats voyaging downstream, and there was little doubt that we would soon be on our way.

Once the lock emptied of traffic and the signal light changed from red to green, we rowed inside. The whole procedure of loading the boats, closing the gate and emptying the lock on the downstream side took about an hour. We emerged on the tidal side of the Thames and rowed past the long queue of boats waiting their turn to go the other direction.

On the downstream side, things didn't look much different at first. Fine homes and parkland lined the shore with boats moored in front of houses and clustered on small wharfs. We were, as we had been for the last 15 kilometres, still in the suburbs. Even though we had just entered Greater London, the city centre was still 17 kilometres away. I was amazed at the city's vastness, and would later learn that Greater London covers an area of 1,579 square kilometres. There are countries that are smaller, dozens of them.

We stopped at a park crowded with people enjoying the sunshine and sat in the grass eating ice cream cones. By the time we were ready to go, the water level had risen substantially, and our boats, which we had pulled onto the grass next to a bench, were already afloat. It seemed a little strange that park benches would be erected below the high-tide mark, but who were we to question those avant-garde Londoners.

As we continued downriver, the water level kept rising, and the path paralleling the river was soon submerged. Trapped pedestrians stood uncertainly on the high ground while others rolled up their pants, removed their shoes and soldiered on, some carrying small dogs and children. Colin rowed above the path behind two cyclists thrashing through axle-deep water.

It all seemed a little perplexing. Beneath a blazing sky, the water kept rising, creating a water world along the river's edge.

Old ladies were trapped on benches, locked bikes were inaccessible to their owners, and parks became lakes.

"Oh, my god, is that a car?" Colin said, pointing ahead.

We rowed up to a submerged brand-new Mercedes-Benz. The water was above the windows, and the leather upholstery was awash.

"Wow. I guess drivers might want to consult with the tide tables before parking in this neighbourhood," I said. "Bummer."

It wasn't all bad. It was now mid-afternoon, and the temperature was close to 30 Celsius. We gratefully rowed up to an ice cream van, its wheels deep in water. Colin took photos while I stood in my cockpit and completed the transaction without leaving my boat. I felt as if I was passing a disaster zone, front-page kind of material, yet everyone seemed to be treating the flood more like a trip to the amusement park than a calamity. The festive atmosphere was fetching.

We weren't sure where we would camp that night. On our map, there was a waterfront patch of green called Wandsworth Park, which looked like it might have potential, but as the afternoon light waned and the park remained a considerable distance away, we began to reassess our options. Besides, it was probably a well-manicured and heavily guarded place where we'd be evicted before we'd put up the first tent pole.

We investigated a mid-river island, but decided against it; its reedy composition and low elevation suggested it would be submerged at high tide.

"What about a pontoon?" Colin said, pointing to one of the wooden docks connected to the shore. "We could pull our boats onto one and pitch our tent."

"You've got to be kidding," I said. "We're in the middle of Hammersmith. If the police don't bother us, I'm sure the drunks will."

"Do you have any better ideas?"

I had to admit that I didn't, and although I had concerns about sleeping in the midst of a pub district, I could imagine things going further downhill when the sun set and we found ourselves on the river without navigation lights and no clue of our destination.

We pulled up to a derelict steel pontoon 50 metres from Hammersmith Bridge. It was about the size of an average sundeck, with a steeply angled ramp leading to the street above. We hopped over the locked gate and explored our surroundings—several thriving pubs, a rowing club and some row houses. We climbed onto the ornate Hammersmith Bridge and observed the panorama below.

"Wow," Colin said. "I never thought I'd be camping within spitting distance of Hammersmith Bridge."

"You can't spit that far," I said.

Colin couldn't resist the challenge, but his efforts fell short.

"Okay, a stone's throw from Hammersmith Bridge," he said.

"You throw like a girl. It must be someone else doing the throwing."

Colin put his arm around me and we savoured the moment. Thousands of lights sparkled on both sides, while the river was a black abyss. Occasional red and green lights marked the presence of passing boats.

We erected our tent in a nonchalant manner, trying to exude the confidence of those who have every right to be here. We waved affably to curious passersby who stopped to stare and went about our usual camping chores feeling like tigers in a zoo. When we slipped into our sleeping bags, I kept all my clothes on, just in case we were woken up by the police or, equally probably, by college kids looking for an after-hours place to drink. Surprisingly, it was a peaceful night, and we awoke to the rumble of London coming alive and sun streaming into our tent.

Rowing through the centre of London is a fabulous experience and should be on everyone's list of 100 Things to Do Before You Die. First of all, there is a pleasing number of old and ornate bridges to slip underneath. There is, of course, London Bridge. It is not particularly inspiring apart from the fact that it is immortalized in the nursery rhyme "London Bridge Is Falling Down," which we gladly sang, loudly and out of tune, as we drifted underneath, while secretly praying it wouldn't. But, really, Tower Bridge is the belle of the ball and well worth serenading. With its twin ornate towers, folding bridge and baby-blue ribbons of steel, it is one of the most enchanting bridges in the world.

Then there's Westminster Hall with its Big Ben Clock Tower and Canary Wharf with its Tower, too—the U.K.'s tallest and put there by Canadians, the three Reichmann brothers. There's the Millennium Ferris Wheel. There's the forty-storey glass Easter egg boringly named 30 St. Mary Axe but more commonly called the Gherkin.

The excitement of passing these and umpteen other famous landmarks in our rowboats caused Colin and me to morph into typical tour-boat tourists, happily snapping photographs, and oohing and aahing at the sights with unabashed abandon. The only problem was we were also the captains of our boats, and navigating the river was becoming increasingly treacherous. High-speed ferries, tour boats, laden barges and police launches abounded, and it was important to remain focused.

Downstream of London, things became increasingly industrial, and it wasn't long before we reached the massive Thames Barrier, a technological marvel that has often been dubbed the eighth wonder of the world. The Thames Barrier is the world's second largest movable flood barrier, after the Maeslantkering in the Netherlands, but it looks more like a futuristic sculpture than a barricade. A row of gleaming metallic piers rise out of the water like giant shark's fins, and divide the 625-metre span of river into six navigable and four non-navigable channels. Hidden underwater lie ten steel gates the height of a five-storey building that can be drawn up to keep out tidal surges.

In 1983, when the Queen opened the barrier, she proclaimed that "London has now been made free of flooding," and while that has been true for over twenty years, climate change has made the future less certain. Initially, barrier closures were predicted every two to three years, but in the last decade, closures have averaged five to six times a year, and the Environment Agency estimates that by 2015 rising water levels and heightened tidal surges will force closures at every high tide, and even then, some tides will surge over it. With 1.25 million people living in a flood-risk zone, not to mention $160 billion worth of property, 26 underground stations, 400 schools, 16 power stations and an airport, this is a major concern.

The gate nearest to the shore was closed, but the other channels were open and we slipped through the adjacent passage. Unseasonably hot weather inland created strong convection winds, which when combined with the 1.5-metre standing waves that formed where the current funnelled between the barriers, made for a rough passage. The Thames was now a different world from the quaint, gentle landscapes we had discovered upstream. Here it was almost a kilometre wide, with windswept waters. The shore was lined with factories, loading docks, cranes and ships. Locating a spot to pull ashore in this industrial world was next to impossible—never mind finding a camping spot. The river was lined with perpetual 9- to 12-metre concrete walls.

We found a long, steep boat ramp entering the river and were able to escape the windswept, choppy waters. We set up camp at the top of the ramp, our tent squeezed between seaweed washed up by the high tide and a gate that protected us from Carlsberg-drinking hooligans hanging out on the Thames Path on the other side.

It was a night of discomfort (sleeping on a slope is rarely pleasant) and interruption. Around midnight, I was awoken by loud drunken voices making disconcerting wisecracks about our tent. The voices were deep and masculine. I clutched the metal pole from our trailer and elbowed Colin awake. We lay silently as their conversation drifted to less troubling topics. Then the high-pitched giggles of two girls joined the exchange, and the quartet moved on to more pressing matters, presumably involving park benches and the exchange of copious quantities of saliva.

The sounds of the rising tide became our next concern. Water gurgled between the wooden rafters beneath us, and passing freighters threw up a wake that sloshed disturbingly close. Another half a metre and we would be awash, but since we had dragged the tent right against the gate, we had few options. I lay awake, exhausted and ill tempered, waiting for water to infiltrate our home, which it fortunately never did.

Usually we wouldn't get up before dawn, but it was crucial for us to be underway to make use of the outgoing tide. At four o'clock we broke camp and readied for departure. We cruised easily at 12 kilometres an hour and, by the time the tide turned, had made it under the Queen Elizabeth II Bridge, the final bridge spanning the Thames. At 812 metres, it was once Europe's largest cable-supported bridge. Here, the clear blue water from the North Sea swirled with the silt-laden water from the Thames.

By mid-morning, the tide reversed and our speed steadily decreased. A strong convection wind continued to hamper our progress. The river was several kilometres across now, but it seemed much larger as the surrounding lowlands and marshes provided an indistinct shoreline. Large waves rolling in from the open sea conspired with the winds and currents, and it wasn't long before we were rowing on the spot. A navigational buoy that we had passed ten minutes earlier drifted in reverse by my starboard side. It was time to get off the river before we lost any more ground.

The low tide exposed a 200-metre expanse of mud and sand that separated us from the shore. It would be impossible to drag our boats over this, so Colin tied our vessels with a long rope to a rusting iron rod protruding from the mud. We squelched through the sucking ooze to shore and settled on a grassy dike that prevented the adjacent pastureland from being inundated.

It wasn't a bad spot to while away the late morning. We lay on the warm grass, eating, sleeping and amusing ourselves with grass whistles and rock-tossing contests. We were only 30 kilometres from Britain's largest city, but couldn't see a single house or road across the flats. Nearby were the concrete ruins of what looked like an abandoned military base, but apart from that, it was just roadless pastureland, criss-crossed with drainage ditches. A herd of shaggy horses wandered among the ruins plucking at grass in the shade.

The water eventually lapped against the dike, and we prepared for our departure as high tide approached. Three hundred metres of swirling brown water separated us from our boats, now floating high above the mud. We had prepared for this and donned our bright red dry suits. Protected from the frigid waters, we swam out to the boats, untied them and continued deeper into the delta. With the tide once again dropping, the current was in our favour, but the headwinds continued to buffet us, and we crashed through large standing waves.

I watched uneasily as the water receded from the shore. We had had trouble wading through the mud during our last stop, and it was likely to get worse as we travelled farther out into the delta. Our destination for the day was a recreational community, and I hoped that they had a dredged channel leading to a beach or marina. It was now six o'clock, and we were making very slow progress into enormous 1.5-metre waves. A beach appeared, fronted by a firm-looking sandbar.

"What do you think?" Colin said. "We could camp there for the night. The tide hasn't gone out too far, so we could probably drag the boats through the mud onto the beach."

"What about water?" I said. "We still need to get drinking water, and there's nothing around here. I think the wind is lessening anyway. Let's keep on and see if we can make it to that village."

Not one to be out-adventured by a girl, Colin agreed, and we kept on rowing. It was still ten kilometres to the community of Allhallows-on-Sea, and I prayed the thin channel marked on our map was passable at low tide. It had been a long, hard day, and with almost no sleep the previous night, I looked forward to leaving our boats in the marina and finding a quiet camping spot.

It was almost nine o'clock when we reached Allhallows-on-Sea, and light was fading quickly. It was hard to discern the details, as almost a kilometre of mud separated us from the community, but it wasn't the quaint seaside town we had expected. First of all, it wasn't situated on the sea, but in a location better positioned for the world mud-wrestling championships, the centre of a massive delta. It could not be called a town by even the most gracious of standards. It was a sprawling trailer park, a caravan holiday resort that had about as much appeal as a swamp in Louisiana. Okay, maybe it was waterfront, but you couldn't get to the water on account of the concrete retaining wall and the expanse of sludge. And the view was equally abysmal: grey, depressing and lifeless.

I couldn't imagine why anyone would willingly choose to come here. Yet they did. And there was more. In the 1930s, it was believed that Allhallows-on-Sea would become the best holiday resort in Europe. They planned to spend millions of pounds to build the largest swimming pool in the United Kingdom, the first artificial wave generator in Europe, an amusement park of epic proportions, not to mention restaurants, cinemas, hotels and all the other hullabaloo that goes into those sorts of things. They managed a railway line and a few pubs, but for some reason, the expected hordes of tourists didn't materialize. Since then, the most promising concept was drawn up in 2004, when plans to build a new airport in nearby Cliffe include paving over the village and turning it into a parking lot.

Despite its lack of appeal as a vacation destination, for Colin and me it represented a sanctuary from the miserable conditions we faced on the water. The water was gushing out to sea, and the dangerous wind-over-waves condition was creating a steep, powerful swell surging over our boats. Where was that channel leading in? We scanned the darkening flats for the passage marked so clearly on our map.

"I don't see anything," Colin said.

I pulled the map out of the dry bag and rechecked its coordinates. "It should be right here," I said, pointing across the mud flats to a dark stretch of shore just beyond the massive trailer park.

We were slipping past the edge of the mud flats as though on a conveyor belt, but there was no opening that would allow us to escape the turbulent water. Instead, the mud flats increased in size, and we were now almost 1,500 metres from shore.

"Look at those buoys," Colin said, pointing to a handful of yellow markers stretching to shore. "I bet they're marking a dredged channel through the mud."

Relief washed over me. "Thank god," I murmured. "It probably leads to the river and maybe a marina for the trailer park."

We rowed towards the markers, following rivulets of deeper water, searching for the channel we pinned our hopes on. But before long we realized there was no passage through the mud. The markers were sitting on exposed shore, and soon so would we. I wanted to cry.

Bump, bump, kerthump. My boat grounded in the receding waters, and I struggled with the oars to free myself. Colin was also stuck 20 metres farther out. We pushed ourselves off and tried to head farther out, but succeeded only in hitting more mud bars. For twenty minutes, we frantically rowed in all directions, bumping and thrashing, and pushing our boats.

"I'm stuck," I said after my prodigious attempts to push free failed.

"Me too," said Colin.

Like a tub with the plug pulled, the water drained away and we were left high and dry. Glistening mud stretched all around as far as we could see in the dusky light. We stepped out of our boats. Mud sucked at my bare feet and I sank to mid-calf. I leaned heavily on my boat to avoid going in even deeper. Suddenly, I felt panicked. The mud was impassable. Any attempt to walk through this would be suicide. We were now separated from shore by well over a kilometre and it was almost completely dark. Colin's boat was at a right angle to mine about 1.5 metres away.

"Hmm, we seem to be at an impasse," Colin said.

It was quiet and calm in the absence of crashing waves. I was happy to be off the dark, treacherous waters, but the stillness of our present situation felt even more ominous.

"I guess we'll just have to sit in the boats and wait for the tide to come back in," I said.

"That won't be too long," Colin said. "It's almost the

bottom of the tide now. Maybe two or three hours."

I played through the scenario in my mind. At about midnight, the water would wash back over the mud. We would once again be afloat in the big waves we could hear thundering in the distance. We would then have to wait another three or four hours before the tide rose enough to reach the shore. In the pitch black, we would attempt to land our boats against the wave-washed, boulder-strewn dike.

All I wanted to do was stretch out and sleep, and I wished I was anywhere in the world other than here.

Britain's large river deltas are notorious for dangerous sinking mud. We had heard numerous stories of people succumbing to the muck—usually becoming completely immobilized, hypothermic, then finished off by the incoming tide. Many fire squadrons near river deltas have special mud-rescue units with appropriate equipment and training. Hovercraft and helicopters are best suited for reaching victims. Special mats are used for walking on the mud, and air pumps are used to break the suction seal around the victim.

"How's this for another option?" I said. "When it was light, I saw a marker buoy about fifty metres towards shore. When the tide comes in, we could drag the boats to it, tie them on and then try crawling or walking through the mud in our dry suits. If we get stuck, we can wait for the tide to wash us free."

I was banking on the fact that the dry suits would prevent us from getting hypothermia, the greatest danger when trapped in mud. We could pack our tent and sleeping bags in dry bags and carry them to shore. I revelled at the prospect of actually stretching out on solid ground and having my first solid sleep in two days.

Trying to make the best of our situation, I fired up the stove, balancing it on the hatch of my boat, and heated up a can of stew. It helped bring normalcy to our situation, and we needed nourishment. We rummaged through the hatches looking for our sleeping bags, tent, breakfast and toiletries, and stuffed them all into two dry bags. We readied the rope, tied our boats together, crawled into our dry suits and waited in our cockpits.

"We're moving," I yelled, jolted awake by the subtle sensation of water rocking my boat.

As the water continued to rise, we made our way to the barely discernible yellow marker buoy and tied *Tantalum* to it. My boat was attached to Colin's stern and would stream nine metres behind so they wouldn't collide in the wavy conditions.

"This buoy clearly doesn't mark a passage," I said. "I wonder what's it's here for."

I shone my headlamp down and noticed the bold letters, "DO NOT ENTER — MILITARY FIRING ZONE." I chastised myself for being so obtuse as to think these marked the safety of a navigable channel. Now we had no choice but to cross over and camp on a shore that was regularly blasted by machine guns, grenades, bombs and other weapons. I was exceedingly unhappy, and my prospects for a peaceful, uninterrupted sleep were rapidly fading.

"Well, at least they're not firing now," Colin said with surprisingly little consternation. "Besides, they probably won't start shooting until the morning and we'll be gone bright and early."

"Isn't nighttime warfare a big part of their training?" I countered.

"I suppose," Colin said. "But it's like deer hunting. They don't just shoot randomly in all directions—they have targets."

"And what if we're behind the targets?"

"Well, I guess we could call it the perfect ending to a very bad day," Colin said flatly.

We each took a dry bag and began crawling and swimming to shore. The shallow pools of water we encountered were much easier to negotiate, and we could easily kick ourselves forward. The mud, on the other hand, was frightening, exhausting and almost impossible to move through. Colin, with his greater weight, seemed to have more difficulty, and twice he had to wait for the rising waters to free himself as his buoyant dry suit pulled him upwards.

While Colin was incapacitated and waiting for rising waters, I discovered I could make reasonable progress by sprinting to the point of exhaustion, then quickly sitting down before I sank too deeply.

"Wait there!" I shouted. I continued my sprint/sit technique until I reached the glorious shore. I dropped off my dry bag and returned to Colin. I carried his dry bag, which equalized our weight, and together we eventually reached shore. We had done it. It was almost twenty-four hours since we had departed the previous morning, and I was exhausted. We erected the tent in the grass and within minutes were asleep. Bombs or not, I was too tired to care.

~~~

"LOOK, THERE'RE COWS OUT THERE!" Colin said, waking me up at seven.

Sunshine flooded our tent, and I was feeling exceptionally grumpy. "Who cares about cows?"

"Think about it. They're not going to put cows where the bombs are dropping. We can go back to sleep," Colin said.

A cow mooed, as if in agreement, and a car rumbled in the distance.

"Someone's herding the cows away in a Land Rover," Colin said, head still poking through the flap.

"So much for that theory," I said. "Let's get up and go."

Colin made breakfast and we discussed our plans for the day. Just as we were finishing our coffee, the Land Rover roared up to us.

"What are you doing here?" a uniformed man asked.

We explained our predicament, pointing to our pathetic mud-covered boats in the distance.

"Just be sure you leave soon. We're starting practice shortly," he said a little more sympathetically, then drove off.

The boats, which had also survived the night, were just beginning to float on the incoming tide. We planned to swim out to them when the tide was a bit higher, hoping to avoid the mud as much as possible. As we splashed through ankle-deep water towards the boats, I noticed mine was listing slightly. I discovered it wasn't holed, as I initially feared, but one of the oars had caught underneath it at an unfortunate angle and was under extreme pressure. We freed the mud-bound oar, which, thankfully, was undamaged, but the oarlock pin was bent at a 20-degree angle.

The rig was still functional, and we immediately began rowing hard towards deeper waters. Within minutes, the retort of numerous firearms sounded. I was relieved when we finally passed between the buoys marking the danger zone.

It was another difficult day. The waves were even larger, and I was overheating in my dry suit, which I couldn't remove because the zipper was stuck. As sweat dribbled down my face, we entered a smaller body of water between the Isle of Sheppey and the mainland. It was an industrial area, and we passed the port of Sheerness, the largest town on the island. The channel further narrowed as we followed the contours of the island. Headwinds gusted at close to 25 knots, and I was thankful for the shelter provided by the island.

Just as we reached the Sheppey Crossing, a four-lane bridge connecting the swampy island with the mainland, my damaged oarlock pin snapped. My boat drifted out of control, and the three-knot current washed me towards one of the bridge supports. Colin quickly tossed me a line and towed me to the shore.

This was also an opportune time to escape my plastic prison, but despite my best efforts, I couldn't budge the zipper. Colin offered help and instructed me to lie on the ground while he sat on top of me. He braced his feet and pulled on the zipper while I yanked on the suit. We were grunting and groaning, making no progress, when a deep voice interrupted us.

"Are you all right?"

I looked up to see the Kent fire-department rescue boat edging onto the boat ramp and a very concerned face peering over the side.

"You looked as if you might be in trouble," he continued.

"Ah, well," I stammered, deeply embarrassed. "I can't seem to get my dry suit off."

This was obviously just the type of emergency the fire department was equipped to deal with, and a crew of fit young men gathered around to offer assistance. While I lay on the ground, Colin grabbed the zipper, a firefighter grabbed my suit, and after an inordinate amount of effort, I was freed.

"What you need is lubricant," another firefighter explained. "Let me see if we've got some." He disappeared inside the boat and returned with a small tube of dry-suit zipper wax.

I didn't even know zipper wax existed, let alone that I should be using it regularly. I thanked them again, and they obliged my request for a photo op with their entire squad. Colin was almost crying with laughter, but I couldn't pass up the opportunity to take a photo I could flaunt to my girlfriends. After all, how often does a girl get rescued by a team of firefighters?

For a day that started with dodging bullets, things were looking a little more optimistic. We slipped down a side slough and, just before the ebbing tide stranded us once again, reached the small village of Conyer, an unexpectedly winsome place. It was an oasis from the swamps, industry and big ships we had endured for three days now. River barges, lovingly converted into live-aboards, sat against the shore, and sailboats were moored in a tidy marina. White houses with verdant gardens overlooked the water. A vivacious woman leaned out her boat and introduced herself as Trish. She took us to meet the owners of the small boatyard, and we were immediately invited to camp on their pleasantly landscaped property. We were free to use the boatyard showers and were welcome to join them for coffee in the morning.

From Conyer, we decided to pedal the remaining 60 kilometres to Dover, rather than rowing the longer coastal route. We travelled through rolling countryside past homes made from shiny flint, the predominant rock found in this area (apart from chalk). Lush orchards of apples, pears and cherries thrived in the warmer climate of England's south. As we pedalled along narrow one-lane roads past forests, gardens and orchards, I felt as if I was following an endless driveway running through a manicured estate. It was lovely, except for the spectacular hills. We had cars pull over and warn us about upcoming rises.

We stopped before another ascent, and I set my bike down to grab a bag of Maynards wine gums from my boat.

"Are you feeling all right?" Colin asked.

What Colin really meant is: Why are you going so slow? I hate it when Colin asks me this, especially as I was actually feeling good, enjoying the scenery and pleased with our progress despite the hills. Colin's comment suddenly changed all of this.

"I'm fine," I said.

"Just let me know if you want me to take some of your bags."

"No, thanks," I said coldly, resenting his insinuation that I couldn't carry my own share.

As we carried on up the hill, I purposely pedalled more slowly—I'd show him what slow was all about—while Colin sped up with equally misguided resolve. He rushed ahead, waited for me at the top of the hill, then rocketed off again when I caught up. We spent the rest of the afternoon like this, pedalling in virtual silence and maintaining a moderate distance between us.

At the end of the day, after we had finished dinner in our tent, I tried to escape to another place through the pages of a *Daily Telegraph* we had purchased that morning. Colin, on the other hand, had made a mess of the tent, emptying the contents of several dry bags in search of something.

"Hey, look what I found while looking for my journal. The last Lindt chocolate bar."

This was getting old. I didn't even respond.

He thrust the bar towards me. "Do you want a piece?"

It did look good, but I declined.

Colin cleared his throat, and I knew what was coming next. "You are my sunshine . . ."

This was so stale. Couldn't he come up with something else?

"My only sunshine . . ."

I didn't want to be cheered but I couldn't help laughing at his attempts. Colin took this as a sign of reconciliation and seemed pleased. He finished off the chorus and pulled out an inner tube to patch.

The next morning, we continued up and down the hills in unison and succumbed to nostalgia at finally approaching the end of Britain. As we rolled down into Dover, wistfulness was replaced with excitement at the prospect of soon reaching France. Ahead lay the English Channel, a formidable barrier, but beyond was the promise of culinary delights and Monet landscapes. And so, with enormous eagerness, I anticipated the next chapter in our journey.

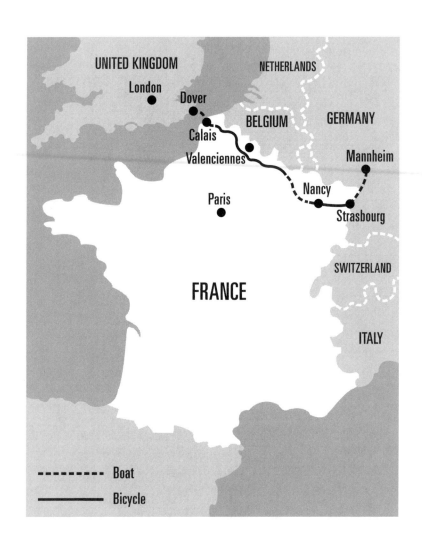

UNITED KINGDOM

London

Dover

Calais

Valenciennes

NETHERLANDS

BELGIUM

GERMANY

Mannheim

Nancy

Strasbourg

Paris

SWITZERLAND

ITALY

FRANCE

- - - - - - Boat

————— Bicycle

3

THE TRAILER VANISHES

FRANCE *(Colin)*

T HE WHITE CLIFFS OF DOVER STOOD IMPLACABLY, a chalk line on the blackboard separating subjects. Like so many before us, we felt they represented the end of our journey through Britain and the start of our voyage to France. Under a blazing sun, Julie and I coasted down a long, steep hill to the base of the limestone cliffs in the port town of Dover.

It was only early May, but an unseasonable heat wave had Dover seething like a disturbed anthill. The streets throbbed with swimsuit-clad vacationers; cars of pimply adolescents leisurely cruised the seaside boulevard; and bodies ranging from pasty white to blistering red carpeted the beaches. Julie and I wove our boats delicately through the throngs, looking for accommodation.

Dover's former position as a seaside retreat had been over-shadowed by its function as Britain's premier ferry terminal, from which goods, people and vehicles were shuttled to and from France. Only one percent of the 18 million people using the Dover ferries each year spent time visiting the town.

I had been to Dover before but, like the other 99 percent, had only been to the ferry terminal and was more familiar with the town through Bill Bryson's *Notes from a Small Island*. Most British seaside towns are shaped by the same cookie cutter, boasting a large pier, tacky stands selling flavourless sugary rock candy emblazoned with the town's name, and carnival-style amusement parks. Gravelly beaches that were once a retreat for the upper class have been sidelined as getaways for those who can't afford to fly to Portugal or the Canary Islands. Dover, however, is slightly different, lacking the ubiquitous wooden pier and end-of-the-road feeling.

Unlike other British coastal towns, Dover seems to have an identity problem as it tries to be both a resort town and one of the world's largest ferry terminals. Its surrounding natural beauty—white chalk cliffs, sandy beaches and rolling countryside—is somewhat muted by the traffic and noise associated with a major ferry port.

We planned to stay in Dover for two days as we prepared for our row across the English Channel. Over the past few weeks, we had heavily researched this leg of the trip, and I was becoming increasingly apprehensive. The English Channel was the busiest waterway in the world, congested with ferries and transport vessels and fraught with storms. The waters were heavily regulated and policed by both the French and British coast guards. The French did not allow human-powered boats to depart from their shores and only reluctantly allowed craft from the other direction. The British were more lenient and allowed human-powered crossings if strict protocol was followed, which included advising the authorities in advance and using a support vessel. The British coast guard then monitored the crossing and continually alerted marine traffic. I was particularly concerned about the difficulty and costs associated with chartering a support vessel, since our online inquiries had not yet netted any results.

At the end of the boulevard, we reached the expansive marina and decided to inquire about storing our boats, rather than continuing to traipse them through the congested streets on our so far fruitless search for a hotel with vacancy.

"That will be no problem," the marina clerk advised us.

"You can keep them in the dry-dock compound for twelve quid a day."

I asked him if he knew of any charter vessels that might be interested in being our support vessel.

"I know a fellow, Nick Streeter, who might be interested. He's accompanied people trying to swim across the Channel with his boat *Suva*. Hang on while I call him for you."

The clerk handed me the phone and a smooth voice answered. I explained that we hoped to row across the Channel in the next couple of days before the weather broke and asked if he would be interested in a job.

"Whoa, whoa, hang on a second," he said. "How long have you been in Dover?"

"We just rolled in half an hour ago. We're pulling our boats behind our bicycles."

"Have you informed the coast guard yet?" Nick asked.

"No, as I said, we just got in half an hour ago. We've been up to our necks travelling through Britain. We planned on organizing the details of this row here in Dover."

"I see a lot of problems," Nick said.

So far, I didn't like his attitude. I already knew what hurdles we faced and was interested in solutions, not a lecture. We had two good boats, planned on following protocol and wanted to take advantage of the unseasonably good weather forecast for the next two days. All we needed was the required support boat.

"I can tell you that we won't be departing before the front rolls in on Wednesday," Nick said. He'd slowed his voice, like a math teacher trying to convey a simple concept to a challenged student. "You can't just pedal into town on your bikes and hop in a couple of boats. You need weeks to prepare for this sort of thing. It's a dangerous crossing. What kind of boats do you have, anyway?"

"They're 18-foot closed rowboats. Tell me, please, why can we not depart in the next two days?"

"You need to contact the coast guard. We need to discuss and strategize how to deal with tides, emergency procedures, etc."

"Look, that can all be done in a day," I said. "As you know, the weather's volatile at this time of year. If we don't depart now while things are good, it could be weeks or even months before we have another chance. Don't stress over this. I'll find someone else who's willing to do the job on Monday."

Nick laughed. "Good luck. It's a small community here, and remember, they have to be registered with the CS&PF."

"The what?"

"Channel Swimming and Piloting Federation. You can't use a support boat that's not registered with them."

"Is this a government requirement? I haven't heard anything about any CS&PF requirements."

"No, but your Channel crossing won't be official if you don't use a CS&PF-certified support boat."

Now it was my turn to laugh. "But we still get to the other side, right?"

Nick harrumphed, and we finished our conversation.

I was a little concerned. Obviously, the charter-boat community was small, and it might be difficult to find an appropriate support vessel. While I was on the phone, Julie was scouring the Internet on a complimentary computer in the corner of the marina office.

"Check this out," she said. "Here's the Channel Swimming and Piloting Federation he was talking about."

I looked at the website and realized it was little more than a collection of Dover charter-boat skippers proclaiming to be official arbitrators of cross-Channel swims, rows and other unorthodox crossing attempts. Seven boats, including Nick's

Suva, were listed as CS&PF-registered, and for a crossing they charged £2,250 ($4,500) or more, £250 for federation fees and the rest for the charter.

It seemed a conflict of interest for individuals with commercial interests to be tied to such an organization. But a quick Google search revealed the importance people placed on having their Channel crossings approved by the CS&PF, and almost all used boats registered with them. Every year, dozens of people cross the 40-kilometre-wide Channel by swimming and in various watercraft, including kayaks, canoes, rowboats and amphibious cars. At almost $5,000 a pop, it seemed a very lucrative business for the charter boats. Julie and I had no interest in having our crossing approved by CS&PF, but I worried that finding an alternative might be difficult in this tight-knit community.

Serendipitously, I had just received an email from another charter company I had earlier made inquiries with. They were willing to make the crossing, and it would cost only £650 ($1,300). I called Mike Williams, skipper of the fishing boat *Firefox*, and immediately liked what I heard. He was professional and experienced, and he offered advice on the most efficient way for us to achieve our objective.

"For us, safety is paramount," Mike said. "I'll have two spotters on deck keeping an eye on you the whole time. We'll plot the most efficient course, taking into consideration tides and shipping lanes, and you can just follow our boat. We'll let the coast guard know of your attempt, so you can focus on getting your boats ready for the crossing."

We confirmed our crossing for Monday, May 12, weather pending, and I was relieved to have this essential component worked out.

As Julie and I further researched the details of our Channel crossing, it became apparent the British were fixated with this 40-kilometre-wide gap separating their island from mainland Europe. It seems any unorthodox vehicle capable of travelling through water or air was not entirely credible until it had crossed the English Channel. For example, most Britons don't remember the truly remarkable feat of the first human-powered flight made by American Derek Piggott in 1961. Instead, the flight of the pedal-powered *Gossamer Albatross* crossing the English Channel in 1979 is the event forever emblazoned in the British consciousness.

The first non-boat crossing of the Channel was made in 1785 by hot-air balloon. It was first swum in 1875, and the first airplane spanned the gap in 1909. In 2008, Virgin Group entrepreneur Sir Richard Branson set a record when he crossed the Channel in an amphibious open-top sports car—not for the first floating-car crossing, but the fastest.

In the last few years, bizarre crossings of the Channel have included a man flying across with a wing and jet engine strapped to his back, a skydiver who became the first to free-fall from one side to the other (falling diagonally from 30,000 feet), and an attempt to pedal a blimp across (thwarted by headwinds).

Swimming has been the most popular unconventional (Channel crossings inspire such oxymorons) means of crossing. Since the first successful attempt in 1875, the trans-Channel Speedo sprint has been made more than a thousand times. Every year, much to the delight of the CS&PF charter boats, hundreds of Britons attempt to swim from Dover to the shores of France.

Yet very few have made the voyage by rowboat. The first known individual to row the Channel was Samuel Osborne, who took thirteen hours to row from Dover to Wimereux in 1888. The record for the fastest time was set in 2003 by British Olympic gold medallist Guin Batten. Guin raced across in three hours and thirteen minutes, but she had to wait all summer for perfectly calm weather. In February 2008, British Olympian James Cracknell tried to break the record, but poor weather left him with a time just over six hours.

We had no interest in trying for the speed record. Our larger boats, combined with our mediocre talent, gave us little chance of beating the Olympians. Instead, our journey across the English Channel was just another essential piece of the mosaic as we moved inexorably towards Syria.

I didn't sleep well the night before our crossing. Regularly I got up to gaze uneasily from our hotel window at growing waves on the water below. A stiff breeze swayed trees, and the sheltered harbour was speckled with whitecaps.

At 4 a.m., Julie and I walked to the marina, where Mike was waiting aboard *Firefox*.

"You still want to go?" he asked, gesturing out into the blackness. "The forecast has deteriorated somewhat, and it's looking a little sloppy."

I knew that the weather would continue deteriorating over the next few days as a large high-pressure system moved east. If we didn't do it today, it would likely be weeks before we could try again. I looked at Julie.

"Let's do it," she said.

Mike's son, Sean, and another man untied the ropes, and the waters surged as the diesel rumbled into reverse. Julie and I tentatively climbed into our boats tied to the side of the dock where we had readied them the night before. Next to our large support boat, *Tantalum* and *Niobium* seemed especially vulnerable, and I shivered as we began rowing through the cold breeze.

It would be an hour before first light. We had chosen an early start to take advantage of calmer morning conditions and to use the tide to our advantage. The tidal current coursing through the English Channel is strong, flowing up to eight kilometres an hour. On the rising tide, it flows towards the North Sea, and it ebbs towards the Atlantic. If all went to plan, our course would be affected by both the flood and ebb tides (pushing us sideways in one direction and then the opposite), giving us a net deviation of zero.

The waters within the port, sheltered by a massive breakwater, were relatively calm, and small waves splashed against our hulls. Within five minutes, we reached the port entrance. The brightly lit *Firefox*, travelling a hundred metres ahead, began rolling, and I braced for the approaching swell.

The combination of a tide ripping northeast against an opposing wind created sloppy one-metre waves. Immediately after passing through the concrete harbour entrance, our boats were awash as we crashed through the swell and were clawed by small whirlpools. Our bicycles and trailers, still packed in their compartments, clattered noisily.

Despite the turbulence, I was pleased with how quickly the boats continued moving. Dover was now a distant array of lights as we moved through a busy black sea. An incoming ferry lit up like a city passed a hundred metres to our left while an outgoing Seacat ferry slipped by our other side. As the ferry increased velocity to its cruising speed of 36 knots (67 kilometres an hour), I was comforted that we had *Firefox* marking our location.

The rough conditions continued, but our speed was a healthy six knots. Water surged over the decks but was deflected back into the ocean by the cockpit combing. After an hour of hard rowing, a pink glow began to fill the sky. The white cliffs of Dover became illuminated, reflecting the salmon hue of the skies above. It was a picture-perfect farewell, but my present efforts subdued any feelings of nostalgia. Julie and I were rowing harder and faster than at any other point on the expedition so far. It was imperative that we cover the 40 kilometres to France as fast as possible to reduce the chances of our plans being thwarted by worsening weather. A failed attempt would be not only humiliating and dangerous but costly. Most likely we would have to resign ourselves to completing the crossing on the ferry.

After about two and a half hours of hard rowing, when France was still invisible over the horizon and England just a thin strip behind us, we heard a jubilant cry from the pilot-house of *Firefox*.

"You guys are exactly halfway there. Halfway to France!" Mike yelled across the water. "Feel free to take a break here. We're between the shipping lanes."

I was saturated in sweat despite the coolness of early morning and removed a layer of clothing. We wolfed down sandwiches and sports drinks while *Firefox* idled nearby.

It had been important up until this point to maintain a constant speed so that the numerous ships around us could plot collision-avoidance courses accordingly. The English Channel is divided into two lanes—ingoing and outgoing— and ships are required to stay within their designated lane. Our present location was the nautical equivalent of taking a break on the concrete median in the middle of a highway.

Behind us, I could see a stream of about a dozen cargo ships bearing towards the Atlantic Ocean. Ahead an equal number were steaming to the North Sea. The Seacat ferries were the most intimidating as they travelled a parallel route very close to ours. Moving at almost 70 kilometres an hour, a speck on the horizon would arrive in minutes, a rumbling, seething monster passing a few hundred metres off our starboard sides.

The winds were decreasing, and the waves began to diminish. We continued our leg to France with renewed vigour, slicing through the eastbound shipping lane. It was the buildings and loading cranes of Calais that first became visible, and eventually I could make out the lowlands they sprouted from. The crew from *Firefox* shouted encouragement as we raced towards the increasingly distinct outline of France.

"Let's head for the beach!" Julie shouted.

"Why?" I yelled back.

"It's closer than the harbour. We've been on the water for four hours and thirty-two minutes. Maybe we can beat five hours."

I've learned that while Julie is not competitive among peers, she is extremely driven to achieve results. I've always attributed her quest for perfection and 110 percent performance to her mother's German influence. Now she was set on rowing the Channel in under five hours, and I knew I'd have to struggle to keep up.

For the last 200 metres, I felt I was competing in the Olympics. Drenched in sweat, we pistoned on sliding seats as our boats skimmed through shallow waters. *Firefox* remained offshore in the deeper water, and sunbathers watched nonchalantly as we sprinted at 12 kilometres an hour towards the beach. Our hulls scraped the sand simultaneously, and Julie leaped onto French soil.

"Four hours and fifty-six minutes!" she yelled.

"Yeeehaaa!" I exclaimed. "We beat the time of an Olympic gold-medallist rower. And I bet he wasn't carrying bicycles in his racing shell."

I felt pleased for many reasons. I was excited that we had crossed the Channel successfully, but I was also thrilled to be in France. We had fantasized about gourmet food and Monet landscapes. The rewards of France had glittered even brighter because of the daunting hurdle in between, but we had reached the Land of Oz and tonight we would celebrate with good food and wine.

~~~

OUR GOOD TIMES IN FRANCE had already peaked as Julie and I finished our celebratory hug and resumed rowing into Calais's harbour. We followed the shore a few metres from the bank, ensuring we would stay out of the way of ferries and other harbour traffic.

High above us on the opposite side of the water, a small figure frantically blowing a whistle emerged from the port control tower. I looked up quizzically. The man disappeared into the office and re-emerged with a megaphone. Garbled angry French filled the air, and we still had no idea what he was trying to convey. I've entered dozens of ports and have never had such an unwelcoming reception. The man's face was now an aneurysm-teasing crimson, and his words were getting faster and louder. Finally, he disappeared back into his office.

Firefox, which had been following several hundred metres behind, caught up with us.

"Any idea what that was all about?" I yelled across to Mike.

"That was the harbour master. I've got no idea what he was on about. His English-speaking assistant called us on the VHF and said we have to tie up at the stone wall over there." Mike pointed to a sheer wall with a heavy swell smashing into it.

"What about that pontoon?" I said, pointing to a floating dock on the sheltered side of the bay.

Mike shook his head. "They specifically said that wall."

Even with all her fenders out, *Firefox* was in peril of being smashed against the wave-washed wall, and Sean and the other deckhand had their hands full keeping the boat from grazing the rock. We pulled our boats alongside, and Mike tossed over several bags they had been carrying for us. It was a precarious manoeuvre, and we almost dropped a dry bag into the oil-slicked waters.

Despite the earlier commotion, no one came down the from the harbour master's office, so we bade goodbye to the crew of the *Firefox* and paddled towards the nearby marina. A sill blocked the marina entrance (to prevent the basin from drying out completely when the large tide receded) and it was passable only between mid-tide and high tide. The water was quickly dropping, and the entry lights had already turned red. Six inches of fast-flowing water now covered the sill, and we made it over just in time.

After tying our boats up, we quickly found a reasonably priced hotel overlooking the harbour and set about looking for a suitable restaurant in which to celebrate.

You may remember that in England when Julie and I were passing through the Lake District we were given a copy of a book called *The Unlikely Voyage of Jack de Crow*. This charming memoir outlines the journey that school teacher A. J. Mackinnon made in his Mirror dinghy sailing from England to the Black Sea. His route paralleled ours, and I had taken to reading his account in the evenings, intrigued to learn of his experiences.

Unfortunately, I had read only to page 196, otherwise we would have done things differently that evening, but nonetheless we opted to have our first meal in France in a pleasant seafood restaurant specializing in mussels. After two steaming bowls of rather bland bivalves and a bottle of wine, we returned to our room exhausted and fell promptly to sleep.

A few hours later I awoke, stomach gurgling ominously. I rushed to the bathroom and spent the remainder of the night on the toilet liquidating my bowels. The following morning, as I lay in bed convalescing, I continued reading A. J. Mackinnon's account. Before sailing across the English Channel, he had received a stern warning from an official with the British coast guard regarding Calais: "Whatever you do, don't have the mussels there. I did last August and I was sick as a dog."

Great. If only I'd reached page 197 before eating out.

Calais is a grimy city with the singular function of transporting people away from it. Tourists pass through quickly, and the only foreigners here for any duration are illegal migrants waiting for their chance to dash across to England. Shops and restaurants are set like driftnets, designed to catch customers not through quality and service but merely by ensnaring them from the passing flow.

We walked to the canal that we would soon be voyaging and discovered it was a world apart from the quaint waterways of Britain. Resources had been put into the concrete channel at some point during the past few decades, but the efforts were falling into disrepair. Garbage and broken glass littered the walkway, and the wooden wharves were thick with guano. Hundreds of homeless lived in the vicinity, their bedding scattered through vacant lots along the canal.

"I'm sure it will be nicer once we get away from the city," Julie said as we stared in dismay at brown waters in front of us.

"I hope so."

We had two options for our journey ahead. We could travel through the canals of France and reach the Rhine River near the intersection of Main River, which leads towards the Danube. Alternatively, we could travel along the coast to the mouth of the Rhine in the Netherlands and row upstream to the Main. We had decided to go through the French canals, reckoning it would offer more varied scenery and allow us to avoid the strong contrary currents of the lower Rhine. Plus Julie loved French food.

A. J. Mackinnon voyaged these same canals in his dinghy. After the previous evening's seafood incident, I made sure to study his experiences carefully. I was pleased to learn that he had no major problems with the lockkeepers, and they allowed him and his three-metre engineless dinghy to traverse the locks by oar.

We visited the small supermarket near our hotel and studied a new range of products, deciding what to purchase for the trip ahead. We returned with backpacks bulging with baguettes, canned stews, aromatic cheeses, cured meats, and fruits and vegetables.

Bright morning sun reflected off shiny yachts as we began our voyage from the Calais marina. With hopeful optimism, we rowed away from the marina basin and back into the main harbour. The canal began just behind the ferry terminal and was guarded by giant sea locks.

Two workers looked down on us.

"*Parlez-vous anglais?*" I asked.

They shook their heads. It was time to dip into my dismal high-school French.

"*Je veux allez à l'écluse. C'est possible?*"

They shrugged uncomprehendingly.

Over the next twenty minutes, through sign language and rudimentary French, we finally made it understood that we wished to traverse the lock. (Really, what the heck else would a couple of boaters pointing at a lock be wanting?) One of the lock employees held up his hand and pulled out his cellphone.

"*Le capitaine de port,*" he said, informing us whom he was about to call.

"Goddamn," Julie said. "If this is the port captain's jurisdiction, we're not going through in a million years."

Sure enough, after a short conversation on the phone, the employee shook his head and disappeared into the office.

Sheer walls lined the harbour, and the only exit was a nearby boat-launch ramp. We paddled to the ramp and began unloading our trailers. A small Peugeot farted to a stop above, and a man in his thirties approached.

"I am from zee 'arbour control bureau. Zee 'arbour master ask me to tell you zat you are not allowed on zis ramp. If you do not move immediately, 'e will call zee police."

"But how else can we leave this harbour?" I argued, "The tide's too low to get back into the marina. We're not in anybody's way here and we'll be gone in five minutes."

"No, you cannot be on zis ramp. Go!" the man said and returned to his car.

Apart from rowing back to England, we had no other options. We ignored his warning and carted our boats a kilometre through the streets of Calais until we could access the canal.

A group of young homeless men watched with interest as we packed our trailers into the boats. It was an awkward launch spot, with a sheer 1.5-metre drop to the water below. At a great disservice to our backs, the boats were finally lowered/dropped into the water, and we were ready to depart.

As we slipped along the canal, the concrete walls became increasingly overgrown with vegetation, and our view of the passing houses and factories was obscured. Brambles, cow parsley, willow and gorse all vied for supremacy along the shore, while aquatic plants thrived in the stagnant, phosphate-rich waters. Duckweed, lily pads and reeds clawed at our hulls and slowed our progress. The air had a faint aroma of sewage, and the water was dotted with small, slimy mooring buoys.

Julie hit a buoy with her oar and shrieked in disgust. "That's a dead animal."

Sure enough, it was a small corpse, bloated and unidentifiable. The canal was littered with unfortunate creatures who had toppled off the concrete walls and had no means of climbing out of the water.

"Not quite the fields of lavender and mustard we envisioned," I mused.

By now, Julie was wagging the bow of her boat vigorously, trying to dislodge a stray grocery bag.

"Not yet, but I'm sure it will get better," she said.

Eventually, the decaying outskirts of Calais were replaced by fields. The high canal banks obscured our view of the flat farmland, and it was only by standing on tiptoe in our cockpits that we could discern our surroundings.

The region we were passing through, Nord-Pas-de-Calais, was composed of low-lying flatlands, barely above sea level. This canal was part of a vast drainage system that made the swampland arable. Small irrigation ditches regularly flowed in from the adjacent fields, introducing more murky water.

The farming in the region was highly mechanized, and the production of flax, wheat, barley, sugar beets and potatoes employed only a small part of the population. During the 1900s, the population had skyrocketed because jobs in textiles, iron, steelworks and coal abounded in industrial centres such as Calais, Boulogne, Lille and Douai. But over the past hundred years, many of these industries declined, and unemployment was now rampant, creating urban decay and desperation. Widespread alcoholism, suicide, industrial wastelands and enormous slag piles had turned the Nord-Pas-de-Calais into the butt of cruel jokes in the rest of France. While the dikes prevented us from seeing much of the surrounding landscape, the murky garbage and corpse-strewn waters conveyed the essence.

We stopped at a tiny village not marked on our map. It was beside a bridge that crossed the canal and consisted of six tired houses surrounding a small pub. Julie waited with the boats while I clambered up the bank to get water for camping.

The only sign of life came from within the derelict bar. Two middle-aged men slumped against the Formica counter, while the bartender counted his meagre earnings. The man graciously filled my empty containers and I returned to the boats.

We soon reached our first inland lock and erected our tent on the grassy verge nearby. There was nobody around, and a sign on the lockkeeper's office indicated they would be away until the morning.

As we dragged our gear up the bank, tiny green missiles assaulted our legs. This plant, I later discovered, was called shotweed and is a type of bitter cress that ejects its seeds up to four metres when disturbed. We marched beyond the reach of nature's artillery and set up camp on a patch of clover and grass.

It was a pleasant evening, and we savoured the lingering daylight. We celebrated our first day rowing in France with a cheap bottle of red wine and beef stew from a can. Cows lowed in the distance, and we retired sleepily to the tent.

France's vast network of canals and canalized rivers crisscross the nation, stretching some 8,000 kilometres in total. These waterways are used for recreation but, unlike in Britain, they continue to be used for transporting cargo, lending many an industrial, utilitarian feel. France also possesses several exceptionally historic canals, including the Canal de Briare, the first European canal to connect rivers from different watersheds; completed in 1642, it joined the Loire and Seine rivers. This project was promptly followed by the ambitious Canal du Midi (completed in 1643), connecting the Garonne River to the Étang de Thau and, very importantly, creating a navigable inland route from the Atlantic Ocean to the Mediterranean.

Despite the antiquity of these manmade waterways, they are by no means the oldest. The first canals appeared in Mesopotamia around 4000 BC in a region that is now Syria and Iraq. These primitive waterways were little more than irrigation

trenches with rudimentary water transportation as their secondary purpose. Beginning around 500 BC, the Chinese used
canals extensively for transportation and made some of the
greatest technological advances. Their early canals used simple
locks that were nothing more than a dam with a gate. Wooden
boards covering the gate were removed when boats needed to
bypass the dam, allowing water to gush through the opening,
making for a quick (and dangerous) passage for boats going
downstream. Vessels travelling the other direction needed to
be winched against the flow and up onto the higher level. These
primitive flash locks used large amounts of water and were not
very practical. Nonetheless, by employing this system, the
Chinese built the first canal connecting two rivers in different
watersheds, the Grand Canal. Completed in AD 609, it
connected Beijing and Hangzhou and was an incredible
1,794 kilometres in length. To this day, it remains the world's
largest and longest canal. It is as broad as a mid-sized river with
minimum widths of about 30 metres. Assuming that the canal's
average width is 40 metres with a depth of three metres, this
means that a staggering 215 million cubic metres of earth and
rock were displaced using hand shovels, which required about
110 million man-days of labour.

The canal and lock we camped beside wasn't as grand,
although the technology had advanced in the last 1,400 years.
It was a straightforward concrete and steel pound lock operated with hydraulic controls. Not surprisingly, the Chinese
were also the inventors of the pound lock (around AD 1000),
which was first used in Europe, in the Netherlands, in 1373
and has been common ever since.

In the morning, we readied our boats and waited anxiously
for the lockkeeper. She arrived promptly at 8:30 a.m. and let us
through without issue, but that was before she knew what kind
of boats we were in. It wasn't until after she opened the

upstream doors and we were in the lock that she came out of the office and peered down at us.

"*Mon dieu*," she said, shaking her head in disbelief.

We soon reached the junction of the larger Canal de Neufossé. Enormous transport barges, waiting to be loaded with gravel, rocks and other cargo, sat at the canal-side loading terminals. Sports fishermen squatted on folding garden chairs placed among the shrubbery, rods hanging listlessly into the weed-choked waters.

Near the town of Saint-Omer, we approached a giant concrete structure that stretched across the water. It was a lock, I suddenly realized, but very different from any others we had encountered. It had a futuristic design; the lockkeeper's office, which towered in a five-storey structure, resembled an air-traffic control tower, and the lock itself was enormous, with a giant guillotine-style gate guarding the entrance instead of the usual double-flap opening.

"Wow, they sure put a lot of money into that," I said to Julie.

But as we neared, the structure transformed. The lower windows in the control tower were broken. The concrete itself was cracked, so much so that entire walls were losing their angular shapes. Graffiti adorned any surfaces that still presented a flat face. Wooden beams, part of a pier along the entrance, were collapsing and dangled in the water. It reminded me of massive industrial projects I had seen in Russia that fell to ruin with the collapse of the Soviet Union.

"Do you think it's still functioning?" Julie asked.

"Beats me. It shouldn't be," I said as we coasted to the derelict pier.

There was no sign of life, so I tried calling the lockkeeper on the VHF radio. We waited in silence staring at the handset. Nothing. The tinted windows in the tower above prevented us from seeing inside. I climbed tentatively over the broken timbers and up a staircase to the base of the control tower. A locked steel door stopped me from going farther, and I returned to the boats.

Everything was silent apart from the sound of a pop can clattering in the breeze. As we deliberated over what to do next, a sudden roaring jerked me from my sleepy state of mind. A wall of water erupted twenty feet from the top of the lock and thundered into the still waters below, transforming our surroundings into a surging and boiling maelstrom.

"They're emptying the lock for us!" Julie yelled.

It was the first lock I'd seen drain in such a dramatic fashion—most others used submerged sluices—but obviously someone in the tower had seen us and was lowering the water level of the inner pound.

As we untied our boats, a man emerged from the tower and picked his way over the dilapidated pier towards us.

"*Non!*" he yelled.

"*Non?*" I said, confused.

He continued in French, and while we understood little, it was clear he was forbidding us from entering the lock. The man pointed to a barge approaching from downstream and indicated he was opening the gates for it, not us. Another man, seeming to possess more authority, joined him and emphatically echoed his partner's protests.

While the two of them continued in French, we resigned ourselves to portaging and began unloading the boats.

"*Non, non!*" the second man screamed.

"*Non?*" I said, more confused than ever.

"*Non, non, non!*" he shouted, rank spittle spraying in our faces.

"*Non* what?"

Eventually we understood that we weren't allowed to

portage either. There was no using the lock and no exiting the canal. Our only option was to turn and row back to where we had come from.

Half a kilometre downstream, we found a quiet bay with a boat ramp. Dejectedly, we dragged our boats from the water and worried about what to do next. It was clear we couldn't row through the French canals as planned. Our choices were to go back to the sea and follow the coast until we reached Belgium or even the Netherlands, or continue on the roads.

"Let's just pull our boats overland," Julie finally said. "I hate backtracking. And who knows, maybe when we get away from this region, the lockkeepers will be more pleasant and we can go back to the water."

We decided to cycle the roads roughly parallel to the canals we had planned on rowing, so we would have the option of returning to the water if circumstances allowed. As the crow flies it was 500 kilometres to the French city of Strasbourg, where we planned on entering the Rhine, but on the meandering course we plotted in our *Michelin Road Atlas*, it was almost 900 kilometres.

As we charted our new route, I felt my spirits lifting. It would be less exciting on the roads, but at least we would no longer be at the mercy of lockkeepers.

The following days passed uneventfully. We averaged about 50 kilometres a day through relatively flat land, passing fields of poppy-peppered wheat and herds of black and white cows. The cows cantered beside us, undoubtedly hoping we'd slip a few buckets of grain through the fence. We'd buy a fresh baguette in the morning and slather brie and tomatoes on it for lunch. Sometimes we'd encounter a café. They tended to be decaying bars that poured more alcohol than café au lait, but we stuck to our caffeine fix.

Often we'd also fill up our water bottles in these café/bars, but in one small village, we delighted in drinking crystal-clear spring water that burbled from a stone dispenser. It was a regrettable choice. By dinnertime Julie was murmuring, "I don't feel so good," and before the sun set, she was dashing into the forest, from which shortly afterwards I could hear disturbing retching and bubbling sounds. A farmer stopped to berate us for our camping choice and request our immediate departure, but changed his mind when he saw Julie's sickly state. Throughout the night, her temperature soared and she spent as much time in the forest as the tent. I worried she would require medical assistance, but fortunately, by morning her fever abated. She was still nauseated and weak, but we slowly carried on.

Eventually, the flatlands gave way to rolling hills and river-carved valleys—more pleasing to the eye but tougher on the legs. We reached the Meuse River and followed its banks to the fortified medieval city of Verdun. This beautiful stone city with cobbled streets and riverfront cafés was the site of one of the costliest battles in World War I. Over the course of eleven months, the Germans and French fought bitterly here, with almost eighty thousand soldiers killed on both sides. The French barely managed to hold on to Verdun, despite its strategic position on the south side of the Meuse and its heavy fortifications. As we passed people relaxing in street-side cafés sipping coffee and munching croissants, it was hard to visualize the violence and destruction that took place here only a few decades earlier.

Farther along the Meuse, in the agricultural village of Saint-Mihiel, we decided to launch our boats. We had been cycling for almost a week and hoped our luck might be better now than it had been on the canal near Calais. The Meuse River is made navigable with locks every few kilometres, and it leads to a channel connecting into the Rhine watershed.

A small park near a bridge spanning the river offered a

suitable launching spot. After packing our bikes and equipment into the boats, we relaxed on the grass and ate a lunch of baguettes, salami, tomatoes and blue cheese. Weeping willows slouched along the water's edge, and a family of ducks eyed our baguettes with interest. I was excited to escape the asphalt and re-enter this tranquil waterway. The Meuse River was infinitely more appealing than the open drains that passed for canals near Calais.

We knew from A. J. Mackinnon's account that the locks in this area were automated, and we hoped this system would work in our favour. Mackinnon described motion sensors near the lock entrances that detected a boat's arrival and triggered a mechanism to open the gates. Optimistically, we reasoned that a vigorous wave of the oar in front of the motion sensor should yield the same results as a jolly Thames lockkeeper.

Unfortunately, our enthusiasm was short-lived. After twenty minutes of rowing against a slow-moving current, we reached our first lock. Julie noticed the sensor, a small box with a reddish lens situated among the trees 100 metres downstream of the lock.

"I'll go ashore and wave my oar," I said. "Let me know when it opens."

Julie continued up the river while I approached the sensor. Trees blocked my view of the lock, so Julie would have to let me know if my efforts were successful. A fisherman watched from the corner of his eye as I stood waving my oar vigorously at the device.

"Anything?" I yelled.

"No."

I waved and waved to no avail. Eventually, I clambered out of my boat, hiked up the bank and vigorously shook my arm in front of the metal box. The fisherman was smirking.

"How about now?"

"Nothing."

Finally I gave up. Our new plan wasn't working. I walked up to a house near the lock and knocked on the door. When the employee emerged, I asked if we could traverse the lock in our boats.

"Where is your remote control?" the young man asked, clicking an imaginary remote with his thumb.

Aha! So I had done my chicken dance in front of a radio sensor, not a motion detector. We were really out of luck. Despite our prior efforts to learn about the intricacies of the French canals, we had been unable to find any information apart from Mackinnon's account. Things had either changed since Mackinnon voyaged the canals ten years earlier, or he had also been waving his oars and arms in vain. Given that he portrays himself as a bumbling, mechanically disinclined traveller, I suspected the latter. He did mention that the motion sensors didn't work very well, and a friendly lockkeeper kept pace with him in a Fiat to operate the gates. We had no such angel in lockkeeper's frocks, and I suspected our pleasant stint of rowing would soon end.

The young man finally relented and let our boats through the lock as he operated the controls, but he warned us there were no lockkeepers farther upstream.

Forests lined both sides of the river as we resumed rowing while discussing our options.

"We could take the bus to the city of Nancy," I suggested, "and try to get a remote from the waterways office."

"Yeah, but they'd never give us a remote if they knew we were in rowboats. Plus they may not even be open."

Both points were valid. We had tried visiting the French waterways office in Calais mid-week. It was closed, and a woman from the adjacent office informed us that no one had been around for a week. We found this situation was common in France, where priority was given to leisure time. You could spend half a day making your way to a public office and more likely than not find it closed for lunch, or an obscure holiday, or workers' appreciation day, or a host of other reasons.

As for being in rowboats, we could be ambiguous and possibly they would assume we were in motorized vessels, but most likely they would ask for our boat papers. Ultimately, we decided, it wouldn't be worth the effort and was probably easier (and less disappointing) to deal with our current hand.

That day we traversed three more locks with great difficulty. Corrugated steel lined the edge of the canal near the locks, and it was about a metre to the lip. Lifting the heavy boats out of the canal and onto the wall was almost impossible, and we damaged them badly in the process. Large gouges scored the bottom of the boats from dragging them over sharp metal, and my oarlock snapped as we manhandled them through trees.

In the evening, we camped in a pleasant meadow beside our fourth lock. A farm road crossed the Meuse River here. This would be the end of our boating in France, we decided. Portaging was just too difficult, and the boats were receiving more abuse than they could handle. We would leave on our bikes in the morning and pedal all the way to the Rhine River.

In the night, heavy rain cleared the muggy air, and we awoke to crisp sunshine. I stretched and left the tent to empty my bladder. I looked around and suddenly froze.

"Uh, Julie?"

"Yes?"

"Did you pack the boat trailer back into the boat?"

"No. Why?"

Julie was now scrambling out of the tent, knowing full well why. Together we stared at the empty spot between the boats and the tent.

"Goddamn," I said. "I should have locked it up. It just seemed so remote here."

We searched through the bushes and peered into the river, but there was no sign of the trailer. We had taken it out to wheel the boats past the locks, but now it was gone. It would be of no use to whoever stole it, but for us it represented our ticket out of here. The trailers had been custom made and were meticulously designed to fit disassembled inside the boats, yet were strong enough for the rigours of hauling up to 100 kilograms. There was no way we could replace the trailer.

"Geez, this sucks," Julie said. "We can't travel on the water, and now we can't even travel on land."

I felt claustrophobic. The past two weeks had felt like a perpetual struggle; just as we'd overcome one obstacle another materialized. Now we were trapped in the middle of a farming region, where the nearest town of any size lay 60 kilometres ahead.

I spent the morning cycling up and down the adjacent roads searching for the trailer, while Julie protected our remaining gear. In tiny, sleepy villages, I peered into open garages and backyard gardens. Elderly residents scowled at me, probably assuming I was a criminal scoping out their homes. I attempted asking a few if they had seen a small boat trailer, but my French wasn't sufficient. Finally, I gave up and returned to the boats.

"I guess our only option is to continue up the river," I said. "We won't get far, but maybe we can find a hotel somewhere. If we can get an Internet connection, we can work on a solution."

"Like what?" Julie mused. "We can't buy a trailer, we can't communicate with the locals and we can't travel on the canals."

We were at an impasse, and I didn't have an inkling of what the solution would be. We pushed our boats back into the river and rowed upstream in glum silence. The locks were frequent, and we made about 10 kilometres progress. The following day we encountered a string of locks as the canal ascended a hill, and we decided it would be more practical to assemble the remaining trailer and bike and shuttle the boats a few kilometres farther up the river. The obvious problem with this option was that one of the boats would be left unguarded for half an hour and therefore vulnerable to thieves or vandals. If a boat was stolen, our expedition would be over. Nonetheless, the alternative was just too difficult, and with heavy hearts, we began the lengthy shuttle. Fortunately, the operation went smoothly, and we transported the boats to a seven-kilometre lock-free section of canal. We were now off the Meuse River on a canal diverging towards the Rhine watershed.

Shortly after re-entering the water, we reached an aqueduct. This 15-metre stone and steel structure allowed the canal to traverse a river valley below, essentially a bridge for water. The aqueduct was wide enough for us to fully extend our oars, although we took our time crossing, staring at the river far below and cherishing the surreal sensation of rowing on a bridge spanning another body of water. From here we rowed seven more kilometres in a pleasantly lock-free stretch of canal. We passed through forests of poplar and willow. Cuckoos sounded in the distance, and momentarily I forgot our troubles.

We reached the village of Pagny, where the tourist information sign near the empty dock indicated a hotel in the vicinity. We decided this was where we would stop and solve our problem.

I'd been considering options all day, and as we ate a snack on a bench beside the canal, I let Julie know my thoughts.

"We have to build a trailer," I said. "It's the only realistic option."

"But how? We don't have tools—and anyway, what would we make it out of?" Julie asked.

"I don't know. We'll have to find a hardware store and see what's available. We'll build a solid trailer, and just pedal on out of France."

The border of Germany was turning into the Holy Grail for us. Julie speaks fluent German, so communication would be as easy as in Britain. Additionally, Germany is a world leader in embracing human-powered transportation and providing adequate infrastructure. All our research indicated that paddle craft are welcomed on their inland waterways.

We assembled the bikes and found the simple but adequate highway hotel about three kilometres from the canal. We shuttled the boats to our temporary home, hooked our computer up to the Internet and began moving forward with our new plans.

Pagny is a village of a couple hundred. The only commercial establishment of any use to us (apart from the hotel) was an excellent, not to mention reasonably priced, buffet for truckers. The gourmet food, ranging from prawns to escargots, was delicious, as was the huge collection of cheeses, breads and salads. Limitless wine, drinks and desserts were included in the €6 ($10) price, and Julie and I were immensely cheered by our find. The place was packed with truckers, and we were exceedingly grateful that the fare demanded by the working people of France was infinitely better than the deep-fried servings offered in North American truck stops.

The next day we rode our bicycles 15 kilometres to the town of Toul. In a large home-supply centre, we spent two hours examining the hardware, tools and lumber selection. Eventually, we checked off all the items on the list, including several lengthy two-by-fours, and loaded the supplies onto our remaining boat trailer. Next stop was the bicycle store, where we purchased two BMX wheels. We carried it all back to our hotel and spent the next two days sawing, drilling, screwing and cutting in the hotel parking lot. Eventually, something resembling a trailer emerged. The result was chunky, wooden and resoundingly primitive but, thankfully, functional, which we confirmed by loading my boat onto it and wheeling it around the parking lot.

"We've done it!" said Julie. We had built a boat trailer in a hotel parking lot in the middle of France.

I continued riding in circles with the boat in tow. "If it can go a hundred metres, it will go a million more."

We departed early in the morning, fully prepared for the journey ahead. We had a working trailer, sound maps and a boatload of food. Our goal was to reach the Rhine River as quickly as possible, before additional hurdles conspired to keep us in France. We wouldn't attempt any more water travel and would just pedal, pedal, pedal. Once we reached the Rhine, our trailer would have served its purpose, and we could, if we wanted, travel exclusively on water.

It was 200 kilometres to the Rhine, a distance we could cover comfortably in four days. A network of country lanes and canal-side roads led us along flat valley bottoms past forests and farms. We skirted the city of Nancy and continued north through monotonous countryside.

The scenery began to transform as we approached the Vosges Mountains, a chain that runs along the western side of the Rhine River. This massif is a mirror landscape to the Black Forest Mountains on the German side of the Rhine and, in fact, had been formed by similar geological processes. The lower slopes are dotted with vineyards, pastures and old stone farmhouses. Forests of beech, maple and pine carpet the upper slopes.

Such pleasing scenery also brought steep hills, and we made our way slowly towards the pass separating the Rhine and Moselle watersheds. Near the village of Arzviller, we pushed our bikes to the summit of Col de Saverne, panting and dripping with sweat. At the top, we sat by the roadside catching our breath.

"Just think, we could have skipped this hill if we were rowing," Julie said.

That was true, but the problem was that the Canal de la Marne au Rhin, which flowed beneath us, negotiated this pass via a 2.3-kilometre-long tunnel. I shuddered at the thought of rowing in pitch blackness through the narrow tunnel and suddenly hearing the ominous rumble of a barge in the distance. Would it be a head-on collision or a steamrolling from behind? Either way seemed less preferable than pushing our bikes in the sunshine.

Dark clouds loomed over the mountains, and thunder rumbled threateningly. A Toyota Land Cruiser stopped and a mustachioed man greeted us in fluent English, introducing himself as Jacques. He gestured towards the approaching storm and invited us to stay in his home in the valley below.

Half an hour later, Julie and I found ourselves on a lumpy track in a forest doing our best to follow the complex directions we had been given. Torrential rain bucketed down and flowed along ruts. Thunder echoed explosively off mountain walls. Jacques had explained that his house was alone in the forest, but we wondered if we had taken a wrong turn—the muddy track we were following seemed more like a disused goat trail.

We rounded a corner and reached an old sandstone home nestled in a crook in the hillside. We felt like Hansel and Gretel. But instead of a wicked witch, it was Jacques who emerged and greeted us warmly. We retreated from the rain, and Jacques showed us our horsehair beds. Dinner included wild boar from the local hills, and in the morning we sampled "honey of the forest" from his bees.

Jacques explained that he was a doctor from Strasbourg, forced to retire early because of a severe heart attack. His new stress-free lifestyle deep in the heart of the Vosges Mountains was good for both his heart and his mind.

From Jacques's house, Julie and I continued cycling along a bicycle path that paralleled the canal leading to Strasbourg and the Rhine River. The path was completely flat while we passed through a dramatic landscape of mountains, forests and pretty canal-side villages. As we neared the Rhine, a lock-keeper looked at us curiously as we pulled up with our boats behind our bikes. He informed us that we were free to travel in the canals and locks. We were tempted, but with the trailers functioning flawlessly and a pleasant, flat bicycle path between us and the Rhine, we decided to carry on overland.

Not only was the landscape dramatically different now, so was the architecture. Buildings were built with the charming German-style timber beam-and-post construction. In fact, this region had once been part of Germany, and the German flavour remained. Many of the town names were German, and most of the older people could speak a German dialect.

At last, we reached the sleepy town of Gambsheim on the banks of the Rhine River. We stopped our bikes at the central crossroad and debated what to do next.

"This calls for a celebration," Julie said. "The trailer made it, and tomorrow we'll be in Germany. Let's find a restaurant that sells flammekueche." Jacques had recommended we sample this regional dish. It is a thin-crusted bread—similar to pizza—topped with onions, bacon and sour cream. We rolled to a stop in front of a tidy bistro and sat down at an outdoor table overlooking our boats. Slanting rays of sunshine illuminated the town as we clinked our wineglasses in celebration.

"You know, it's been pretty pleasant ever since we passed the Vosges Mountains," Julie said.

"Yeah, it *has* been a contrast to the first half of our journey in France," I agreed. "The scenery is beautiful, people pleasant. Must admit, though, I'm still looking forward to having my first bratwurst and pilsner."

The flammekueche arrived, as though to remind us of the good food we had enjoyed in France. The wood-oven-baked crust was cooked to crispy perfection, and the simple topping of traditionally abundant ingredients was delicious. We devoured our meal while reflecting on our journey to date. It was now mid-June, and we relished the prospect of having so much still to explore with all of summer still ahead.

After finishing our meal, we climbed on our bikes and began pedalling the final few kilometres to the banks of the mighty Rhine.

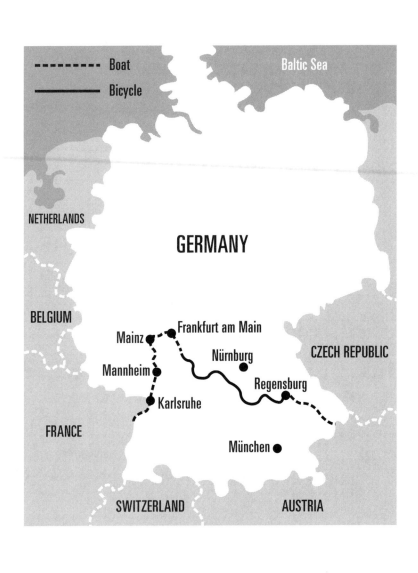

4

MAINZ ATTRACTIONS

GERMANY (*Julie*)

W E SPENT OUR FINAL NIGHT IN FRANCE camped in a pleasant park, hidden from the road by a jungle of trees flourishing in the rich, damp soil. The mighty Rhine River pulsed only a few hundred metres distant, obscured by an earthen dike. In the morning, we broke camp in record time, urged on by the most voracious mosquitoes we'd yet encountered.

We followed a gravel track over the dike to a small private marina, but since it hadn't yet opened, we went in search of another launching spot. (It was either that or climb over a high fence with all our gear.) A rutted track meandered between trees along the river side of the dike. Most of the bank was unapproachable, guarded by a thicket of brambles, willows and beech, but eventually we reached an exposed section.

The river was about 300 metres wide, and thick forest lined both sides. The slate-coloured water moved quickly, roiling like a Druid's cauldron. The Rhine is arguably the most important river in Western Europe. It begins in the Swiss Alps and flows through Liechtenstein, Austria, France, Germany and the Netherlands before spilling into the North Sea near Rotterdam. It is certainly Europe's busiest river and also one of its longest. Despite its rather modest world-ranking as the 111th longest river, its strategic location as a transportation corridor and as a defensive barrier has had an immeasurable influence on the development of modern Europe and, in many ways, the rest of the world. On average, 2,000 cubic metres of water are discharged every second, and currents of five knots (10 kilometres an hour) are not uncommon. Even the name Rhine (Rhein in Germany, Rhin in France, and Rijn in the Netherlands) connotes speed: it is derived from the Celtic word *renos*, meaning raging flow.

A light breeze stirred the leaves, and we busied ourselves on the dappled bank. We lifted our boats off their trailers and executed the familiar routine of packing our gear away. The only difference this time was that Colin's homemade trailer would no longer fit inside the boat. We removed the wheels and placed them in the middle compartment, but the bulky wooden frame had to be strapped on the deck with bungee cords. It wasn't quite as streamlined or as seaworthy, but it would have to do.

By ten we were finally ready to depart from the shores of France. We wrestled our boats into the water and gently rowed to the edge of the eddy line. I broke into the current, where the rushing waters accelerated my boat downstream. I was barely working, but the trees slipped by as though I were on a high-speed conveyor belt. This was the fastest flow we had yet encountered, and I was relieved we weren't going upstream. It was delightfully exhilarating. The water churned, bubbled and swirled with great gusto, and I grappled to control my boat. Great upwellings shouldered *Niobium* from side to side, making it difficult to travel a straight line. Pebbles clattered on the river bottom, and the sound was conveyed through the hull like the crackle of static electricity.

Colin rowed hard towards the centre of the river.

"How are things over in France?" he yelled back. "I can smell bratwurst and hear oompahpah music playing over here."

We were having so much fun that we didn't want to get

off and opted to take our breaks on the water, all the while making spectacular progress. We lounged in our spacious cockpits, admiring the limitless expanse of trees, then jumped overboard to escape the daytime mugginess. We didn't even land for lunch, but transformed the flat portion of our outrigger into a plate and cutting board for assembling cheese sandwiches slathered with mayonnaise and French mustard.

By mid-afternoon we reached an imposing concrete hydro-electric dam that blocked the river. We pulled out beside a string of bollards and nestled the noses of our boats between algae-coated boulders. Since I was now the official communicator, it was my job to trek 300 metres to the lofty lock tower in hopes of gaining passage, while Colin minded the boats. A formidable steel fence and locked gate thwarted my plan to converse with the lockkeepers. This was the Fort Knox of locks.

I perused the large and comprehensive placards detailing the history and importance of the Rhine and the electricity it provides, and suddenly noticed there was a specially built canal for human-powered boats to circumvent the dam. As I returned to our boats, a fraught-looking man without a shirt began yelling at me.

"Halt!" he screamed, his face red and distorted. "You can't go through the lock!" Before I could reply he continued. "I watched you arrive in your canoes. You can't leave your canoes there," he fumed, pointing to our boats in the distance.

"I didn't know," I muttered, hastening my pace to widen the distance between us.

He leaped off his bench and began following me, his staccato diatribe about everything I was doing wrong getting ever more loud and intense. That's when I suddenly remembered: when a German yells at you, it's a gesture of friendliness and goodwill. It's when he takes on a hushed voice that you need to worry. Or at least that's what Colin had relayed to me from our guidebook. I had never really noticed this during my previous visits, but why else would this man be simultaneously yelling and offering help?

We reached the boats, and our new friend belted out instructions to Colin, woefully unaware that his words were falling on uncomprehending ears.

"*Nein, nein!*" he screamed as we lifted our boats onto the grass. "You must use the stairs." He mimed how one would carry a boat up the steps.

"Our boats are too heavy," I protested.

But he could not allow such blatant flouting of rules and with steely determination insisted on helping us do things the right way. Eventually and with great difficulty, the three of us carried our boats up a grassy slope and slid them down the other side into a metre-wide channel. We thanked him and quickly rowed away. He continued to bark out directives until we were out of earshot, when no doubt he climbed the dike to reclaim his park bench and wait for the next round of transgressing tourists.

The narrow channel was an impressive bypass. It wound through a forest thick with dragonflies and overhanging trees, meandering for several kilometres until finally rejoining the Rhine well past the lock and dam. I couldn't believe the effort the government had made to create this convenient bypass for our boats. Things were looking promising for a pleasant journey through Germany.

When the river was clear in both directions, we would slip into the middle and rocket along at speeds of 15 kilometres an hour and sometimes more. But since the Rhine was the busiest river in Europe, we shared that space with quite a few hulking river barges carrying coal, sand, cars and other weighty objects. Many consisted of two or even three barges, connected like a great water train and pushed from behind by a thundering tug.

As well, we shared the water with river cruise ships, dredgers, police vessels and (very occasionally) pleasure boats. Initially, the prospect of a collision terrified me, but it didn't take long to realize that to get hit by one of these behemoths would require the greatest level of ineptitude and obliviousness. It was practically impossible not to see these boats, and getting out of their way took nothing more than the few shore-bound strokes required to exit the navigable mid-river channel. Like that of many larger rivers, the Rhine's deeper water was marked with green and red buoys (red on the left, green on the right when facing upstream—the opposite of North America).

We spent our first night on the river camped on the banks of a side channel under a lush canopy of poplar and willow. Just as we finished our canned coq au-vin and the last of our French wine, the hot humidity of the day broke with a torrential thunderstorm. Lightning blazed across the sky and thunder detonated. It was a delight to observe from our dry tent, and I was glad we weren't still on the river.

The following day we rowed an impressive 66 kilometres, one of our farthest days yet. The morning was full of sleepy villages, forested parks and the occasional isolated *gasthaus*. Near lunchtime, the alluring scent of grilled meat foreshadowed the appearance of a riverside café squeezed into a break in the trees. A small ferry terminal accompanied it, and we landed our boats behind the ferry ramp. We ordered bottles of Dunkel (dark beer) and their daily special, a seemingly atypical German meal of various salads and chicken skewers. Then we seated ourselves at a stout table on the balcony. The numerous diners around us all spoke in German, and there was something reassuring about being back in the country where I had spent so much of my childhood.

We stopped again in the afternoon, this time at a small town to buy groceries. Colin stayed with the boats while

I perused store aisles, finding treasures such as muesli, Tetra Pak milk and instant dumplings, but failing at more basic staples, like ground coffee without added caramel. Speaking the language was a great boon, but even then I couldn't understand the clerk's explanation about this particular taste preference.

I returned weighed down with enough groceries to sink a small boat, but as it turned out, I was already too late. Clothes lay draped across rocks, equipment was piled haphazardly on the bank, and Colin was in the midst up dragging my boat to higher ground.

"A fast tug came by and sent up a huge wake," Colin explained. "The cockpits flooded and everything in the open hatches is wet."

We collected stray water bottles, sodden maps and granola bars, inspected our boats for damage (there was none), and repacked. Then we drowned our sorrows in two pails of rice pudding and continued on our way.

The next day, the rural landscape gave way to a more urban one. Long bridges spanned the river and factories lined the banks. Loading cranes and noisy conveyor belts worked continuously emptying and filling barges. We passed through Mannheim, described by our guidebook as a sprawling industrial city that wouldn't appear on anyone's top 100 German tourist destinations, which, from our river perspective, seemed an accurate description.

As we passed the seemingly endless row of factories, I couldn't help but wonder about the quality of the water. Noxious gases were pumping from red and white smokestacks, while water intake and outflow systems were cordoned off and marked with danger signs. Add swaths of farmland leaching nitrogen fertilizers and other agricultural runoffs, not to mention the effects of 58 million people who live in the catchment basin, and you've got the making of an award-winning cesspool.

In the mid-twentieth century, the Rhine was one of the most polluted rivers in Europe. Almost all the fish had died, and its rank odour was sufficient to dissuade even the most enthusiastic of swimmers. Modest rehabilitation efforts suffered a catastrophic setback in 1986 when a chemical plant in Switzerland burned down and flushed 30 tonnes of pesticides into the upper Rhine. The resulting devastation spurred an unprecedented commitment to safeguarding the river, and the Rhine Action Programme was created. This organization set the lofty goal of returning salmon to the river by 2000. Salmon, long considered the hallmark of healthy watersheds, repatriated the river three years ahead of schedule along with pike, perch, trout and dozens of other species. Things still aren't what they used to be, but the transformation of the Rhine has been called miraculous and is a tribute to the resilience of waterways when they are given a chance.

Worms, the next major city we encountered, was infinitely more appealing. It is one of Germany's oldest cities, and its skyline is dotted with fetching spires and domes. We pulled into an unfinished marina, and just as I was about to go off in search of groceries, a canoe joined us. It wasn't much bigger than one of our boats, but based on the table-cloth-sized Union Jack billowing off its stern and assortment of camping equipment stored within, we deduced the three young men weren't locals.

"Where are you going?" I asked as they tied their vessel to the pontoon next to us.

"All the way to the North Sea," a youthful fellow with a broad-brimmed hat answered. "We started at the source in Switzerland a few weeks ago."

Another of the men added, "This is our holiday. We had this Canadian canoe left over from a previous expedition and thought we'd do the Rhine this time around."

The "Canadian canoe," a Wenonah, was actually made in the United States, but Europeans call any open paddle craft a "Canadian canoe." The Germans actually shorten it to just "Canadian," as in, "I fell in the river and was hit on the head by a Canadian." Our decked boats, on the other hand, were usually labelled as just "canoe," without the Canadian prefix.

Their high-sided, well-built boat had a rich history. The previous summer, they had paddled down the entire length of the Mississippi. Travelling nearly 4,000 kilometres by canoe is a remarkable feat, and we were doubly awed when we realized one of their team members was paralyzed from the waist down. The men were from Staffordshire, England, and planned to reach the Rhine mouth in two weeks. They were the first long-distance paddlers we'd encountered since starting our own journey four months earlier.

We left Worms about the same time as they did, and their three-person craft gradually moved into the distance. Although they were slightly faster, their penchant for drunken evenings and hungover mornings gave us the tortoise's advantage. As a result, we saw the trio again the following day before we reached Mainz.

The large city of Mainz was located at an important juncture for us. Here, we would turn onto a major tributary of the Rhine, the Main River, and voyage upstream through the heart of Germany. The Main River leads to the Rhine-Main-Danube Canal, which joins the Rhine and Danube watersheds.

This part of Germany was romance central. Our course would take us to the Romantic Road, an ancient trading route with lots of scenic castles and walled villages. Had we continued on the Rhine, we would have found ourselves on the

Romantic Rhine, a gorgeous section of river flanked by precipitous slopes covered in Riesling vineyards and medieval
castles that is a UNESCO World Heritage Site. I had already
been to the Romantic Rhine. Eight years earlier I had travelled
by train and boat, visiting villages of half-timbered homes and
staying in clifftop castle-cum-hostels. So I was looking forward
to visiting a new amorous area.

In the heart of Mainz, we pulled our boats onto a rowing
pontoon, serendipitously positioned next to the Mainz
Campingplatz, where we planned to stay. We towed our boats
to the campground, paid a modest fee for the night and prepared to revel in the amenities provided in a commercial
campground. And it must be said that the campgrounds in
Germany are a cut above. For example, this campground,
which wasn't particularly noteworthy on a national level, had
a restaurant serving schnitzel and bratwurst, a beer-stocked
store, laundry facilities and an abundance of showers and
toilets, all of which gleamed with hospital sterility. You could
spend a lifetime searching the campgrounds of North America
and not find amenities built and maintained to such fastidious
standards.

We drove our tent pegs into the perfect lawn and, in stark
contrast to the meticulous spaces of our fellow campers, encircled our tent with a cornucopia of equipment. We truly became
the trailer trash of the park when we next draped our tent with
wet and fusty clothing and pulled out an extensive array of fibreglass, paints and tools to carry out some minor repairs.

Colin sat on the picnic table eating licorice and watching
two cyclists who just arrived.

"I've never seen such a nation of perfectionists. Check
these guys out."

The older German men unclipped their panniers
and double-locked their bikes to a tree. They enclosed their

bicycles in custom rain covers before carefully examining the ground where the tent would go. Leaves, tiny twigs and what looked like stray grass clippings were removed, and an improbably tiny tent was erected. The two men climbed inside what looked like a one-person bivouac shelter and flattened out their sleeping bags, running their hands repeatedly over the surface, smoothing out any creases. Finally, they ran trip lines from their bicycles to the tent as added security.

It was now mid-July, and this was almost the halfway point in our expedition—day 89 and kilometre 2,750. Here, we planned to give the boats an overhaul and touch up the numerous nicks and bangs. *Niobium* and *Tantalum* had so far endured endless abuse, including being driven into cement canal walls, smashed against lock barriers, crashed onto jagged boulders during portages and dragged over countless rough surfaces. Nonetheless, they still floated and, except for a hefty wad of duct tape plastered on *Niobium*'s bow, looked pretty good. We sanded the areas that were heavily gouged or damaged and patched them with the epoxy resin and fibreglass that we carried in our tool kit. After a few hours of work, the boats were good as new and ready to complete the second half of our journey.

~~~

THE OTHER REASON FOR OUR HIATUS in Mainz was our plan to visit my German relatives, who lived in Meppen, a small town not too far from the North Sea. We stored our boats in the secure campground and boarded a high-speed train. After three months of travel at a pace rarely exceeding a cantering coyote, zipping along at 200 kilometres an hour gave me a new-found respect for the marvels of modern engineering.

My parents, like one-fifth of Canadians, are immigrants. At the age of twenty-four my mother moved to Toronto to live with her sister, who had immigrated there two years earlier. My Syrian-born father immigrated to Toronto in 1973, met my mother through mutual friends and within a year they were married with a newborn: me.

According to the 2006 census, there are 6.2 million immigrants in Canada. These are people who are or once were landed immigrants (now called permanent residents), which usually means they were born abroad, moved to Canada and were granted permission to live here permanently. Many, like my father, become Canadian citizens, while others remain permanent residents, like my mother.

For a country with 31 million people, 6.2 million is a large figure. Per capita, Canada grants more citizenships than any other nation. Every year, more than 200,000 immigrants become Canadian citizens. As a result, Canada is full of first- and second-generation Canadians, like Colin and me, curious to learn more about our family origins. Sometimes the roots are obscure and distant, while for others, their roots are like a second home. This is what Germany has been to me. I first visited Germany with my mother when I was one. Later, when my father joined the military and had to be away for training exercises, we moved to Germany for over a year, and I attended junior kindergarten. I learned the language, and when we returned to Canada, I refused to speak English. I understood my teachers' questions, but much to their dismay, I replied in German. In total, I have been to Germany more than a dozen times. I have also learned how to cook bratwurst, red cabbage and schnitzel, which makes me about as German as a foreigner can be.

Yet most of my experiences in Germany were as a child, and I absorbed my heritage through a child's eyes and innocence. I knew almost nothing of the hardships my family endured during the war. I knew little about my deceased grandparents and nothing of earlier generations. All I knew were the warm embraces of my uncles and aunts and the secret hiding spots for the sweets they lavished upon me. On this visit, I planned to learn the details of my German heritage.

My uncle Herbert and my mother, who was visiting from Hamilton, Ontario, were waiting for us at the station. They are both in their seventies, bespectacled, and of the typically German sturdy stock. After a profusion of hugs and greetings, there erupted a cacophony of concerns about our health, primarily how skinny we were and how hungry we must be, and they hustled us into the car intent on fixing those maladies.

In my family, life revolves around food. Any visit is preceded by weeks of shopping, preparation and strategizing. Colin enjoys a good meal and can pack away substantial quantities, but he was completely unprepared for the pending consumption bonanza that defined our family gatherings.

"This is very nice smoked halibut," he'd say, genuinely enjoying the football-sized wedge of fish overflowing his plate.

"You like it," my uncle would reply, beaming with joy. He'd then find an even larger piece and lay it on top, adding, "And there's more where that came from."

Colin would protest, feebly and ineffectually, and the flow of food would continue at an unrepentant pace. If Colin inadvertently murmured an "Mmmm" as a spoonful of potato salad entered his mouth, my mother would act with lightning reflexes, loading another serving onto his plate. I couldn't help but find great humour in the lavish attention laid upon him. Over the days, Colin acquired a few tricks, eating at a profoundly unhurried pace, ensuring there was always food on his plate, and when queried about his dawdling consumption—"What's wrong, don't you like my cooking?"—he'd simply claim it was his third helping and didn't know how they could have missed his gluttony.

My aunts and uncle took to my new husband quickly, appreciating his efforts at speaking German and his eagerness to help with chores. They, like my parents, had some reservations about the dangers of our adventuring career and whether it would pay the bills, but they were happy that this trip brought us to them and that more than made up for it. If they had one gripe with Colin, it was that he didn't eat enough, although it would take someone like Takeru Kobayashi, the world hot-dog eating champion (he can eat more than fifty hot dogs in twelve minutes), to satisfy that condition.

Our family visit was a pleasant and relaxing break from rowing. We stayed in my uncle's immaculate brick house, the same home I lived in during my childhood trips to Germany. At the back of the yard was a gate that opened into the property of a home shared by my mom's sister Waltraud and her widowed sister-in-law Maria, so it was easy for the whole family to be together. For three days, we did little more than eat, chat and watch soccer. It was the start of Euro 2008, a three-week tournament between sixteen of the best European teams. Germany was doing well, and the nation was engrossed.

When the TV was off, I pried into my family's history, trying to extend the branches of my family tree, but nobody could offer any information beyond their grandparents. Unlike Colin, who had traced his roots back to the seventeenth century, thanks largely to his dedicated sister Betti, we couldn't dig beyond the twentieth century. My family is disconnected from their place of origin and unable to search records normally available in churches. Besides, their past is heavy, and full of memories they don't wish to dwell on.

My mom, Helga Wilfriede Sadowski, grew up in western Germany but was born in a state that no longer exits: East Prussia. Once part of the Kingdom of Prussia, East Prussia was then a state of Germany and considered to be the nation's bread basket, but after World War II, East Prussia was divided between the Soviet Union and Poland. Her parents and grandparents were farmers, and anything earlier is a mystery. When she was seven months old, her mother died, and her father, unable to look after an infant while running the farm, entrusted his daughter to his brother's family in a neighbouring village.

My mother was brought up with her cousins Herbert and Irmgard, and for two years she enjoyed the most stable and carefree years of her childhood. They lived in the small farming village of Friedrichsthal near the Baltic Sea (in what is now Poland). My mother became close to the two cousins she lived with, and they became her surrogate siblings. Biologically, they were also close, since my mother was related genetically to both her uncle and his wife—not for any sinister reason, but because two sisters had fallen for two brothers. My grandmother's sister married my grandfather's brother. Then, to further complicate matters, after my grandmother died, my grandfather married her other younger unwed sister. It's a bit of a brain twister, which is why I call all my mom's relatives over fifty uncle or aunt.

Her family's was a typical subsistent farming life. They owned cows, horses, rabbits, ducks, pigs, chicken, turkeys, cats and dogs, and grew wheat, corn, potatoes, sugar beets and fruit trees. My mother watched her uncle plough the field by horse and harvest wheat using a scythe. Her aunt baked ten loaves of bread at a time in a stone oven and afterwards used the leftovers to make what my mom called *Brotmann* (breadman), a bready sugar-glazed version of a gingerbread man, for the children. They sold butter, milk and flour at the market and bought buckets of small fish caught from the Baltic Sea.

In 1939, when World War II started, my mother was almost three. Her biological father was conscripted in the early stages of the war, but her uncle, who cared for her, stayed home until the final moments of the war because of his poor eyesight and profession: as well as farming, he logged trees, which were needed for building bridges. Her life went on quite normally for a few more years. There were food rations and fear, but it wasn't until 1945 that things became really grim.

Nazi propaganda assured the Prussians they would be safe from the advancing Russians and decried evacuation, denouncing such actions as defeatism and ordering fleeing civilians to be shot. And so people stayed, even as bombers flew overhead, the Soviets penetrated the border and the Red Army advanced west. Then one day, my mother's uncle came home with an ill-fitting uniform and a rifle and hugged his family goodbye. In the throes of defeat, the Germans launched the Volkssturm, a national militia that conscripted the old, the infirm and anyone previously deemed unsuitable. It was obvious the Germans would soon be defeated, and it was time to leave.

On Friday, January 19, 1945, the schoolmaster's daughter ran to the homes of all her classmates and relayed the message that they would evacuate the next day. Another relative, Willy, who hadn't been conscripted on account of his lame leg, spent the day building a protective cover for their wagon, and my mom's aunt packed and readied the horses. The next day, a massive bombing attack began, and Russian tanks rolled into their village. Convoys of horse-drawn carriages departed throughout the day, but Willy was worried that they would make a tempting bomb target in the daylight, and my family, along with many others, delayed their departure until midnight.

It was a caravan traffic jam fuelled by fear and tempered by chaos. They travelled three kilometres the first day. My mother and the other children were not allowed out of the caravan, but caught snippets of conversation: the cows they had set free were following; there were dead bodies strewn along the road; grenades were exploding nearby. Sometimes they stopped to rest in houses and abandoned factories, but were always fearful of bombings during the day and soldiers slitting their necks at night, both of which occurred with alarming frequency. Eleven days later, they were captured by Russians and forced back home.

They returned to devastation. Their farm equipment was stolen, their animals were dead or dispersed, and their home had been ransacked by soldiers. Four months later, in May 1945, the Soviets had complete control of East Prussia and made life insufferable. The Russian soldiers, intent on revenge for crimes committed by the Nazis during the invasion of the Soviet Union, pursued a campaign of violence and mass rape. "It started as soon as the Red Army entered East Prussia and Silesia in 1944, and in many towns and villages every female aged from 10 to 80 was raped," wrote Antony Beevor in his book *Berlin: The Downfall 1945*. My mother tells of how soldiers broke into houses demanding women and girls to rape. Some girls tried hiding in piles of hay, but soldiers threatened to set the mounds ablaze. My mother's family dug a hole in the dirt of their cellar where the women could hide.

After two years of unbearable life under Russian rule, my mother's aunt and her three children finally escaped on November 13, 1946. They walked 18 kilometres to the train station and began what would be a two-and-a-half-month 1,000-kilometre journey by foot and train to West Germany. Her uncle survived the war and joined them in Germany, but her father was not so fortunate. He was, according to a letter from the Red Cross, captured and sent to a Russian labour camp, where he died and was buried in a mass grave.

My mother has never returned to see her birthplace, her childhood house or the cemetery where her mom is buried. "There is nothing left," she says with a dismissive finality.

I, however, am curious and gently pry further, trying to balance sensitivity with a desire to understand where I come from.

I wonder how all this has affected her. What does witnessing such atrocities do to a child? Does the raw triumph of survival offer any compensation for the loss of your father, your home and all your possessions? I wanted to take these pains away from her, erase her history and replace it with the kind of carefree childhood I had. But of course I can't, and I can't even pretend to understand because it is horrific beyond imagination. All I can do is look at my mother with the respect she deserves and feel slivers of shame for the times I have been a bad daughter.

Recently, I had asked my mother what she planned on doing with a small sum she had hoarded from her meagre government pension. I was surprised and a little dismayed when she said it was for her funeral. Live a little, I wanted to tell her. Enjoy life while you're here; take a cruise, buy a bicycle. But suddenly, as I sat at the dinner table in Meppen, hearing dark stories of the war through tight lips, it became clear. My mother was brought into a world with death as a close companion. She witnessed human beings stripped of their rights and their pride, abused, raped, beaten and sent to the grave in the most inhumane manner. Now, in her adopted homeland of Canada, she took great comfort in ensuring that when her own death came, it would be with dignity.

~~~

COLIN AND I RETURNED TO MAINZ, launched our boats and rowed one kilometre against the Rhine's current to the confluence of the Main River. The Main is one of the Rhine's biggest tributaries, pouring some 17.3 billion litres into it every day. The river begins 524 kilometres away, in Bavaria, but we were not following it to its source. Instead, we were using it as most transport vessels did, as a means to reach the Danube River on the other side of the continental divide. Connecting the Rhine and Danube rivers was a long-standing ambition that stretched back to the eighth century, but was only fully realized in 1992, when the Rhine-Main-Danube Canal was completed. It is a 171-kilometre-long artificial waterway stretching from the city of Bamberg, which lies on the Main, to Kelheim, on the Danube. If we wanted, we could follow these interconnected waterways all the way to the Black Sea, which is exactly what thousands of barges and a handful of pleasure boats do every year.

Our plan was a little different. Since the trailers still were working well, we chose to combine land and water travel to experience some of the exceptional bike paths Germany is known for. We would follow the Main River until it elbowed north and would then travel overland through a series of bike routes to Regensburg on the Danube River. Our course would take us through some of Germany's most spectacular scenery, including the celebrated Romantic Road.

Although the Main is a river, it has been canalized to make it more suitable for ships. We encountered our first lock, a large industrial complex, within half an hour. I pulled out the VHF radio, tuned into Channel 20 and called the lockkeeper.

"We are in two rowboats, *Niobium* and *Tantalum*, and are requesting permission to travel through the locks," I said in German.

I held my breath. This was the first of many German locks we needed to go through. Nervously awaiting the reply, I looked up at the control tower atop a mass of steel and concrete.

Suddenly, an affirmative response crackled through the radio, and within moments, the lock doors folded open and we rowed in. This was a big lock, about 350 by 25 metres, designed for multiple barges carrying thousand-tonne loads. We looked exceptionally diminutive as its only occupants. Nonetheless, the lockkeeper seemed more than happy to usher us through, and given the recent downpours, we were unworried about water levels. We relaxed in the middle of the compound, free drifting, while two acres of water around us began rising. Fifteen minutes later, the far gates opened, and we waved goodbye to the lockkeepers and continued on our way.

The Main was an entirely different creature from the Rhine. While the Rhine was powerful, almost daunting, the Main was slow and sleepy. In some ways it reminded me of the Thames. It was a river conducive to recreation. We frequently passed day kayakers or club rowing teams. Farms, vineyards and tidy villages lined the banks. Even the barges were less frequent, and often we found ourselves rowing in complete silence apart from the *squeak-clunk* of the oars.

We passed through two more locks just as easily as the first before pulling ashore in a manicured park for the night. We set up our tent in a discreet spot between weeping willows in the pouring rain. As lightning split the sky, we felt confident that few people would be using the park before our early-morning departure.

The following afternoon, we reached Frankfurt, Germany's financial hub. Glass high-rises speared the troposphere, groomed parks dotted the waterside, and everyone seemed handsome and well dressed. We pulled into the Westhafen Marina, a newly built waterfront complex that advertised moorage for €16—about $25—a day. The office was unoccupied, so we pulled our boats onto a dock, packed our essentials and hopped over the locked gate to the street. We were moving quickly so as not to be late for a special dinner invitation.

It was a fortunate coincidence that friends of ours from Wallace & Carey, a Canadian distribution company that had been integrally involved in our expeditions, happened to have a layover in Frankfurt the same day we were passing through. We took the train to the Sheraton Hotel at the airport and looked forward to our unlikely reunion in an unexpected locale.

We met Frank Carey, the company's owner, and his colleagues Jackie and Nick in an upscale restaurant serving German cuisine. I displayed an utter lack of restraint with the Riesling, not to mention the potato dumplings and pig knuckle, which is fabulous despite its unappealing title. Jackie, Frank and Nick ate and drank with equal gusto, and they shared stories of their experiences in Turkey, where they had just been. It was somewhat surreal, knowing that our friends had just come from Istanbul, and we were heading there. The only difference was they had stepped out of a comfortable jet, and we would be continuing in our worn rowboats docked seven kilometres away.

The next day, we rowed through the heart of Frankfurt, admiring the combination of old architecture juxtaposed against modern glass and steel. Hot sunshine brought hordes to the riverside paths, parks and umbrella-adorned beer gardens. The opposing current was slow, and we made good progress towards Istanbul.

By now, we had discovered that Germans loved to row as much as, if not more than, the English, and clubs and practising teams were strewn along the Main. Speeding shells packed with panting, glistening rowers would often slow to inquire about our peculiar craft. They would listen with interest and invite us to their clubhouse for juice, coffee or snacks. Since most of the rowers spoke good English, Colin had no trouble communicating.

At one such club, we relaxed on the pontoon drinking apple juice mixed with sparkling water. The rowers took turns describing the local wildlife, including an unusual goose from Egypt that had just recently expanded its range into the region.

A young man with short-cropped hair tapped Colin's boat and ran his finger along a deep score made during a collision in France.

"Have you had any trouble operating the locks?" the man asked.

"Not at all," I said, thinking he was referring to whether the lockkeepers were letting us through. "I just call them up on the VHF radio and they open the gates."

The rowers chuckled, and another man said, "There's actually a second set of locks built for rowboats and other sports boats. They're manually operated. They're very small and hard to see, but most of the dams around here have the sport locks. Just look for the arrow with the sport boat symbol when you arrive."

I was thoroughly impressed that the German government placed such priority on paddle craft that it had commissioned a secondary lock system for small boats. I was also amazed that the lockkeepers were so laid back that they happily ushered us through the giant commercial locks while we could have been going through the smaller systems.

Just upstream of the rowing club, we encountered another weir blocking the river and searched for the smaller lock. Just as the rowers had described, there was a tiny opening on the left side of the main lock. I disembarked on a small wooden pontoon fronting the lock and climbed the concrete stairs to the stainless steel control panel. Colin tied my boat to his and rowed through the open gates.

In the giant commercial locks, the rise of water had seemed quite minimal relative to the size of the compound. This lock, however, was more like a crevasse in a glacier of concrete, and I peered down six metres to see Colin and the two boats in the shadowy depths.

"Are you ready?" I yelled.

"I guess so."

The controls were straightforward, and I pushed the button operating the hydraulic gate. The doors silently closed.

"Okay, I'm going to flood the chamber," I yelled.

I pushed the button that operated the upstream sluice and walked over to the edge. This was by far the highest small lock we had ever negotiated; at the bottom of the two-metre-wide abyss, Colin and the boats looked like toys. The sluices slowly opened and water began gushing in like a filling toilet. The water swirled and boiled more vigorously than ever. Colin wrestled with the boats to prevent them from slamming against the concrete wall. Finally, the water neared the top and the turbulence abated.

"Wow, that was exciting," Colin said as he rowed out the far side.

Our destination was Aschaffenburg (or "Ass-chafing-burg" as Colin liked to pronounce it). The name means castle by the Ash River, named after the Aschaff River, a tributary of the Main. Unlike its name, it is a beautiful city, dominated by the seventeenth-century castle Schloss Johannisburg, which stands imposingly above the Main River.

From there, we began a cycling route outlined in our guidebook that began by following the Main River until the town of Wertheim at the confluence of the Tauber River. The paved cycle route then traced a narrow valley carved by the Tauber and merged with the Romantic Road, an ancient trading route meandering through remarkably well-preserved walled medieval towns. We looked forward to exploring an area described as having some of Germany's most beautiful architecture. After the town of Rothenburg, the path veered from the Tauber Valley, crossed the continental divide, and then followed the Altmühl River down to the Danube. Though it passed through mountainous terrain, the trail was quite level.

My chafed derriere was grateful for the switch from paddling to pedalling, as was my lower back, which was beginning
to bother me with sharp, jolting pains. With the aid of a few
aspirins, I could still row, but we had over 4,000 kilometres of
waterways ahead and things were not getting better. I tried
stretching, rowing straighter, rowing slower, but nothing
seemed to help. During our 10,000-kilometre row across the
Atlantic Ocean, I didn't feel a twinge of lumbar discomfort,
which made me wonder if I was getting too old for this.

Cycling seemed to lessen the pain, and my spirits were
buoyed by that and by the fabulous condition of the bike path.
Even though it was wide enough for a car and paved, it was
strictly for non-motorized travel. Regular signs marked distances
to upcoming communities, while fruit trees and park benches
appeared with regularity. I was happy to see the path was amply
used by dog walkers, stroller-pushing mothers and touring
cyclists, almost all of whom seemed intrigued by our road boats.

Barely a kilometre passed without someone stopping us.
Unlike the British, who displayed their amicability through
passing wisecracks about rain or Noah's ark, the Germans were
overtly curious about what we were doing and wanted to learn
about the mechanics of our boats. It seemed as though they
were considering the practicality of acquiring a similar set-up
for themselves. We fielded questions about the boats' construction, our daily mileage, seaworthiness and the trailer
construction. People wanted to know how to build a system
like ours, and I wouldn't have been surprised if we had
returned in a year to find a few boat-toting cyclists on the trails.

Cycling is big business in Germany. Every year millions of
touring cyclists pedal along the nation's 50,000 kilometres
of bike paths. Not only is cycling an excellent way to discover
a country, encouraging you to experience hidden gems away
from typical tourist itineraries and to eat hearty meals with

complete justification, it fosters a host of mom-and-pop businesses catering to the visiting pedaller. Small villages that would be overlooked by tour buses have bustling cafés, bicycle shops and accommodation geared to passing cyclists. The bed and breakfasts are wholesome and inviting, the kind of place where the hosts would yell at you in contented bliss and topple oversized swaths of fresh bread and farm cheese onto your breakfast plate. The pleasure of lengthy cycling trips on roads exclusively for human-power traffic is a foreign concept for Canadians. While we have the gorgeous scenery, long-distance cycle-touring in Canada involves sharing the roads with cars and trucks. The noise, fumes and danger detract from the trip, and our experience in Germany made me realize what we're missing. On bike trails, you can let your imagination wander without worrying about straying into the path of a semi, the birdsong comes through strong and undiluted, and it is easy to chat idly as you pedal side by side.

It took a day to reach Wertheim, and there the scenery changed dramatically as we veered away from the broad open valley created by the Main River. We now followed a much quieter (but still paved and broad) bicycle path that wove through a canyon carved by the Tauber River. Thick forests surrounded us, and we pushed our bicycles over a set of ever-steeper hills. After a few kilometres, the canyon widened into an agricultural valley, and we passed between the mountains through fields of wheat and orchards. We crossed the Tauber frequently on old arched stone bridges and passed the remains of many paddlewheel water mills that had been used in the past to mill wheat, saw logs and perform any other tasks requiring brute energy.

This part of Bavaria was a real-life museum. The well-built homes and buildings had been maintained through the ages, and now strict regulations ensured the villages and towns retained their heritage charm. On our fourth day of cycling, we reached Rothenburg, a walled city perched on top of a very high hill. To say we struggled does not do our efforts justice. These were the sort of switchbacks Lance Armstrong trained on. All but the hardiest cyclist would dismount and push or, as we saw one group do, load their bikes into a car and drive up. We strained upwards, thighs burning, locked arms pushing against handlebars and, between every incremental inch forward, gripped the brakes with white-knuckled ferocity to avert a downward free fall. Rests were out of the question, as there was no way to prevent the boats from rolling back. Eventually the road levelled, and we arrived at the great walls of the medieval city.

Rothenburg is one of Germany's hidden gems, not obscured from public knowledge but veiled behind a 2.5-kilometre stone wall that has protected it for centuries. We crossed a moat on a cobblestone bridge, passed the watchtower, slipped under a stone arch in the city wall and finally entered the community. It was like stepping back into the Middle Ages. Half-timbered homes lined narrow cobbled streets, geranium-filled flower boxes spilled from equally colourful houses, grand fountains and statues adorned the airy central square, and clip-clopping horses pulled camera-toting tourists. The preservation orders here are the strictest in the country, and apart from a few cars and residents chatting on cellphones, the year could have been 1750. Nowadays, most of its inhabitants cater to tourists, and the town is one of the highlights on the 350-kilometre-long Romantic Road. We bumped along cobbled streets past throngs of tourists, shoehorned our boats through the crowded central square and parked in front of an open-air restaurant.

"What are you going to have?" Colin said as we settled under a red umbrella.

"Kasespaetzle and Schneeballen," I said excitedly.

"Uh-huh. I think I'll have the chicken sandwich," said Colin as he studied the menu.

"Do you know what Kasespaetzle and Schneeballen are?" I asked, feeling slighted that Colin hadn't even absorbed what I said.

"Huh?" Colin's eyes darted to the boats as a group gathered around taking pictures. "Isn't it like coleslaw or something?"

"It's two different things. Kasespaetzle is one of my favourite German dishes. It's made from dumpling-like noodles slathered in a rich, cheesy sauce and topped with fried onions."

"Mmmm, sounds good," Colin said enthusiastically, perhaps sensing my indignation.

"And I read about Schneeballen in the guide book. They're a local delicacy. *Schneeball* means snowball. Imagine a pie crust cut into thin ribbons, rolled into a hollow baseball shape, deep-fried and dusted with powdered sugar."

"Sounds a bit like a pie without the filling. I think I'll have the carrot cake for dessert," Colin said.

The spaetzle was as good as I remembered. The schneeballen was visually captivating, but, as Colin hypothesized, it tasted as exciting as a banana cream pie without the banana cream.

With full stomachs, we rolled down the hill leading out the other side of town and began another steep ascent, this time to the continental divide separating the watersheds draining into the North Sea and the Black Sea. It was a long, steep climb, but not too bad considering it would be the geographical pinnacle of our journey. The path meandered through a forest of beech, fir and pine. Cow parsley crowded the sides of the track. At four in the afternoon we finally crested the hill, and we stopped our bikes beside a stylized blue and white sign. The somewhat cryptic image displayed a series of lines parted in the middle like a 1980s hairstyle.

"This is it!" Colin yelled. "We've reached the continental divide. It's all downhill from here."

Behind us, any precipitation that didn't evaporate would flow a convoluted route all the way to the North Sea. Ahead, it would flow thousands of kilometres to the Black Sea and then into the Mediterranean.

"I have a tradition," Colin said and looked around furtively. "It's for good luck."

Colin unzipped his fly and with little effort divided the contents of his bladder between the North and Black seas. I had to pee anyway, so in the name of luck, I added to the flows of both watersheds.

~~~

THE SLOPE DOWNWARDS WAS GRADUAL, and we made good progress into the valley of the Altmühl River (a tributary of the Danube). We emerged from the forest and pedalled through peaceful farmland and enchanting villages. We had diverged from the primary bike path, but this one was just as well maintained. Touring cyclists were now infrequent, and it was more often farmers tending the fields whom we nodded to. Camping spots were easy to find, and we tucked ourselves into the corner of farms, between trees off little-used roads and, when possible, in commercial campsites, which were becoming more common.

In Treuchtlingen, a modest-sized town with abundant amenities, including (importantly for us) a kebab takeout and ice cream shop, we asked directions to the campsite. The man we queried noticed us taking a wrong turn and chased after us by motor scooter. He led us to a small collection of riverfront tents. A beaming hippie with long dreadlocks, a tie-dyed shirt and a colourful knitted hat welcomed us and chatted idly as we unpacked our gear. He was a relic from the 1970s who lived with two toddlers and a beautiful wife half his age in a tiny trailer augmented with a hammock and picnic table.

When I praised the quality of German cycling paths, our host related the origins of their cycling movement. In the 1970s, a group of students spearheaded a drive that ultimately led to a pace of bike-path construction exceeding that of roads. Since 1976, the total length of cycle routes in Germany had quadrupled from 12,911 kilometres to by some estimates about 50,000.

Canada has a few quality bicycle paths, but they are not interconnected, and for most randomly chosen A-to-B trips, a cyclist is forced to follow busy roads. Whereas in Germany, a pleasant bicycle path can be found connecting most towns. In 2007 Colin and I cycled in the Pacific Rim National Park on the west coast of Vancouver Island, a world-class tourist destination, and we encountered some of our most dangerous cycling conditions ever. We've cycled through Third World countries with a better shoulder for cyclists than those found around Long Beach. When we queried the park officials, they insisted the environment couldn't take the extra burden of a track catering to fossil-fuel-free vehicles. The highway and numerous vehicular parking lots are the limit of what the park can handle. The Canadian government could learn a lot from the Germans.

Germany's abundance of cycling paths is a case of "if you build it, they will come." In Münster, Germany's most cycling-friendly city, bicycles are used for one in four trips. By comparison in Canada's most pedalled city, Victoria, B.C., only one in twenty trips are made on bicycle. On average, 10 percent of trips in Germany are pedal-powered, which is five times higher than in Canada and ten times higher than the United States or United Kingdom.

I wasn't surprised so much to find that more people cycle

here as to discover it hadn't always been this way. The advent of the automobile led to a precipitous decline in cycling in Europe, which would have undoubtedly continued if it hadn't been for concerted efforts. In the 1950s, cycling in England was more popular than it was in Germany, as the Germans fully embraced the automobile industry, building world-class autobahns and mass-producing cars. Interestingly, grassroots efforts in Germany began breathing life back into cycling as an alternative, while Britain continued catering almost exclusively to the car. It's hard to say what cultural forces spawned such differences, but these two European nations, both with strong economies, now have distinctly different cycling habits. The Brits are tied with Americans in their rejection of the bicycle, while Germany is a world leader.

The thing is, people don't want to ride their bikes if it elevates their chances of dying or being maimed, and that is a real likelihood in the U.K., U.S. and Canada. If you ride your bike in the States, you are seven times more likely to be injured and 2.5 times more likely to die than if you ride in Germany—a factoid that may help explain why in America 75 percent of cyclists are male, while in Germany and the Netherlands, the number of women on bikes is equal to or surpasses that of their male counterparts.

We were usually the only foreigners on the bike paths and felt as though we had discovered a national secret. The same was true with the campsites, including this one, which was, excluding us, populated by Germans intent on celebrating the summer solstice with fireworks and a few bottles of pilsner. Colin and I joined in the festivities, bumping plastic mugs of white wine, cheering not only the start of summer but travelling our greatest distance in one day: 77 kilometres, a feat that had less to do with extended daylight hours, or athletic prowess for that matter, and more to do with the absence of hills.

But the landscape was beginning to buckle, and in the morning we passed an expanse of limestone cliffs jutting skywards. The calcium carbonate had been weathered into a series of contorted hoodoos, and a handful of climbers clung to an exposed face. Above them, paragliders circled on updrafts. Our free-spirited friend from the campground had told us these were the Zwölf-Apostel-Felsen, or Twelve Apostle Rocks, a place of grand dinosaur discoveries. We stopped in a lookout area, and I tried to decipher the German placard to satisfy Colin's curiosity, but all I could tell him was that the limestone had been formed during the Jurassic period and was an abundant source of fossils. The cliffs were clearly of great national interest, a point that was emphasized by the appearance of a dinosaur museum and tyrannosaurus-inspired tourist trinkets in the next town.

Between the cliffs, the Altmühl River had carved a meandering path, which was flanked by apple orchards and cool forests. By mid-morning, the mercury had soared and we were tempted to launch our boats into the cool, inviting waters. But numerous weirs blocked the small river and as it wasn't used for transportation, there were no locks, which meant frequent portaging and we decided that would be too difficult.

We had a new indulgence to help us beat the heat and fuel us forward. In the sleepy communities en route, we'd stop in open-air cafés and order iced coffees, a decadent concoction of ice cream, whipped cream and espresso—more dessert than drink. Thankfully, there were ice cream cafés, or *Eis Cafés*, everywhere, all filled with treats of the most tempting indulgences, often disguised under unassuming and unusual names. When I first peered into an *Eis Café* menu, I was dumbfounded by the presence of dishes one would expect in an Italian restaurant, such as spaghetti, pizza and lasagna. These were places with only the barest of kitchens or none at all. Plus, they were obviously not run by Italians, and I could only guess at the quality of Italian cuisine served in small-town Bavaria. Then I realized they were ice cream facsimiles.

I never quite dared to order one of these, but studied the menu photos and keenly observed my fellow diners. I deduced that spaghetti, one of the most popular dishes, was created by squeezing ice cream through a press to look like long noodles, which were then topped with strawberry (marinara) sauce and white chocolate shavings (Parmesan cheese).

As Colin watched pizza-shaped slabs of ice cream being delivered to the next table, he mused: "Fruit salad replicas might make you feel less guilty."

"Or how about a vegan raw-food special—alfalfa sprouts and some cubed raw vegetables," I said. "That would be a healthy-looking ice cream treat."

"And why is it always Italian?" Colin asked. "They could go local—sauerkraut and bratwurst."

"Not exciting enough," I said.

"How about Yorkshire pudding and roast beef?"

"Too English. Nobody wants anything to do with British food."

"Okay, pemmican, smoked salmon and maple syrup," Colin said.

"That's not a dish—or a cuisine—it's Canadian gastronomy that exists only in the pages of a tourist brochure. Anyways, what does pemmican look like?"

Besides ice cream, there were other things that captured our attention, namely fairy-tale steeples and, not as colourful but equally suited to children's tales, storks. In this part of Bavaria, church spires were often bejewelled with brightly coloured roof tiles arranged in a mosaic pattern. Diamonds of orange, blue, green and white were visible from several kilometres. Storks' nests were also perched at great heights, table-sized wreaths of sticks adorning lampposts, treetops, chimneys and just about anything capable of accommodating such a load. The proliferation of nests was not surprising, as storks are a common bird in this part of Europe, but never had I seen such avian adoration. There were placards lauding the stork's history and biology, birdhouses annexed onto rooftops and attics converted into avian sanctuaries, not to mention bird feeders galore.

While my head was in the clouds, Colin's was unequivocally terrestrial. He had his gaze firmly fixed on the hillside, searching for aberrations that might betray a cave or fossil waiting to be discovered. In England, we had tromped around in marshy fields, my sodden feet fostering disinclination towards lectures on geological formations and underground caverns, and here we perused dark crevasses in the karst landscape.

"Do you want to crawl inside this dark, minuscule hole and see what's inside?" Colin would ask cheerily.

"No, thank you," I'd answer, equally pleasant. "But you go right ahead." At this point I'd pull out a handful of snacks or fiddle with the camera, while Colin went spelunking.

Occasionally I'd hear an "Ohhh, I think I found something," and he'd emerge with a weighty rock of no particular interest that neither one of us was willing to carry. But this time was different. He disappeared into an inky gash in the rock as I chatted to an amicable foursome of German touring cyclists. Moments later, a loud thud echoed from the cliffside, and I turned around to see Colin's tightly lodged backside engaged in a desperate bid for freedom.

"Are you all right?" I asked.

"Fine," he said in a strained voice. Moments later, he was free, albeit dirty and dishevelled.

"Spiders," he said, taking off his shirt and brushing at his remaining clothes. "It was full of big spiders and they dropped onto me when I wiggled in."

That was the last German cave Colin explored.

Later that day, we arrived at the Rhine-Main-Danube Canal. If we'd stayed on the water, we would have followed this flow in our boats. We paused on a bridge spanning the 75-metre-wide channel and watched two barges enter an upstream lock.

Our pathway followed the canal for about 30 kilometres. In the town of Kelheim, we mounted a large dike and finally saw the mighty Danube River, which was a goliath compared to the thin canal that fed into it. The Danube is the largest river originating in Western Europe and is 2,880 kilometres in length. Its first trickles originate near Donaueschingen in the Black Forest, 470 kilometres upstream from where we stood. The Danube used to be significantly longer, with its source in the Swiss Alps, but the buckling landscape diverted those waters into the Rhine, where they flow to the North Sea. Even water that falls within the Danube watershed is lost to the Rhine River via vast underground caverns near Tuttlingen, where the water disappears through sinkholes and flows under the continental divide.

Ten countries border the Danube, and there are many variations on the name, including Donau, Duna, Dunaj, Donava and Tuna. The river is named for its fast currents—from the old Celtic word *danu*, meaning to flow or run and the headwaters of the river are still extraordinarily fast, even though they have been slowed with the implementation of dams and hydroelectric projects.

Contrary to the title of the popular waltz, "On the Beautiful Blue Danube," the Danube's waters are anything but cobalt. Its sediment-laden flow ranges from milky coffee to it's-time-to-toss-the-Christmas-tree green depending on the water level.

Our path continued along the banks of the Danube atop dikes built to contain the river, and after pedalling 25 kilometres we reached Regensburg. With a population of 150,000, this was the biggest city we'd encountered since leaving Frankfurt some 550 kilometres and thirteen days earlier. We cycled into the busy city centre, negotiating our 7.5-metre-long contraptions through throngs of tourists and vehicles. Despite our trouble navigating, we were charmed by the architecture and lively atmosphere. Regensburg is yet another gorgeous UNESCO World Heritage city, vying for the title of best preserved medieval town in Europe. The core is crowded with an abundance of stone and half-timbered structures. Pedestrian bridges punctuated with wrought-iron lampposts spanned the river, and alluring restaurants swarmed with tourists. I knew exactly where I wanted to go: the Historische Wurstküche, a place that claims be the oldest bratwurst house in the world. I studied the map in our guidebook and enthusiastically led Colin to the outdoor restaurant fronting the Danube.

It was obscenely crowded, and after an eternity of hovering with growling stomachs, we shoehorned ourselves onto the end of two already overflowing benches. There was a short menu, but everyone was having miniature bratwurst, and the only question seemed to be how many. Our middle-aged waiter was snooty and inept, as though he had seen one tourist too many, but the long wait and bad service were worth it. The crispy sausages were cooked to perfection, with a delightful array of spicing and accompanied with honey-sweetened mustard and a dollop of zesty sauerkraut. The meat was high quality, and I had to admit they were the best bratwurst I had ever tasted.

Our bratwurst diner was born in 1142 when the Steinerne Bruecke, or Stone Bridge, next to us was completed and a construction office was converted into a place to feed stevedores. The 336-metre arched stone bridge was, during its heyday, an engineering marvel and the only bridge to span the Danube River for hundreds of kilometres. It was in a very lucrative position as a crossroad of trade. Tolls were extracted from both

And they're off: Colin and Julie begin their expedition in Caithness, Scotland's most northeastern corner.

A castle near John o' Groats built by Colin's grandmother's clan, the Sinclairs.

Colin lines *Tantalum* and *Niobium* through locks on the Caledonian Canal, in the company of a fishing boat.

Julie half-expected to run into Mr. Toad or Jemima Puddle-Duck as she travelled the Oxford Canal.

Locks, clock and paddle: The Thames is like a canal, says Colin—a very wide canal.

Colin and Julie camped by the Meuse River in France. Their trailer was never seen again…

…which meant building a replacement.

Julie closes the hatch on the compartment where the bicycle and trailer are stored.
Camping equipment is kept in the compartments fore and aft.

Colin finds himself in deep water in a lock on the Danube's Serbian side…

…and in heavy traffic in Bulgaria.

While waiting for the weather to improve in Turkey, patio-building helped pass the time.

Made it!

At the olive farm,
"a collection of names
in a faraway land"…

… become family.

river traffic and bridge traffic, while labourers were employed to transfer the goods. Our voyage over the bridge and into the river would once have cost a fortune, but now it was all maintained by the German taxpayers.

On the far side of the bridge, we found a pleasant riverside park in which to prepare our boats for the water. The Danube roiled and surged and promised a speedy journey for our remaining 35 kilometres or so in Germany. We had spent twenty-five days in the country and travelled some 900 kilometres on her waterways and bike paths, but for me the journey contained more personal discoveries than physical ones. This trip was about exploring who we were as much as the lands we travelled through, and Germany was at the heart of my history. I couldn't claim any monumental personal revelations, but I felt more connected to my past and to the circumstances that led to my existence. I knew my mother better, not only as a parent but as a person who'd led a complex life and had her own struggles. And now I was en route to discovering my other side, my Syrian heritage.

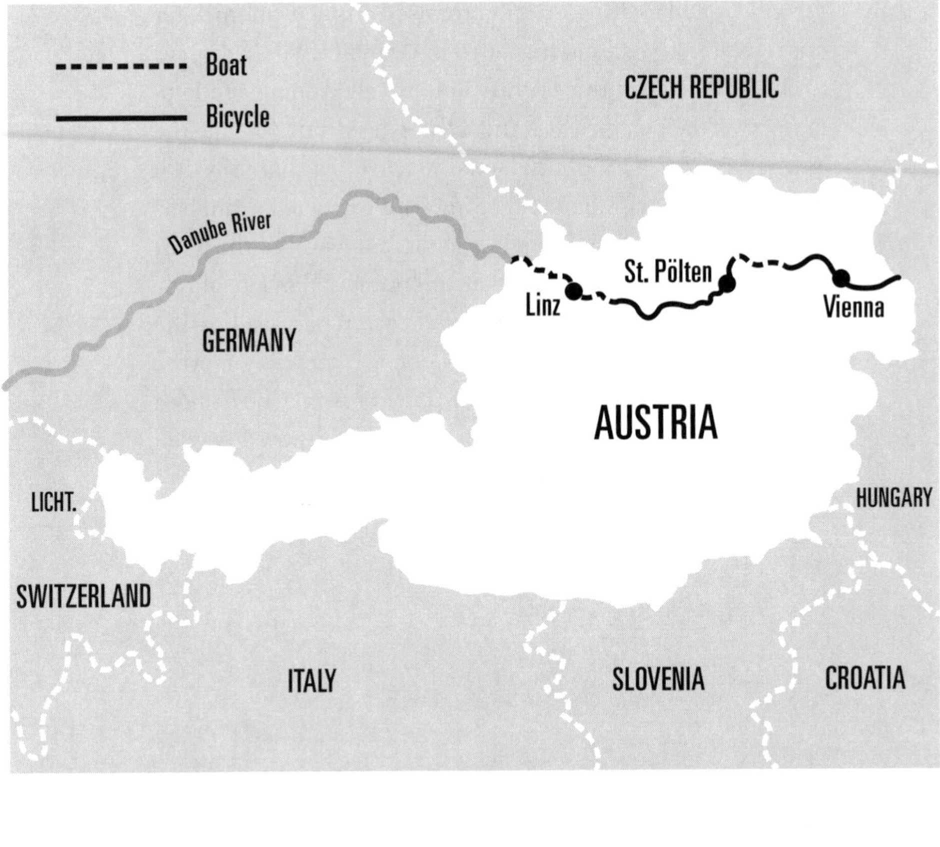
Boat
Bicycle
CZECH REPUBLIC
Danube River
St. Pölten
Linz
Vienna
GERMANY
AUSTRIA
LICHT.
HUNGARY
SWITZERLAND
ITALY
SLOVENIA
CROATIA

5

IS IT A DOG? IS IT A BEAR?

AUSTRIA (*Colin*)

I STARED IN FEAR AT THE MECHANISM. Leave it to the Germans to create something so functional, so straightforward and yet so terrifying. The liability-fearing Canadian and American governments wouldn't in a million years create such a device.

I was looking at a paddle-craft bypass sluice at a large hydroelectric dam on the Danube River. There was a six-metre difference between water levels, and the engineers had created a convenient one-way system to transit boats from the reservoir to the river below.

It works like this: You paddle away from the concrete structure to a chain dangling over the water. A forceful jerk of the chain (a bit like the ones on old-fashioned toilets) triggers a hydraulic mechanism that lowers a gate at the entrance to the sluice. The thunder of turbulent water filled the air, and the paddler is expected to commit himself to a 60-metre ride down the world's wackiest waterslide.

At least that was how I thought it functioned. That's what Julie told me the sign said. (There were no directions in English.) But perhaps it was simply an overflow chute to spill excess water when the river was high, and nosing one's boat over the edge was a one-way ticket to oblivion. Maybe Julie had misread the sign (her technical German is a little more limited) or was extracting retribution for my efforts to convert her to spelunking. We had, after all, already decided that I would go first, since I was the dispensable member of our two-person team. Julie enthusiastically offered to cheer and take pictures as I flushed myself down the drain.

With sweat dribbling down my brow, I manoeuvred under the chain and tugged. Slowly, the giant steel door lowered and slick water disappeared over the edge. Like the view from the brink of a waterfall, there was no water to be seen, only the roar of disturbed liquid below.

My distinctly not-built-for-whitewater rowboat drifted to the edge before accelerating down the liquid roller coaster. The walls zipped by in a blur, and gravity rocketed me through the churning waters towards a rooster tail at the bottom. In thirty seconds it was over, and I was at the base of the dam, heart pounding, but unscathed.

Julie jogged down to the bottom, video camera still rolling. "You looked a little nervous up there. How was it?"

"Good. It was fun," I said, feeling thoroughly exhilarated, "and a whole lot easier than portaging our mountain of gear."

I still couldn't believe the infrastructure the German government provides for its cyclists, rowers and paddlers. This sluice system must have cost millions to build, but it was a priority for the German people.

There is a series of hydroelectric dams on the Danube in both Germany and Austria. They are relatively small dams, and the reservoirs are contained with dikes along the banks, so the surrounding land is not inundated. Upstream of the dams, the current is slow, almost non-existent, while downstream it rockets, occasionally reaching 12 kilometres an hour. We savoured these swift waters, relaxing and letting the river do the work, while observing the breathtaking scenery. Orchards, vineyards and forests lined the banks, and people rode their bikes or walked along the riverside paths. To the north, the hazy blue form of the Sumava Mountains could be seen—the great Bavarian Forest.

We reached the medieval city of Passau, one of the most beautiful cities along the Danube. This Bavarian community of fifty thousand is placed strategically at the confluence of three rivers near the Austrian border. We drifted quickly along the base of a stone wall protecting the city from the river. Fine-cut stone buildings painted assorted pastels faced the Danube. Hundreds of tourists milled along the top of the wall, snapping shots of the river and the fetching architecture.

As we reached the city centre, large tour boats were moored against the wall, rocking gently in the swift current. On the other side of the river, steep cliffs and fortifications protected the city. It was immediately apparent that this location was perfect not only as a trading hub, with three rivers converging, but also from a defensive standpoint. The swift waters of the Inn River flanked the other side of Passau, shaping the town like a pizza slice, vulnerable only on the crusted edge.

Early Celtic tribes first settled in this spot, and later it was colonized by the Romans. In the fifth century, a monastery was established, followed two hundred years later by the creation of the largest diocese of the Roman Empire. From this period on, the city prospered, benefiting from its strategic location. Tolls were extracted from passing boats, and terminals were built for storing salt, grain and other goods shipped along the river.

On the north bank, we passed the confluence of the Ilz River, a relatively small flow originating in the mountains of the Bavarian forest. A high, craggy ridge divides it from the Danube right to the point of entry. Heavy fortifications and a wall run along the length of the summit. A few hundred metres farther along the south bank, at the terminus of the city, the

Inn, joins the Danube. Really, it is more like the Danube joining the Inn. The Inn, carrying frigid silty water from the Alps, has a greater volume than the flow we were emerging from and its thawed-ice waters had an air-conditioning effect, suddenly chilling the warm day.

"Shall we stay at the Inn tonight?" Julie said.

"Huh?"

"Check out that little island just below the entrance of the Inn," Julie said. "That looks like the most perfect camping spot I've ever seen." She pointed to a sandy beach fronting a thick forest. The emerald glacial waters of the Inn hadn't yet merged with the Danube at this point, giving the location the feel of being on a completely different river. Best of all, this wild, pristine location offered a panoramic view of Passau's best angle.

We dragged our boats up the beach and set our tent on level gravel. A group of swans waddled up and preened themselves a few feet away. We admired the view of Passau only a kilometre away, bejewelled with green-domed cathedrals and round watchtowers. High on the hillside across the Danube, a heavily fortified castle overlooked the valley below.

"I think this is the nicest camping spot on our expedition so far," Julie said as she buried her feet in the warm sand.

I had to agree. Passau marks the end (or the beginning) of a world-famous cycling route that follows the Rhine 350 kilometres to Vienna. It is the exclamation mark completing a sentence of endless superlatives. We knew we could expect enchanting scenery for the duration of this route, and I was excited about the week ahead.

The Austrian border lay 400 metres to the south of us, and it merged with the Danube just over a kilometre downstream. For about 22 kilometres, the Danube marks the border between Austria and Germany, before veering entirely into Austria.

Later that evening, I lay against the boat, the rhythmic waves swooshing over the sand just a few metres away. An open journal on my lap was more of an excuse to relax than a tool of industrious productivity.

"So how's the writing going?" Julie asked.

"Great. I'm outlining the lessons we've learned on maintaining our relationship. You know, the marriage-therapy stuff."

"Are you going to read it to me?"

"I haven't written anything yet; I'm still trying to distill the key points."

"Maybe we get along so well because I'm so cute and nice," Julie said. "And because I'm so good at putting up with you all the time."

"Yeah, I think that's it," I said. "And even though I can be an inconsiderate lout, you're so tolerant and forgiving that it all works out."

"And don't forget what a good cook I am," Julie added.

"I think it's the Lindt chocolate bars. They say chocolate is the catalyst of love."

"Maybe you could surprise me someday with a different treat than Lindt," Julie said. "There are lots of better chocolates. French truffles would be nice."

"That's it—surprise and spontaneity. That's the underlying theme in our relationship."

Julie looked mildly surprised. "When was the last time you surprised me?"

"How about last night after dinner? I bet you didn't know there were any chocolate bars left."

Julie looked unimpressed.

"Well, when's the last time you surprised me?" I asked.

"This afternoon when I put the whole chili pepper in your sandwich."

"That's not exactly what I had in mind."

The next morning we departed our camping spot with optimism, excited to be following a stretch of river we knew very well. During our previous journey, travelling around the world by human power, we had cycled along the Vienna-to-Passau path, and it was the highlight of our trip through Europe. Now we would be travelling through the same valley, but this time we would be on the river we had looked upon so many times, with a few pedalling excursions for the full experience.

The swift current pushed our boats along while huge boils shouldered us like boisterous but mellow-tempered elephants. We followed the distinct, swirling line separating the coffee waters of the Danube from the lighter green of the Inn. It took several hundred metres for the rivers to mix completely.

"We're in Austria now," Julie said as we passed under a bridge.

"Well, I am, but I think you're still in Germany," I said. "The line runs down the middle of the river."

Julie paddled around to my starboard side, then started nudging my boat towards the left bank.

"I think you're in Germany now," she said cheekily.

Thick forests of pine and fir with a peppering of maple and ash lined both sides of the river, and we occasionally saw pannier-toting cyclists when the path neared the water's edge. Woodlarks, orioles and shrikes twittered in a perfect forest symphony.

We intermittently passed barges, heavily laden with gravel, sand, coal, scrap metal or other dense materials that were still economically viable to transport by water. These rusting hulks seemed incongruous in the painted landscapes around us. Sporadic breaks in the forest provided settings for villages that could have been inspired by Hans Christian Andersen.

The eye-catching homes were constructed in the Germanic style of beam and plaster, with finely crafted shutters and window boxes displaying impeccably nurtured geraniums. The occupants could usually be seen working somewhere on their property—weeding, painting, planting, pruning—maintaining their little oasis.

And then we would be whisked back into thick, jungle-like forests, listening to the songbirds, or the repetitive, but never irritating, call of the cuckoo. Occasionally, we would encounter small ferries, loaded with cyclists, criss-crossing the river.

It was pleasant travelling, but I was worried about Julie's back. She didn't say much about it, but I noticed her regularly taking Aspirins and massaging it whenever we stopped. I wondered why she was feeling such discomfort now but hadn't throughout our entire Atlantic row; was it something about the design of the boats? Her boat was exactly like mine, except the position of the rowing seat had been customized to her dimensions.

"Can I try your boat?" I asked during one of our hourly snack breaks. "I want to try your rowing set-up."

"There's nothing wrong with it," Julie said. "But sure. Just make sure you bring it back."

We slipped into the water and into each other's boats.

Julie's rowing system was slightly different. I had forgotten that in Dover she had screwed her shoes onto the footplate so that her feet wouldn't slip when she rowed. Her shoes were a little too small for me, but I placed my feet on top of them. I rowed for a few minutes, then stopped. It felt uncomfortable and awkward.

"I think it's your rowing shoes," I said. "They're too high."

"If that's all it is, that would be great," Julie said. And it was. That night she repositioned her shoes, and over the following days, the pain in her back subsided.

~~~

WE WERE PASSING THROUGH a mountainous region now, with the Alps stretching away to the south and the Carpathians to the north. The steep-sided valley often terminated in granite cliffs that plunged down to the river, with only a few pines clinging tenaciously to their flanks. On one such precipice, we passed Krempelstein Castle, a simple, square fortress without lavish buttressing or turrets. Other, fancier fortifications dotted much of the river, once collecting tolls, offering protection and defending borders. The river itself made an excellent barrier, and its southern banks marked the northern frontier of the Roman Empire, offering a natural defence against the fierce Germanic tribes to the north.

In total, there were nine locks between Passau and Vienna (about one every 35 kilometres), which slowed the flow considerably. This section used to be one of the fastest on the Danube River, and during higher flows, transport vessels were unable to make headway into currents that could exceed 20 kilometres an hour. Today, that energy has been harnessed and is used to power the lights and computers of Austria. Seventy percent of Austria's electricity is hydroelectric, with most of that coming from rivers within the Danube's watershed.

Unlike those in Germany, the Austrian hydroelectric dams didn't have small self-operated locks for sport boats, or the more exciting sluice-chute bypasses. They did, however, allow us to go through the giant locks along with the river barges. They also had portage routes with complimentary trailers available, but once when we tried using this system, none of the staff knew where the key was to unlock the trailers, and instead directed us to follow two gravel-laden barges through the locks.

We passed a series of castles perched on clifftops before reaching the famous Donauschlinge, one of the most photographed features of the Danube. Here, the Danube travels in a massive S-bend as it is shouldered mightily by unyielding granite mountains. A hotel with a small marina was situated in this dramatic location, and we stopped to have a coffee while savouring the view. The ruins of Haichenbach Castle were perched on the summit of the ridge overlooking the river flowing along both sides. The steep slopes were carpeted with pine, contrasting with the tawny waters of the Danube rushing below.

Our coffees arrived, and we toasted, clinking our espresso cups.

"Here's to uniting paths," Julie said.

I clearly remembered this location from our previous trip along the bicycle path three years earlier. I had scrambled up the steep valley wall, hoping to find a clear view of the Donauschlinge to photograph. It was a bittersweet period. Our days cycling through Austria were enjoyable, but in the town of Linz (which we would reach again shortly), I had learned my mother had terminal cancer with an estimated six months to live. It was a tenuous period in the expedition, and Julie and I had almost returned to Canada. Fortunately, my mother defied the odds, and to this day, three years later, remains in good health. Only a few weeks earlier, we received an email from her saying she had not only completed the Vancouver Sun Run (a ten-kilometre race with over fifty thousand competitors) but was in the top 10 for her category.

At Linz, the Danube widens after being channelled through precipitous valley walls upstream. Like Passau, Linz prospered from trade on the river, but it lacks the same charm. While Passau's connection with the river trade is more historical, Linz maintains its position as a hub for river commerce to this day, which gives it an industrial feel. Nonetheless, medieval buildings still abound in the city core, and it is a vibrant, rich community. Most of the industry is located just downstream, where a string of factories producing chemicals and steel sit next to the water.

We drifted past large, square compounds and enormous mounds of coal and steel ore. Smokestacks belched clouds of irritating gases, causing both Julie and me to cough. It was a stark transition from the fairy-tale landscapes we had passed through only a few hours earlier.

After passing the industrial zone, we searched for a place to take our weekly day off. Our map showed the small town of Enns coming up two kilometres off the Danube, and it likely offered the facilities we required. It was on the banks of the Enns River, a small tributary. At the base of a hydroelectric dam, we pulled our boats from the river, assembled our bicycles and began the short ride into town. The sun was low on the horizon, enriching the already vivid colours of tan wheat fields and lush orchards blanketing the outskirts of Enns. In the town centre, we found a hotel, and the manager graciously offered to store our boats in the safety of his friend's barn across the street.

Enns is the oldest town in Austria, having been granted its official town charter in 1212. The location has been inhabited for four thousand years, and like most towns in Europe, it has been influenced by many ruling cultures from Celts to Romans to the Habsburg monarchy. The town is now a pleasant, quiet community, its economy based on surrounding agriculture and tourism. Its centre is perched on the top of a hill dominated by a vibrant central plaza encircled by immaculately maintained buildings dating back through the ages. We explored the open square and strolled through narrow peripheral streets, easily finding adequate facilities to complete our weekly chores of resupplying, mailing and communicating.

From Enns, we decided to take a break from the river and

cycle along the adjacent pathways. The industry of Linz was now behind us, and the paved cycle path, smoother than a waxed whale, wove between the river and the adjacent slopes.

Austria possesses one of the most exquisite sections of the Danube River. The nuanced landscape combined with the Austrian knack of gracefully incorporating human presence in nature creates a perpetually changing but visually pleasing landscape. From the path, we had a very different vantage. On the river, the lack of interaction had made our surroundings seem like a succession of picture postcards. What used to be a resplendent village gracing the river's edge was now a maze of cobbled roads to be negotiated. The smell of freshly baked bread would spill from the bakery while the postman would nod as he completed his early morning rounds. Passing pedestrians would smile and say "*Grüss Gott*," which literally translates as "Greet God," and was markedly more religious than the "*Hallos*" and "*Guten Tags*" extended to us in Germany.

We returned to the water for a day, then pedalled into Vienna on the path, still pleasantly shaded and enshrined with abundant vegetation. Our main clue that we were approaching Austria's capital was an increase in the number of cyclists and rollerbladers. Even so, the city engineers had created three parallel riverside paths to accommodate the large numbers wishing to enjoy fresh air by the Danube.

Vienna is situated where historic overland trading routes meet with water. Amber, spice and salt moved through this region, and Austria prospered as a trading hub. The city is graced with rich architecture from different periods, including medieval, baroque and modern. Unlike Passau, it doesn't present itself to the river; instead the centre and the most striking buildings are placed a few kilometres west of the Danube. Development near the river is a bland combination of modern subdivisions and warehouses.

We didn't spend long in Vienna, preferring to avoid the logistical issues of being in a big city with two rowboats. We continued along the riverside path to the southern outskirts and found a pleasant camping spot where the trail re-entered the thick forest. We pulled our boats along a deer track that dead-ended in a windfall.

"Perfect," Julie said happily. "We'll have a peaceful evening here."

This was our favourite time of day. Within minutes, we were relaxing beside the tent while madras curry bubbled on the stove. We munched on multi-grain bread fresh from Vienna and sun-dried tomatoes for starters. We toasted with mugs of Riesling while the sun slipped behind the trees. This was probably our last day in Austria. Tomorrow we would reach the former Eastern bloc country of Slovakia.

We fell asleep shortly after dark, tired from an extra-long day cycling through Vienna. In the middle of the night, I suddenly woke up. I knew I had been woken by something, but I didn't know what. I listened intently, but heard only the sounds of the forest. Leaves rustled, crickets chirped and a mosquito hummed within the tent's confines.

And then I heard it. A snarling growl sounded from within a few feet of the tent. It was deep and resonant, sounding like a cross between a bear, a wolverine and a bull. Julie was instantly awake.

"What is it!?" she said while fumbling for the headlamp.

I didn't have the foggiest notion. "It must be a dog," I said at last.

Suddenly it sounded again—even louder and fiercer. If it was a dog, it had to have been dreamed up by Stephen King.

"Maybe it's a bear," Julie said. "Get the knife!"

I grabbed the knife and unfolded the blade. We both knew it was unlikely to be a bear, but at the time in a pitch black forest it seemed all too likely. Slovakia was only a few kilometres away and we knew brown bears lived there. Perhaps they had expanded their territory into Austria.

Rooaaaaaaaaarrrrrrrrrrr!

I clutched the knife and waited. Nothing. Five minutes later, the noise sounded again, much farther away.

"I think it's going away," I said, trying to reassure Julie.

We heard a few more muted snarls and then silence. Fatigue overwhelmed my fear, and I soon fell back to sleep.

Bright light filled the tent at seven o'clock, and Julie shuffled over to the vestibule to ready our breakfast of muesli and coffee. She peered through the small window and suddenly froze.

"Honey, check this out," she said.

I crawled over to the window and looked into the forest. A small deer about the size of a German shepherd was asleep in the shadows of a tree.

"The poor little thing had to spend the night in the forest with the monster," Julie said tenderly.

The deer, hearing our voices, peered at the tent. It stood up on short legs and opened its mouth.

ROOOOOOOOAAAAARRRRRRRRR!

We burst out laughing. The mystery of the forest monster had been solved. I couldn't believe the fearful cry this pint-sized creature could make. We later learned that we had encountered a roe deer, a diminutive barking/growling creature that lives in the European woodlands.

~~~

WE DECIDED TO CARRY ON along the bicycle path, which continued into Slovakia. Downstream was a massive hydroelectric project that backed up the river in a broad reservoir. Descriptions of this vast manmade lake were unappealing, and the frequent headwinds would make rowing difficult. The bicycle path, on the other hand, travelled through forests, farmland and the outskirts of Bratislava, the capital of Slovakia.

Below Vienna, the Danube River valley was much less dramatic. The land is flat, and most of the area adjacent to the river is wetland forests and farms. Enormous dikes prevent the lowlands from being flooded, and for a long section our path ran atop a dike set a kilometre back from the river. The thickly forested land between us and the Danube was part of an overflow basin, allowing the river to widen during floods, thereby reducing the rise. If the dikes were right next to the river, the waters would rise higher and be more likely to breach the artificial barriers.

There were fewer touring cyclists now, and often we found ourselves alone, pulling our boats past green fields and poplar forests. Frequently, the path diverged, but small signs indicated the correct route to Bratislava.

After pedalling 35 kilometres without encountering a single town or village, we finally reached the community of Hainburg an der Donau. This walled city of about five thousand was on the Danube's banks next to the ancient Roman camp of Carnuntum. A large stone wall protected the community from the Danube, and whitewashed buildings with ochre ceramic roofs surrounded an impressive church. Behind the town was a castle, perched on the only hill we had seen that day.

The late-July sunshine blazed down as we dragged our boats up the hill and past the castle. At the summit, vast wheat fields rustled in the noon breeze, and beyond we could clearly see the city of Bratislava on the far side of the river. We were still in Austria, and the Soviet-built architecture was a stark contrast to the domes, turrets and finely crafted stone

buildings we had become accustomed to. Rows of characterless concrete apartment blocks were arranged like an old
hockey player's teeth.

A few more kilometres of pedalling brought us to the
Slovakian border. It was no longer manned, now that Slovakia
was part of the EU, but the buildings remained—unoccupied
and decaying. Even without the manmade border distinction,
it was immediately obvious that something was different. The
manicured landscapes of Austria transformed to weed-filled,
untended boulevards, and everything seemed unkempt.

Austrians are probably tied with the Germans for being
the world's greatest perfectionists. From a slovenly North
American perspective, it is almost beyond comprehension how
an entire nation is able to maintain such impeccable standards
of cleanliness, precision and style. Slovakia, on the other hand,
had, until recently, been dominated by socialist policies.
Individual input had been erased from regional styling, and
unfortunately, Big Brother tended to overlook the finer details.

Recently, however, Slovakia has joined the European Union,
and it is rapidly rejecting the culture that the Soviet Union had
forced upon it. I was excited about exploring this country and
about finally reaching the border of Eastern Europe.

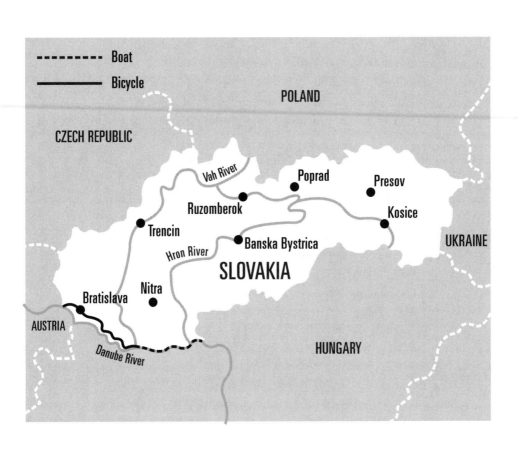

6

A PEST-INFESTED VESTIBULE

SLOVAKIA *(Julie)*

WE HAD EXCHANGED A NATION DECORATED with hilltop castles and farmland serenity for one scarred by crumbling concrete monstrosities. Slovakia's capital, Bratislava, was a Soviet metropolis of tired apartment blocks that pierced a horizon of golden wheat. Colin called it "an urban design nightmare." For both of us, this was our first trip to Slovakia. Collectively, we had visited four of its five neighbours (Ukraine, Hungary, Czech Republic and Austria) and spent at least a year in Russia and countries that were once behind the iron curtain, but Slovakia was still a mystery to us.

Like most Canadians, I suspect, we didn't know much about this tiny country, which was only a smidge larger than Vancouver Island. I couldn't think of a single Slovak food I'd ever eaten, a song I'd heard or any famous landmarks. For me, more than anything else the country's name inexplicably conjured up visions of skewered lamb dipped in tzatziki. And as far as I know, souvlaki is not a Slovak dish. Colin's opinions on Slovakia were embryonic, but Bratislava's jarring and objectionable appearance was rapidly advancing them.

We reached the border control office, which squatted between the bicycle path and adjacent road. Roof-mounted pictographs promised food, coffee, information and money exchange, but the guards were long gone and the building had a shuttered appearance. Slovakia had been part of the

European Union since 2004, and at the end of 2007, it had joined—with Poland and Hungary—the Schengen area of free movement, which then included twenty-five European countries that had done away with border controls between each other.

Nonetheless, a collection of parked cars suggested some amenities remained on offer, and I wondered if we should try to exchange some money. Slovakia's currency, the koruna, or crown, had recently been fixed at about 30 Sk to a euro, which Slovakia would adopt in January 2009. We had heard from a handful of people that most places here already accepted the euro, and so when Colin said, "Naw, it looks closed," I was all too happy to keep pedalling.

"Look at the difference between Austria and Slovakia," Colin said, pointing to a bed of garbage and bedraggled plantings. "Why can't everyone take pride in their surroundings like the Austrians?"

A maze of highways in various states of disrepair and construction surged beside us, bordered by scrubby, unloved trees and towering billboards promoting everything from kitchenware to high-end watches. The change was striking, but at least the path remained wide, smooth and free of motorized traffic, a peaceful corridor carving through chaos. As we neared Bratislava, crowds of rollerbladers and a smattering of cyclists flooded onto the path. It was a sea of scantily clad bodies, some clumsily teetering forward but most hurtling along at breakneck velocity. Our boats occupied much of the path, and we delicately wove our way forward, frantically shouting "Ahoy"—which according to our phrase book meant hello—when a collision seemed imminent.

The heart of Bratislava lay on the far side of the Danube, and we paused at a riverside parking lot to absorb the vista. It was markedly prettier than the decaying high-rises that formed our first impressions, but was still nothing to write home about. Several ochre-roofed buildings of semi-grandness overlooked the water, and apparently, within the old city centre, which lay out of sight, sat baroque castles and other pre-Soviet non-prefab gems. Slovakia's capital, like the country, had been fought over and changed hands as often as a basketball in a game of pickup. The Celts, Romans, Huns, Ottomans, Hungarians, Austrians and Soviets all had their go at running the country. Bratislava itself has had a few different monikers and still goes by its historic names Pressburg and Pozsony in Austria and Hungary respectively. It has been affected by a broad range of influences and cultures, caused not only by its tumultuous past but by its position amid a melee of nations. Bratislava is the only national capital in the world to border two countries (Austria and Hungary).

We passed a series of bridges that looked like art-class experiments. One sprouted a UFO-like orb atop a tower—it was a restaurant fittingly called UFO—and another had baby-blue staircases and ramps that spiralled like a fairground roller coaster. We stuck to the cycling path and crossed the Danube on a less inspiring albeit more pedestrian-friendly structure tacked onto a rail bridge. On the northern side of the river, the concrete was less perfect, but deft rollerbladers effortlessly navigated over the cracks, and we followed suit. We passed a series of homes, each encased in barbed wire and guarded by large, menacing dogs, and a makeshift restaurant made of unpainted plywood. Colin ducked inside to buy two cold drinks and discovered that euros were not readily accepted.

The path veered away from the roads and into increasingly peaceful surroundings. A marina appeared, then a sports club, where I filled our water bottles. Recreational enthusiasts flocked here, but skaters far outnumbered any other group. The path was alive with crowds of beautiful, fit people, many wearing only bikinis—including a few of the barely visible string kind—and Speedos. A muscular man in skin-tight shorts strode by, not a rare sight, except when his face revealed he was at least in his seventies. All this scantily clad activity seemed as much a pursuit of fitness as an opportunity to flaunt, although other people didn't seem to be ogling.

Colin was now enjoying Slovakia, and any initial grumbles about Soviet disarray had faded. He was full of praise for a nation that despite years of oppression had fully embraced outdoor recreation and fitness. It seemed the entire city of Bratislava was on rollerblades, and Colin offered superlatives like "Wow" and "This is great" and "Incredible" with lengthier morsels of praise like "Why can't other countries promote physical activity like this?" and "Look at how fit these people are—this is a population with discipline and dedication" and, of course, the inevitable comparisons to the belt-busting nation across the Atlantic. "This is what fat Americans need to do instead of eating buckets of diet food."

This was, without a doubt, a spectacular recreational path. We had heard from an American tour guide leading a cycling group through Austria that the Danube trail would improve in Slovakia, though improving on perfection seemed unlikely. But the Slovaks did, one-upping their neighbours with wider and smoother pavement. According to our map, they also built the path in triplicate, with two comparable routes on the other side of the river, one exclusively for inline skaters.

What impressed me was not that they valued physical fitness and human-powered transportation—most European nations do—but that this expensive infrastructure was supported by a country that emerged from communist rule less than two decades ago and has a per capita GDP—a measure of a country's prosperity—less than half Canada's. Slovakia is a nation in transition. The year they joined the European Union, the World Bank singled out their business environment as undergoing the fastest transition in the world. Investment poured in, especially from Volkswagen, Kia and Citroën, and Slovakia soon made more cars per capita than any other nation, which thankfully did not compromise their affinity for human-powered transportation. Two years later, their GDP growth was the highest of all Organization for Economic Cooperation and Development (OECD) countries, which included thirty developed nations spanning North America, much of Europe, Australia and Asia. This improvement is reflected in un-employment rates, which have plummeted from close to 20 percent a decade earlier to a more modest single-digit number. Undoubtedly, there are issues tied to the country's progress, from rising costs to corruption during privatization, but the people around us looked happy, healthy and very fit.

The only problem was that there were so many of them. Even now, 15 kilometres from Bratislava, there wasn't enough of a break in the skaters to allow us to slip off the path un-noticed and find a private place to camp. But the sun was edging low in the sky, so when we found an opening in the trees, we took it, deeming the scantily clad passersby unlikely to return to rob us in the night. The ground was flattish and covered in fine sand that blew into our dinner pot, our tent and our eyes and ears. A scattering of toilet paper clumps suggested that this was not a wholly private place, a theory confirmed when a man on a mountain bike stopped to say hello and tell us about a beautiful lakeside camping place not too far away. But we were already settled, plus the route he pointed out was an off-road dirt path with an abundance of protruding roots and stumps.

Our first night in Slovakia was quiet and restful, a trend that continued throughout the morning. The rollerblading hordes had dispersed, and we sped along the dike-top path.

Occasionally, advertisements appeared painted on the pavement beneath us, a stencilled or spray-painted invitation to a restaurant in an upcoming town or to a botel. We didn't know what a botel was, until we passed a floating hotel and realized it was an amalgamation of hotel and boat. The Slovaks have a way with words: at one point we passed a tiny town called Horny Bar.

At Cunova, the Danube took on a lakelike appearance because of a hydroelectric reservoir. Here, Slovakia diverts much of the Danube into a reservoir and funnels it through a concrete canal where it eventually flows through turbines and generates electricity. Hungary, on the other hand, allows the remainder of the river to flow unaltered. This was and still is a source of contention.

The Gabcikovo Dam began as a joint project between Hungary and Czechoslovakia in 1977, but more than a decade later, and before the project was completed, Hungary had a change of heart and withdrew. Hungary cited environmental concerns, although critics suggested more self-serving interests linked to a changing energy policy, the initiation of other power projects, and ambitions to trigger the collapse of Hungary's communist regime by fostering controversy and civil unrest. The European Commission tried to mediate, and then the International Court of Justice in The Hague intervened. In 1997, it dished out a ruling that faulted both parties and did little to resolve the issue. In the meantime, Slovakia built a smaller dam exclusively on its own territory.

There are unarguably serious environmental issues with hydroelectric dams. This dam diverts 80 to 90 percent of the Danube, dropping water levels by as much as three metres and narrowing the river. This change increases sedimentation, causes groundwater levels to drop and compromises the quality of underground drinking water reserve. The river no longer has the same ability to rid itself of pollutants like agricultural runoffs. Fish biodiversity and numbers have declined. But without the dam, Slovakia would be more dependent on other sources of energy—nuclear, gas, oil and coal—and they have their own conundrums.

Near lunchtime, we reached the concrete monolith, which bustled with activity. Two barges chugged into a lock, while construction workers banged in the belly of another. Tourists milled about, moving between the restaurant, lookout tower and descriptive placards. We opted for the tower first, choosing it for its lofty vantage and as a pleasant stop for lunch. It's hard to imagine a hydroelectric dam, especially such an unlovely one, having much tourist appeal, but the tower was crowded and we had to edge aside an entwined young couple to get a spot with a view.

The water downstream swirled and bubbled, the current markedly faster than before the dam but at nowhere near the speeds we had anticipated. Downstream of the dam, the river flows uninterrupted for some 900 kilometres until reaching the Iron Gate Dam spanning Romania and Serbia, making it the longest unobstructed section of the river. The sluggish velocity was troubling. We still had 1,860 kilometres to go to reach the Black Sea and needed any extra oomph the river could offer.

"It's probably because the Danube is divided here," Colin suggested. Eight kilometres downstream of the dam, it would merge with the remainder of the river, which flowed in natural channels that braided their way through Hungary. "Once the flows combine, it'll be faster," Colin concluded.

I nodded in agreement and privately hoped he wasn't being overly optimistic.

"Why don't we stay on the bike path until we find a place to buy food?" I said.

The river unified and broadened into a network of channels and marshland. With this expansion, our route migrated inland, and a buffer of trees and shrubs graced our right side. Things were pleasant, serene and smooth—until the infrastructure budget ran dry and we found ourselves bumping along dirt ruts and suboptimal tracks. Bright red and white barriers dotted the route, presumably to deter cars, but unlike other cyclists, we didn't fit through the narrow openings and had to dismount, gingerly manoeuvre our boats down the grassy slope of the dike, bypass the structure, then heave upwards again. The countryside was verdant and sparsely populated, with fields of corn or sunflowers, water towers that jutted skywards like oversized sewing pins, and a few forlorn villages.

We stopped in one such place in search of drinking water. A row of identical beige houses lined the road, all single-storey and modestly sized, with brick chimneys protruding from the roofs and sturdy metal fences encircling the yards. The town was empty except for a grey-haired woman tending her roses. We knocked on her gate and held up our water bottles, a gesture she immediately understood. Her two dogs, friendly knee-high creatures of mongrel lineage, jumped on us in search of head strokes while she took our bottles and pumped water into them from an outside well. She didn't look faintly bemused or crack a glimmer of a smile, but instead maintained a stoic look that those behind the iron curtain were renowned for. Yet fulfilling the same stereotype, she did not hesitate to offer help, and I remembered from our previous journey it had annoyed Colin that people often mistook the stony faces of Russians as a sign of coolness when in fact they were some of the kindest people in the world.

As we resumed cycling, the sky intensified to a brilliant, threatening collage of colours. A blanket of deep blue-black unfurled, promising a shift to more tumultuous weather. The wind blew with a sudden ferocity, trees groaned menacingly and leaves hurled downward. Storks blew across the inky sky, thrown from their perches and set adrift on the wind.

"Woohooo!" I yelled, my voice barely audible over the tempest.

The wind hammered my back, pushing me forward at tremendous speed. Without pedalling, I cruised at a pleasant pace and with a few cranks on my pedals I charged forward like a racer. We sped along for a short while but then the path degraded again, returning to a narrow rut carved through the grass. Our speed diminished, and suddenly the wind and rain were no longer quite as exhilarating. We inched forward until my stomach protested that dinnertime had passed.

The forest was an impenetrable mass of trees and shrubs with sporadic trails snaking through it. Intent on finding a private, out-of-the-way place to camp, one that wouldn't be visible to the occasional groups of teenagers who cruised by in old souped-up cars, we took one such detour. It was like stepping into a bug-breeding program. Clouds of bloodthirsty mosquitoes and horseflies descended upon us, ravaging unprotected epidermis while we frantically searched for the DEET-heavy repellent packed at the bottom of one of the panniers. After significant blood loss, we launched an aerosol attack, which momentarily dispersed the mob, and swiftly set up our tent.

"I don't want to go back out there," I said, swatting at a mosquito with its proboscis buried in my arm.

Making dinner in the pest-infested vestibule seemed like the worst chore in the world, and I pondered what I could assemble from our meagre reserves without going outside to use the stove. As it turned out, nothing, which really was a moot point because after mere moments of sanctuary, we heard a rustling and peered outside to see a man and his son cycling towards us. Their moderate speed was enough to keep the bugs from devouring them, but unfortunately it turned out that we were camped in the middle of the trail, completely blocking their path. We hurried outside, murmured apologies, and hastily pushed our tent aside.

This camping spot was clearly not well chosen, and so we moved our settlement out of the forest and onto the grassy meadow, a highly visible spot but one that was less obstructive and, equally important, less buggy. Making dinner wasn't as bad as I feared. A stiff breeze kept the bugs at bay. I cooked *Knödeln*, a type of Austrian dumpling, which were pleasantly tasty. Throughout the night, the wind escalated, relentlessly rattling our tent fly, and intense deluges of rain hammered on our nylon ceiling. That night I dreamed our tent was forced airborne and floated across the sky like storks blown off a treetop.

In the morning, we ate the last of our Austrian muesli and set off to find a town with food and accommodation. Mid-morning we stopped in Zlatná na Ostrove, a village of 2,500 that had, according to our guidebook, a campsite and two churches, which seemed a windfall of amenities. The village was markedly more prosperous than others we passed, with cared-for homes, intensely cultivated gardens and brick sidewalks. We found the *panzion*, an unassuming house that not only rented rooms but also served meals. An assortment of antique farming tools decorated an outside wall, and an expansive pigeon house commanded the roof of an adjacent building. It was charming and I wanted to stay here.

A bald, mustachioed man came outside and told us in broken German that there were no more rooms, but that we should wait as his wife spoke English and would be right out.

"We have no rooms," she repeated apologetically, "but there is a large hotel on the highway, about five kilometres away."

"Do you know if they have Internet?" I asked.

"I think so, but I will call to find out." She rushed inside and after a few moments returned crestfallen. "They do, but because of the big storm last night they've lost all their power."

"What about Komarno?" Colin asked. "Would they have a hotel?"

"Yes, yes," she gushed. "You should stay at the Sports Hotel. It is big, surrounded by trees and not too expensive. You will like it."

This sounded good to us, and Komarno was only about 15 kilometres away.

"It is easy to find," she continued and delivered a monologue of directions that I immediately forgot and I suspected Colin did too.

As a parting gift, they gave us a postcard of their Hege Bar. It was a collection of photos of plain but clean rooms, a well-stocked bar, a row of casks and a harnessed horse pulling a wooden carriage containing our host and another man—both bald, mustachioed and stony-faced.

Komarno is a city of nearly forty thousand that stretches across the Danube; on the Slovak side, it is called Komarno and on the Hungarian side, Komarom. It used to be contained within one country, Austro-Hungary, but after World War I, that empire crumbled and the Danube River became the divider between Czechoslovakia (which separated into the Czech Republic and Slovakia in 1992) and Hungary. Most of the city is located in Slovakia, but ethnic Hungarians outnumber Slovaks by almost two to one, and the city is considered the cultural centre for Hungarians living in Slovakia. We paused before the bridge leading into the city—turn right and cross into a new country or turn left and enter Komarno—and were gripped by indecision. It would be exciting to be in a new country but there was the lure of the Sports Hotel, big and affordable, and since the Slovak side was larger, we stood a better chance of finding the amenities we required. A man passed by en route to his car, and I asked him for directions.

"Do you know where there's a *hotel*," I said, stressing and elongating the word. I pushed my map in front of him and repeated "Hotel," giving my shoulders a slight shrug that I hoped conveyed it was a question I was asking. I had forgotten the smattering of Slovak I had practised and was talking in the annoying manner of tourists who can't be bothered to learn a few words of the local language.

"I am sorry for my English," he said politely. "It is not so good." It was perfectly understandable, and I blushed with shame at my ignorance, appearance and odour (the last time I showered or changed my clothes was a week ago). "The Sports Hotel," he said and pointed to a spot on my map.

And so we entered the Slovak side of the town and sought out the well-recommended Sports Hotel.

It was actually called the Panorama Hotel, but as it had a track circuit in its backyard, therapeutic thermal pools across the street and sat on Sportova Street, it was obviously the right place. Just as the couple in Zlatná na Ostrove had promised, it was big. And ugly. It was a tribute to the Soviets' reverence for pragmatism over aesthetics. We entered the cavernous lobby, complete with a bar, sofas, an adjoining dining room and a dimly illuminated reception counter staffed by a brusque woman of later years. She spoke German, not English, a notable characteristic of that generation, and checked us into a room for about $45 a night including breakfast. We established the particulars—Internet access (available in the room), breakfast times (7 to 10 a.m.), and where to park our boats (in the neighbouring covered garage)—and trudged up the spiral staircase clutching our dry bags.

The room was also Soviet style, which meant no double

bed but a collection of single beds—however many could fit into the room—accompanied by nightstands and a lamp or two. Our room had three beds and two lamps, neither of which worked. There was a closet, a bathroom with a shower, and a clothesline strung across the balcony. It was completely sufficient without the slightest hint of excess; it was perfect.

I stretched across the bed, kicking off my shoes and flooding the room with noxious fumes.

"Wow," Colin said and followed suit.

"Glad I don't have to wash those socks," I said.

Colin grimaced. "Are you sure I didn't do the laundry last week?"

While Colin washed our dirty clothes in the bathroom sink, I disembowelled our dry bags. Everything damp had to be hung up to dry. Sleeping bags needed to be aired, food inventoried, shopping lists written, electronic equipment charged and so on. Within moments of arriving, we had transformed a neat and tidy room into chaos. Clothes and shoes blanketed the radiator; our tent and sleeping bags were draped over the clothesline and balcony; dirty clothes sat in the sink and on the bathroom floor; and all three beds were crowded with various bits of equipment from cameras to plates to toiletries.

"I think we should just leave this all for later and explore town," I suggested.

"That sounds like a brilliant idea."

It was a short walk to downtown—across a park, past a condemned apartment block and down a street of pleasant houses and fruit-laden plum trees—but it seemed as if we had entered a different country. Soviet-era designs were replaced by pastel-coloured buildings with columns and wrought-iron balconies, clock towers and spires, pedestrian-only streets of elaborate stone and brick designs, and an open square lined with benches and trees. We wandered happily, pleased that we had decided to stop here and not some river botel or highway motel. The downtown was surprisingly empty, with cheerful shops beckoning but no one to entice. We were perhaps the only other tourists and certainly the only English-speaking ones.

In a trendy but quiet café, one of many, we drank espresso and marvelled that it was better than any we had had for a long time. Just to confirm our findings we ordered two more drinks, cappuccinos this time.

"I hate this part," Colin said when his cup was empty. "Maybe we should have one more, just one."

Colin ordered another espresso, a double this time, and finished it in two sips. We settled our bill and continued down the street. Besides cafés, there were an inordinate number of ice cream bars, another addiction. The flavours ranged from the typical—melon, strawberry, mango, vanilla, chocolate—to the trendy, like Red Bull. At 8 Sk (Slovak korunas) a scoop, which worked out to three scoops for a dollar, it was an inexpensive treat. My first cone was one scoop of mango and one of coconut. It was delicious, more gelato than ice cream, full of flavour and delightfully smooth.

"Do you think we could move here?" I joked. "Rent a little apartment, write books and eat ice cream?"

"That doesn't sound too bad, except we'd stop fitting into our clothes pretty soon."

We vetoed the relocation but did decide to stay an extra day, a decision based on more than just the food, delightful architecture and spa. We had piles of work to do for our website updates and for our *National Post* and *Los Angeles Times* travel blogs, in addition to the standard grocery shopping, laundry and equipment maintenance we did every week. And so, fuelled by plenty of caffeine and ice cream, we spent the next two days intertwining chores with sightseeing.

I am not generally a fan of museums. I find them sterile,

and my eyes glaze over too easily, but there is something about small-town museums that is more tempting. Their scale is manageable, and they're casual and lightly staffed with people who are keen to share their ample knowledge and who often trumpet obscure but intriguing stories you would normally never hear.

We were the only visitors in the *Muzeum*. The first floor contained a display of black-and-white photographs, mostly close-ups of faces I didn't recognize. We were bored and about to leave, but what we thought was an exit turned out to be a stairway leading to the second level, which held a more captivating collection. It was a hodgepodge of archaeological discoveries, including Bronze Age tools and Stone Age rock chisels and axe heads. There were plenty of Roman finds—pottery, coins, belt buckles, hairbrushes, frying pans—as well as muskets and swords from the following millennia. Large maps showed the excavated areas, accompanied by grainy black-and-white photos of trenches dug into rock and soil. There were signs, which, although bilingual, were in Slovak and Hungarian. Nonetheless, there was something appealing about being alone amid a collection of artifacts that had come out of the nearby ground and represented the cultures that lived and died here for thousands of years. We returned to the blinding sunshine, bought two more ice cream cones and walked back to our hotel, wondering why more people didn't holiday here.

After working up a tremendous appetite doing little more than writing updates and uploading photos to the website, we headed to town in search of a restaurant. There were lots to choose from, and I was being particularly indecisive. I wanted our first Slovak meal to be good.

"It's entirely up to you," Colin said, sensing my fussiness and wanting to ensure that he would not be held responsible for any bad decisions.

I perused menus, glanced inside to judge popularity and finally found a place in which to order halusky, the national dish. Halusky is basically a variant of dumplings, spaetzle or gnocchi; it is Slovakia's version of the ubiquitous dough morsels that are popular in Europe. My halusky came topped with cream and blue cheese, making it rich, decadent and the ultimate comfort food. Colin ordered wood-fired pizza, which also looked good and worth trying.

"Do you want to try a bite?" I asked, hoping for a reciprocal offer.

"It looks a little like—" he paused, his lips pursed thoughtfully, "that dish you had in Germany. Remember? The sneeze ball one."

"Schneeballen," I corrected. "That was the dessert. Spaetzle was the meal." I took another bite. "It tastes a lot like spaetzle too, except with blue cheese instead of fried onions."

Colin reached his fork across the table and scooped up a mouthful. He chewed contemplatively. "Mmmmm, that is good," he said, his empty fork en route to my plate for seconds. "Do you want to try my pizza?"

If Slovakia's food is comforting, I don't know what you'd call its thermal pools: comatose-inducing perhaps. The spa across from our hotel was more like a community centre than an upscale resort. The building was squat and utilitarian, with peeling paint and public washroom decor. A portly matron collected 160 Sk from us, about four dollars each, and pointed us to our respective change rooms. I was already wearing my swimsuit under my shorts and shirt, and quickly stripped off my outer layer and rushed outside. There were half a dozen or so pools, one large and intended for swimming laps, another of comparable size but lined with seats and covered with a mostly open retractable glass roof, and various smaller tubs of diverse temperatures. I slipped under an outside shower and headed straight to the roofed pool, which, based on its popularity, was clearly the star attraction.

The water was warm, perfect bath temperature, and had a slightly green tinge. I inhaled deeply, searching for a sulphurous odour but not finding it, instead breathing an earthy scent, like the dust of disturbed gravel. Jets drove a stream of bubbles into my lower back, and I melted with delight.

Colin joined me in the pool, smiling broadly. "Wow, this is great," he said, his shorts billowing wildly, inflated by the aerated jet firing into his back.

"What do you think that is?" I said, pointing to a row of underwater chaise longues.

"I don't know, but they look pretty relaxing."

The recliners were occupied, but we moved closer to a series of water cascades that massaged our neck and shoulders. Across from me was another curiosity, an underwater metal bench with pinhole jets. The seat was cool and the water hot, providing an interesting contrast of temperatures that was surprisingly pleasant.

"I think this is the treatment for gynecological disorders," I said.

"What?" Colin said, poking his head out from under the waterfall.

"Gynecological disorders!" I yelled. "At least that's what their brochure said."

The English promotional materials had provided a few chuckles, being full of misspelled words, awkward sentences and endearing enticements like, "Hot spring water have favourable effects of locomotor disorders, rheumatic disease and follow-up treatments of gynaecological illnes."

Colin sat down next to me. "It feels interesting, but I don't see how it's going to cure gonorrhea or syphilis." Then after a moment's thought, he added, "Doesn't that seem a bit troubling? I mean, who knows why the last person was sitting here."

It was a good point and not one that I wanted to test too thoroughly, and so we moved to the submerged chaise longues, which were now free. A metal plate ran along most of the recliner, and just like the previous station, it was pin-cushioned with tiny jets. Their propelling force buoyed me upwards, and I pulled myself down to feel the cool metal plates against my body. It felt astounding, and I wondered what potential therapeutic benefits it touted.

Balneology, the therapeutic use of baths, was popular in this part of Europe and had been for over two thousand years. In this country alone, there were over a thousand mineral springs and nearly two dozen spa resorts. But like these thermal pools, they were generally not the resort destinations often associated with spa culture. The Slovak spa was more clinical than recreational, a trend that was accelerated during the twentieth century when the Czechoslovak government nationalized and "modernized" them. Often this meant bulldozing elegant Habsburg architecture and replacing it with concrete monoliths. The philosophy was that spa treatments should be available to all, and they were. Until 2005, the state paid for them, and doctors prescribed one- to three-week spa therapies. Now there were small surcharges, but they still felt like places where someone with a serious ailment might spend a few weeks following a regimen prescribed by a white-coated specialist. And based on the clientele's advanced years, I suspected many of them came here for just such reasons. However, the therapeutic value was not lost on us, and we left feeling energized.

Our mini vacation in an undiscovered spa town was just what we needed before commencing our lengthy row to the Black Sea. From here on, there would be no side excursions by bicycle. The roads were simply too busy, narrow or dangerous to navigate with our hefty boats, and besides, once we were on the river, roads would mostly be inaccessible. We would spend the next month or so exploring the Danube River exclusively from the water.

In the morning, we pedalled to the Vah River, which borders the eastern side of Komarno and flows into the Danube. We readied our boats on a cement ramp near a floating restaurant and slipped into the river. In a kilometre, the Vah joined the much wider and faster-flowing Danube. Forests, farmland and small towns slipped past. Hungary was on our left side and Slovakia on our right, but soon we would be entirely in Hungary. A small river, the Ipoly, marked the border between the nations, and we searched for it, not wanting to miss this significant landmark. But before we knew it, we had travelled more than the 70 kilometres it was to the border, and without noticing the river or any discernible shift in scenery, we had said goodbye to Slovakia.

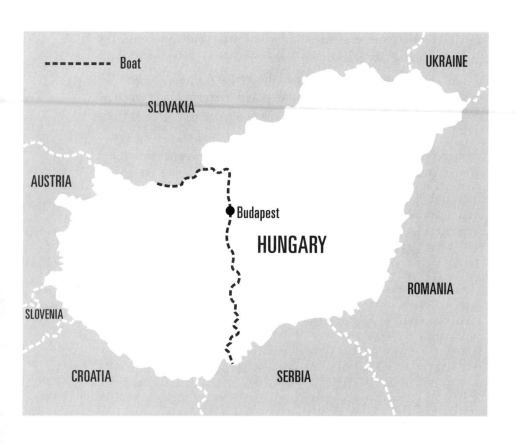

7

SEEING GOD

HUNGARY *(Colin)*

A VOYAGE DOWN THE DANUBE RIVER used to be the test of a boater's skill and patience in dealing with bureaucracy. Ten national borders criss-crossed the river, and each required dealing with customs, immigration, border guards and other officials. We heard of a traveller in the mid-1990s who found the bureaucracy so gruelling that he turned his power boat around and returned home.

Now things are different. Most of the countries along the Danube's banks are part of the European Union (the exceptions being Serbia, Ukraine and Croatia), and as a result, borders are opening up. Our passage from Slovakia to Hungary was as simple as relaxing in our cockpits and allowing the current to carry us from one nation to the other.

In Austria and Germany, the Danube is contained within the immovable folds of the Alps and Carpathian Mountains, giving it the vigour of an oversized mountain stream coursing between walls of bedrock. Within Slovakia and beyond, the Danube flows through the vast Pannonian plain, offering the river no guidance. It braids and meanders, creating semi-submerged islands and shorelines that flood during high water. From our river vantage, this resulted in a monotonous panorama. The flood plain was unsuitable for building, so villages were scarce. Instead, an unbroken swath of trees, almost jungle-like, lined the fertile shore.

Fifty kilometres into Hungary, the landscape suddenly transformed. The Hungarian Median Massif reared from the vast plain, creating an unexpected and awe-inspiring backdrop. The river negotiated these mountains through a narrow valley, dramatically altering our world.

We reached the city of Esztergom, perched on a hillside dominated by a vast cathedral that looked like a close relative of St. Peter's in Rome. The sprawling remains of a palace and splendid heritage buildings created a visual delight. It is one of Hungary's oldest cities and was the nation's capital for three and a half centuries in the early second millennium, retaining its prominence afterwards and becoming an important cultural mecca. The sun was setting, and we decided this would be a perfect location to spend the night.

Just downstream from Esztergom, we reached an un-inhabited, thickly forested island with a view of the palace and cathedral. We dragged our boats onto the sandy beach and congratulated each other on finding such prime waterfront real estate. Julie procured a bottle of Slovak red, and we relaxed in the sand, admiring the view illuminated by the last rays of sunshine. It had been a good day's travel. Without locks to contend with and aided by a reasonable current, we had travelled 87 kilometres. Downstream, for more than 800 kilometres, the river ran free, with no dams or locks, and we looked forward to finally drifting freely like a couple of Huckleberry Finns. The only obstructions between us and the Black Sea were the enormous Iron Gates Dam between Romania and Serbia and a smaller sister barrage just downstream of it.

The main reason that there were no hydroelectric dams along this section is the flood plains through which the river flows. With no valley walls to contain rising waters (the massif we were currently travelling through is only a short section), vast tracts of agricultural land would be flooded if a barrage were erected. The Danube's waters flow much more slowly through the plains (averaging about three to four kilometres an hour), but we would make good progress with no obstructions.

The following morning was a treat as we continued through the low mountains. It was obviously a popular recreational destination for Hungarians, and we could see vacationers hiking in the hills, relaxing on the beaches and paddling in small watercraft. Kayaks, canoes, inflatables and other recreational boats were popular in Hungary, and we would continue to see them throughout the country. Later, after crossing the Serbian-Croatian border, we would not see a single local in a recreational paddle craft in the remaining 1,500 kilometres to the Black Sea.

The mountains grew in size, and they shouldered the river left and right. I felt as if I was back in Austria, with the mountains slightly more subdued and the river much larger. We reached the great Danube Bend, where the river is forced back on itself, changing from a northeasterly course to southwesterly. A group of school-aged kids splashed in the sunshine as their camp leaders taught them to row and kayak.

"This is lovely," Julie said as she peered at the map to see what was ahead.

"Yes, a little piece of heaven," I agreed. We had stopped rowing and were letting the current do the work.

"And soon we'll be seeing God," Julie said.

I peered around to make sure no barges were bearing down on us. A commuter hydrofoil was in the distance, but it was steering well clear of our boats. "And why would that be?"

"Because God sits just downstream of us."

"Hallelujah!" I cried, although unsure what she was talking about.

Julie passed the map over while munching a chocolate bar, and I noticed that a small village named God was coming up on the left bank. We could already see it, a collection of buildings and a small ferry terminal servicing the large agricultural island of Szentedrei-sziget.

It was mid-afternoon. We had already passed through the mountains, and the land was levelling out. With Budapest only 30 kilometres distant, towns and villages appeared more frequently, and the arable land was intensively farmed.

After our break, we tested an idea to make things more efficient. We connected our boats with a bungee cord, and I began to tow Julie's boat. She lashed her oars on deck, draped the padded life jackets in the cockpit for cushioning, and relaxed with a book. Her boat tracked quite well under tow, and the bungee's elasticity ironed out the irregular force of rowing. I glanced at the GPS and was heartened to see our speed had only dropped from nine to eight kilometres an hour.

"This is perfect," Julie said, looking up from her book.

"Well, I'm afraid your highness will have to trade positions with the hired help in an hour."

It worked perfectly. We had discovered a much more efficient way of travelling down the river. Instead of rowing for eight hours a day, we could now spend half that time reading, writing, eating, taking photographs and enjoying the scenery. We came up with the term "princessing" to describe our new mode of travel, a tribute to the royal treatment received by the towee.

The Danube cycling path is said to extend all the way to Budapest, but we knew that the reality was a little different. In Austria, the path was a dream: smooth asphalt, no vehicles and spectacular scenery. In Slovakia, it was mediocre; the scenery was much less dramatic and the path was reasonable (though the second half was gravel). In Hungary, it was not so much a bicycle path as linked roads that often travelled far from the river.

On previous visits we had cycled the best sections of the bicycle path, and as far as we were concerned, our launch point in Slovakia was the end of pleasant pedalling conditions. The roads in Eastern Europe were busy, narrow and often in rough shape. It would be much safer on the river, and we planned on staying on the waters of the Danube all the way to the Black Sea.

Unlike Vienna, Budapest is situated right on the river and is a splendid sight. We hadn't seen such a magnificent array of architecture from the water since passing through London. Churches, spires, domes, clock towers and great cathedrals graced the river's edge in a seemingly endless display. It was such a contrast from Bratislava that it was hard to believe that Hungary had also been a part of the Soviet empire. Of course, these buildings were built before the arrival of Communism, but it was miraculous that they hadn't been replaced by the faceless concrete blocks the Soviets were so fond of.

We had hoped to stop in Budapest, but quickly realized this wasn't possible. Sheer walls ran along the edge of the river, and there was nowhere to pull off. Additionally, the waves were bigger than any we had yet encountered on a river. A strong headwind, combined with busy river traffic and walls that reflected the waves back into the centre, created extremely choppy and erratic conditions. Progress was difficult, and we were unable to relax and enjoy the panorama.

We passed under a series of busy overpasses, including a famous chain suspension bridge built by Scottish engineer Adam Clark in 1840. Ferries, tour boats, barges and other ships plied the Danube here, and we hugged the shore to avoid being run down.

As always, the industries lay downstream, so as not to steep the city in poisons, and after passing Budapest, we were treated to a duck's-eye view of the manufacturing district. Eventually, the factories, belching smokestacks and loading terminals were replaced by forests, and it was time to find a place to camp.

The Hungarian section of the Danube has extraordinarily beautiful beaches. Vast tracts of fine beige sand line the banks, creating shorelines that could rival Venice Beach in California. The beaches were covered with bronzed Hungarian bodies— sunbathing, swimming, playing volleyball, roaring in Jet Skis or speedboats or paddling small watercraft. We passed beach after beach carpeted with bodies.

"This is ridiculous," Julie said finally. "Where do all these people come from?"

It really was a mystery. The beaches were bordered by thick forests. It seemed the entire population of Hungary was holidaying on the banks of the Danube, even though there were no resorts or hotels and few other buildings.

At last we found a section of beach on a small island free of sunbathers. We slipped into the refreshing water to escape the oppressive heat. Once adequately cooled, we set our tent on the sand beneath a giant leaning poplar.

The clean, fine sand we were enjoying, in the company of millions of Hungarians, was the result of the river's erosive forces. Upstream, where the water flowed faster through the mountains, we had often heard the clacking of thousands of rocks being rolled in the current. Eventually, these rolling stones are ground into fine sand and carried down the river and deposited in the slower currents, such as at the edge of a river. I wondered if the dams built upstream, which slowed the current and prevented sand from being washed down-river, would eventually cause these beaches to disappear.

The next day, we drifted past endless forests lined with inviting beaches. A rickety café, clad with particle board, mate-rialized in a gap in the trees, and we decided to stop for a rest. We had no Hungarian forints, and hoped Hungary's entry into the European Union would enable us to pay in euros.

The café had little to offer apart from a selection of soft

drinks, potato chips and a small freezer of ice creams. We grabbed two Cokes and two frozen bars from the freezer.

"Do you speak English?" Julie asked the woman behind the counter.

She shook her head and looked imploringly to her husband and two teenaged children standing nearby. They too shook their heads.

Hungarian is different from most European languages, related only to Finnish and Estonian (very distantly). Greek, Italian, French, German, English, Romanian and most other European languages are from the Indo-European family. Hungarian is a Uralic language, more specifically Ugric, which is still spoken by indigenous people living in Siberia east of the Ural Mountains. Today, only 15,000 Ugric speakers remain in Siberia (where it originated), while there are 14.5 million native Hungarian speakers. Hungarian has been separated from its Ugric mother tongue for three thousand years, and the speakers can no longer understand one another.

Because Hungarian has so little in common with other European languages, it is a tough tongue to master. And by the same token, Hungarians seem to have a tough time mastering anything but Hungarian. On our previous expedition cycling through Hungary, we found it to be the most monolingual of all European countries we encountered. We tried communicating with people in German, English and Russian, but with very little success. Nonetheless, the people were warm and friendly and were willing to take the time to play charades.

In this remote café on the riverside, it was time to refresh our acting skills. Julie pulled out a few euro bills and pointed to the goods we intended to purchase.

The woman picked up the money and studied it very closely. She then beckoned for the rest of the family to examine the bills before handing them back.

"Good?" I said.

With a pencil and a piece of paper, the woman wrote the number of forints our purchase would cost.

I pointed to a one-euro coin and wrote on the paper, "1=300." Our bill came to 780 forints. I held out three euros along with a thumbs-up. "*Jó?*" (Good?)

She didn't know. Her husband and kids spent time tapping on a large calculator, coming up with an assortment of numbers. Our ice creams were melting. Finally she nodded, and we paid our three euros. We relaxed on the balcony in sagging chairs around a varnished particle-board table and enjoyed our treats.

~~~

IT WAS EARLY AUGUST, and the heat was almost unbearable. On the river, we tried to escape the sun with hats, glasses and polypropylene clothing, but still it got to us. We were developing heat rashes and sweat sores on our bottoms and in our armpits. We took frequent breaks and plunged into the cool water. Next to the boats, things seemed stationary, but like the undetectable movement of our planet hurtling through space, the current propelled us inexorably downstream. Within minutes of hauling ourselves back into our boats and resuming our toil on the oars, we would overheat again.

Thunder squalls threatened frequently, and black clouds spilled great sheets of rain, but the mini tempests usually missed us. By afternoon, strong convection winds blasted up the river, slowing progress as we ploughed into steep, powerful waves. The river was half a kilometre wide now, and when it ran straight, the swell exceeded one metre.

Our new towing set-up never ceased to draw attention from passing boats and spectators on the shore. When I towed

Julie, interest was moderate, but when I relaxed in the cockpit, reading a good book or munching a sandwich while Julie sweated and strained on the oars, people took notice. Generally, the reaction was amusement, and people would laugh and offer encouragement. Others seemed to find my apparent laziness offensive. While we couldn't understand what they were saying, their expressions and tones clearly conveyed the essence.

I'm afraid I goaded them. *"Elősegít!"* (Faster!) I would yell to Julie, before giving our audience a regal wave.

The oppressive 38-degree-Celsius heat slowed our metabolisms and dulled our brains. We stopped in the town of Dunaföldvár, a sleepy community where the only sign of life came from the water park. We were in dire need of two things: gasoline for the stove and Hungarian forints. After our previous efforts trying to use euros, we realized it was essential to acquire Hungarian currency.

This small town of about ten thousand is next to a large bridge spanning the Danube. Julie stayed with the boats, and I walked down the empty main street looking for a bank. It was Saturday and most stores and banks were closed, but fortunately I found a bank machine that dispensed 10,000 forints.

As I peered around in a sweaty daze looking for the gas station, a friendly young woman who spoke good English offered me directions. I must have appeared confused because she suddenly gestured for me to get in her car and kindly drove me to the gas station, then back to the boats.

We continued downstream in the sizzling heat and past the riverside town of Paks. Just downstream of this sizable community, a waterway diverged from the river fronted by a massive metal gate. Behind this barrier were the intake and discharge pipes for Hungary's only nuclear power plant. Forty percent of the nation's energy was created within this fenced compound.

"Keep an eye out for two-headed glowing fish," Julie said as we passed the nuclear plant.

In April 2003, the power plant suffered a "level 3 event"—code for a serious incident. While one of the reactors was shut down for its annual cleaning and refuelling, some uranium fuel pellets escaped from their holding container and accumulated on the bottom of the cleaning tank. This led to a radioactive discharge from the plant and the potential for a chain-reaction explosion. Fortunately, the situation was brought under control, resulting in only a slight discharge of radiation from the plant stacks.

The original thirty-year life expectancy of the power plant would be reached in just a few more years. However, revised estimates now expect the plant will be able to safely generate electricity for an additional twenty years with moderate refurbishing.

We continued through the endless Pannonian Plain. The waters moved at about three kilometres an hour, and the shore was an unchanging strip of forest apart from occasional towns and villages.

Originally, this region was a vast tract of wetlands. The river would have carved a meandering path of oxbows and loops, and the adjacent forests and marshes were inundated during higher waters. Over the centuries, humans straightened the river by dredging and hemmed it with enormous dikes to make the surrounding land suitable for agriculture.

The transformation of the river to suit human needs decimated the original ecosystems that were a part of the Danube. Fish once spawned in the reeds, and otters thrived in this wetland habitat. Fortunately, in recent years, Hungary, Croatia and Serbia have been making a concerted effort to revitalize these wetlands. Just downstream of the town of Mohács, we entered one of the largest wetland preserves in all of Europe.

Within this park, which extends across the borders of three countries, the Danube has been allowed to return to its natural state. The adjacent forests and reedlands are again saturated with the Danube's nurturing waters during the three flood months as engineers reopen the side channels and oxbows that once acted as nourishing capillaries. Storks and herons abound, and the wetlands act as a natural filter, helping to clean the Danube's waters.

The river travelled through a maze of islands and channels, and each night we were able to camp on a remote sandy beach on our own island. The dense vegetation, sparse habitation and muggy heat felt more Amazonian than Eastern European.

Finally, along this wild, jungle-like stretch of river, we reached the border of Croatia. The changing political state of this region rendered our research obsolete, and we were unsure of the proper protocol for entering this non-EU country. It was late evening as we drifted uneasily towards the border, placed amid thick forests. Suddenly, Julie spotted the red, white and blue horizontal stripes of the Croatian flag painted on a sign among the trees.

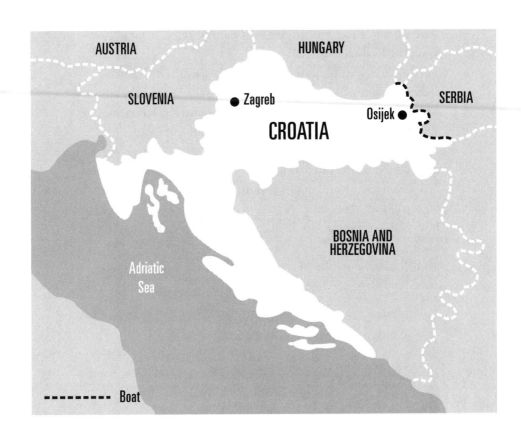

8

MINEFIELD

CROATIA *(Julie)*

U NTIL NOW WE'D BEEN IN THE EUROPEAN UNION, freely crossing
borders without the need of visas or passport checks.
When we entered Croatia, all that changed. There was
no guard posted on the bank, no police boat patrolling the river,
only a set of three signs: the Croatian flag; the kilometre distance marker, 1,433; and the monitored frequency, VHF 16.

For the next seven kilometres, we would be in Croatia. Then
the Serbian border curves towards the river, and the Danube
becomes the dividing line between the nations for five kilometres, then we would return fully to Croatia, followed by a short
stint in Serbia, and so on. The border between Serbia and
Croatia zigzags like a cardiogram, mostly following the Danube
but sometimes looping away so that the river flows entirely
within one nation—chiefly Croatia. Geographical descriptions
of the area generally ignore these deviations, referring to the
Danube as the border between the nations, with Croatia on
the west and Serbia on the east. It zigzags like this for the first
135 kilometres after leaving Hungary, but then the border and
river part ways and the Danube flows entirely within Serbia.

We were a little unsure about border protocol. We carried
an assortment of reference books with us, but those that
addressed this border crossing were too dated to be of value
while the more recent ones didn't mention it. Would there be
a sign on the river indicating where boats should stop for

immigration and customs clearance? Should we go ashore at the next town to inquire? Did we even need to worry about entry and exit stamps? After all, most of the countries on the Danube were part of the European Union, including those downstream, Bulgaria and Romania, so perhaps for simplicity's sake they allowed boats to travel freely through Croatia.

A kilometre after entering Croatia, a metal lookout tower peeked out above the trees. We approached hesitantly, expecting soldiers to wave us off the river, but it was empty and we slipped by. In fact, the river had been deserted since we entered Croatia, the banks lined with a thick forest of deciduous trees and shrubs. A thin band of pale sand rimmed the water, sometimes widening into a beach, other times disappearing completely under the overhanging vegetation. Since it was now nearly seven o'clock, we searched for a spot that could accommodate our tent.

"Over there," Colin said. "It's a perfect beach."

We crossed to the east side and bumped our boats onto the gently sloping sand. My feet sank into its fine white grains, still warm from the intense afternoon heat. The beach was empty, but not undiscovered. Flowers were drawn in the sand, watermelon rind littered the beach, and a whole watermelon lay smashed open like a post-Halloween jack-o'-lantern.

"Let's go for a swim while it's still warm," I said.

Colin was a step ahead of me. He had stripped off and was wading into the water.

"What if someone sees you?" I joked. "I hear public nudity is punishable by death in Croatia."

"Come on in," Colin said.

I undressed down to my underwear and waded in. The water was just cool enough to be refreshing and quickly washed away my fatigue and accumulated grime. Afterwards, we set up our tent, cooked ravioli and dined under a cloudless sky bright with stars. On a hill across the river, lights from a handful of Croatian homes twinkled. We washed up, recorded our daily mileage (88 kilometres) and the day's events in our notebooks, and then delved into the ship's library.

Despite our desire to travel light, we were carrying a full 30-litre dry bag of books, including travelogues, all our journals since Scotland and an arsenal of guidebooks. We had a set of four German map books outlining cycling routes along the Danube, which also offered excellent detailed maps of the river and surrounding towns. Then there were two books specific to boating on the Danube. One, published by the German Canoeing Association, contained everything an über-organized German paddler might find of value, which is to say it was invaluable to us, illustrating the locations of locks, campsites, restaurants, stores, as well as monitored VHF radio frequencies, speed of current, distance of lock portage routes and so on.

The other was *The Danube: A River Guide* by Rod Heikell, which is arguably the most detailed English guide to the Danube. It is, however, slightly dated, having been published in 1991. The Danube was a very different place then, both physically and politically. The Main-Danube Canal and the Slovakian hydroelectric dam didn't exist, and Croatia was not an independent nation. In fact, Serbia, Croatia, Slovenia, Macedonia, Kosovo and Montenegro were all grouped together as Yugoslavia.

We also carried heavy conventional tourist guidebooks detailing each of the twelve countries on our route. The towns and areas we travelled through were rarely mentioned, but the guides contained good historical overviews of the countries and up-to-date cultural information.

As I thumbed through maps of the upcoming river, Colin reached into the small blue dry bag and withdrew a roll of toilet paper.

"I'm about to explode," he said. "I'll be back in a bit."

I cringed at Colin's choice of words; mines were a real risk here.

"Be careful," I said. "Don't go too far into the forest."

Our guidebook to Croatia offered the assurance that as long as you stayed on well-trodden routes, you'd be safe from blowing up. We, however, were anywhere but in the tourist areas, and these forests between Serbia and Croatia were one of the most heavily mined areas.

In the early 1990s, two million land mines were laid in Croatia, and over half of those had been placed in this region (Eastern Slavonia). Since 1991, these land mines had killed 430 people and injured three times more, including a Dutch tourist who lost a leg in 2003. The mines were laid during the Croatian War of Independence by a trio of armies, the Yugoslav People's Army, the army of the Republic of Serbian Krajina and the Croatian Army.

In 1990, Croatia sought to separate from Yugoslavia and made changes to their constitution that eroded the rights of ethnic Serbs, who accounted for one-eighth of the population. Ethnic hatred flourished, and the Serbian community sought to create their own state within Croatia. Meanwhile, Croatia held a referendum on separating from Yugoslavia, which showed 93 percent of the population (predominantly Croats) were in favour of independence. The Serb minority was against breaking away from the predominantly Serbian-controlled Yugoslavia and boycotted the referendum. Instead, they held their own vote, which overwhelmingly favoured seceding from Croatia and creating their own autonomous territory.

In June 1991, Croatia, along with its neighbour Slovenia, declared independence from Yugoslavia. The Yugoslav People's Army attacked both countries. In Slovenia, the assault lasted only ten days, after which the army withdrew and Yugoslavia acknowledged Slovenia's independence.

In Croatia, the story was much different. The Yugoslav People's Army backed the Croatian Serbs, who had taken control of regions of Croatia, and by August, it was a full-out war. Croatia's army was inferior, and they quickly lost control of a quarter of the country. Approximately half a million people were displaced and ten thousand died within the first six months of the war. International pressure mounted, and in January 1992, a tenuous United Nations–brokered ceasefire was signed. Croatia was internationally recognized as a sovereign country, yet the war simmered on for three more years.

The Serbs in Croatia proclaimed their own autonomous entity, the Republic of Serbian Krajina, which was not recognized by the Croatian government or the international community. It included a crescent-shaped region that straddled Bosnia and Herzegovina and the area bordering the Danube through which we were travelling, a total area about half the size of Belgium. They created their own currency, postal system, government and army, but the republic was not economically viable, with its 90 percent unemployment and inadequate agriculture—not to mention an overwhelming dependence on Yugoslavia, which was tiring of the burden.

In 1995, the Croatian Army, which had strengthened considerably, launched a massive offensive and in several days overtook most of the Republic of Serbian Krajina and ended the war. The war saw genocidal atrocities on both sides of the battlefield, and tensions between Croats and Serbs still run high, especially in Serb-populated regions like those bordering the Danube.

And so we worried not only about travelling through a minefield but also about navigating a border between such disparate nations. Which is why, when we heard two deep voices outside our tent at 11:30 p.m., we were a little nervous.

"I don't think they're close," Colin said. "Maybe even on the other side of the river. Sound travels easily over water."

We listened intently. The voices came nearer and were definitely on our side of the river.

"Don't worry," Colin said. "They're probably just fishermen."

Colin withdrew his multi-purpose tool and unfolded the blade, tucking it into the flap of the tent near his head. I gently zipped open the tent door and peered out. The moon cast a faint glow over the river, illuminating a small aluminum boat and its two occupants sitting on the shore. They seemed harmless enough, probably fishing and having a drink after a day's work. In about an hour, they left and we were alone again.

Just as I was drifting off to sleep, a loud bang hit our tent, like a hand striking it.

"Who's there?" Colin shouted.

No one answered.

Colin unzipped the tent and lunged outside, intent on surprising the intruder. I was relieved to hear him burst out laughing.

"It's a fox," he said. "He must have smelled the food and was hoping for a free meal. He dragged the toiletry bag down the beach."

The fox could still be seen next to the water below. Moonlight reflected off the river, silhouetting the slight creature, and I couldn't believe the fear he had caused. It seemed that small furry creatures had a remarkable ability to terrify us. The last time I had been this scared was when the roe deer in Austria howled outside our tent.

~~~

THE MORNING HERALDED a change in weather, and rain drummed down on our tent. Thunder rumbled ominously, and it took extreme willpower to extract ourselves from the cozy interior. We took solace from the change in wind direction, which gave us a rare tailwind. Within an hour, we reached the Croatian town of Betina and the bridge connecting it to Serbia. It was a farming and fishing community with tidy riverfront homes with whitewashed exteriors and ceramic roofs clustered amid the trees. Aluminum runabouts were tied up to the dike. A statue of a person holding a star commemorating a victorious World War II battle against the Nazis towered above the trees. Several barges were tied up next to the bridge, and a sign lettered in both Cyrillic and Roman marked the eastern shore as Serbia.

We considered stopping to inquire about clearance procedures, but decided it was easier to ask for forgiveness than permission and opted to leave that can of worms firmly shut. After the town, we returned to a long, monotonous stretch of river with little more than flat, forested shores.

"No wonder the cruise ships speed through here at night," I said, referring to two brightly lit boats that had passed our tent the previous night.

"It's pretty dull," Colin said, "and slow. Why don't you try rowing closer to shore. The current there should be stronger as we round this corner."

I edged away from the centre, towing Colin's boat behind me. We had been taking turns towing one another since Hungary. From the rower's perspective, it felt very sluggish, and the boat no longer glided through the water. Instead, at the end of an oar stroke, the bungee cord tightened and arrested the momentum. And the movement was much more jerky, as the boat in tow tugged and strained like a cantankerous filly.

Although the rowing was less enjoyable, I loved my time in the towed boat. It was possible to eat, read, sleep, have cups of coffee and tea, take photographs and even dance, while making reasonable time down the river. And overall we did make better progress, as we were able to travel longer hours without becoming fatigued. As a result, I quickly grew to enjoy the towing system, except for one thing: Princess Colin had picked up the irksome habit of backseat rowing.

"You'll want to move over for the freighter, but not too much because of the back eddy," he said. He pointed to the rippled water near the shore. "See the eddy line."

"Okay." Why couldn't he just sit and read his book?

"You're too far over. The current will be stronger in the middle." Colin checked our speed on the GPS. "Not much of a current here."

"I know," I snapped and changed my direction again.

Colin's advice was sometimes useful, and at first I appreciated it. But eventually it just became tiresome and finally I exploded.

"Well, if you're so great at this maybe you should do all the rowing."

"I was only trying to help."

"Well, it doesn't help," I continued. "It makes me feel as though you think I'm incompetent."

"I'm sorry," Colin said. "I didn't mean to do that. You're the most capable person I know."

It was hard to stay angry after that, and I decided to give our eleven-month-old marriage a second chance.

Colin made a concerted effort to make fewer recommendations and I accepted them with more grace, a strategy that worked well for about four hours.

We stayed on the water all day, switching places every hour. No one here, unlike in Hungary, laughed at our towing set-up or teased Colin about his lack of chivalry. Maybe this was because there was hardly anyone on the water to do so. We might see the occasional fisherman, dipping his rod or net into the water next to a fishing camp, a small cluster of semi-permanent tents, but there wasn't a single recreational boat or person lounging on the many beaches. The river was up to a kilometre wide, with frequent islands of white sandy beaches. To our left lay a watery land of braided channels running between scrub-covered shoals, a humid environment that fostered prolific avian wildlife, including egrets, cormorants, herons and storks. Before the war, this spot was popular for fishing and camping, but now it was deserted.

When the sun touched the trees, we made plans for our nightly accommodation.

"How about an island retreat?" I suggested as Colin rowed. "There are a couple near the town of Vukovar, and we can stop in Borova beforehand to get water."

Surprisingly, our German guidebook indicated that Borova had a canoeing and kayaking club, which seemed rather incongruous for such an impoverished and war-torn region. I was curious to see the club. When we reached the nine-metre-high dike fronting the small town, Colin stayed with the boats and I clambered up a brick staircase with my empty water bottles.

At the top of the dike, I looked around the nondescript town. At this point, I had no knowledge of the events that had taken place in this small community which had led to the 1991 Croatian War of Independence. Nor was I aware of the atrocities that had taken place nearby when men, women and children had been dragged from their cellars and killed.

Instead, it was just an ordinary-looking town with simple houses and a few multi-storey brick apartment blocks. There was no sign of the canoe club, so I asked an older woman carrying a bag of groceries. "Canoe club?" I tried again in German.

I have no idea if she understood me, but the woman launched into an endless tirade of directions in an indecipherable tongue with copious hand-waving. Wherever she was describing, it was a long way off, so instead, I knocked on the door of a nearby house. A man in his mid-thirties appeared, wearing overalls and a tool belt. Music poured out through the open door, an unusual but pleasant blend of opera and polka. I held out my empty two-litre water bottles, and he led me to a tap in the backyard. In a few moments, his wife came out. She spoke a little English.

"We are fixing the house," she said, pointing to a crumbling wall.

"*Dobro*," I said, recalling the Croatian word for good.

"No, no dobro. Bad." She said firmly.

"I mean *good* that you are fixing it."

The woman was confused.

"Bad, very bad," I finally said.

The woman smiled. "Yes, bad."

After exchanging a few more halting phrases, I thanked her and said goodbye: "*Dovidenja*."

I wasn't sure if my choice of Croatian was correct. Although this was Croatia, much of the population in this city was Serb. It was like that before the war of independence, too, and as a result, this was one of the first places where violence erupted. In May 1991, twelve Croatian policemen and three Serbs were killed here in a gun battle that fuelled the ensuing violence in Croatia and set the stage for conflict in other Yugoslav regions.

At the time of the wars in Croatia, Slovenia and Bosnia, I heard about them through the news and also from my father, who was in the Canadian military and working as part of the UN effort to provide humanitarian aid. He flew missions bringing food and medicine into Sarajevo in Bosnia and Herzegovina and taking out wounded. To me, they were terrible conflicts unravelling in faraway places I never expected to be in. To be here now seemed surreal.

The rain resumed as we continued rowing, and we camped on a Serbian island within sight of Vukovar. It was low and marshy with a carpet of plastic pop bottles farther inland that had been deposited by floodwaters. Thunder cracked and the deluge intensified. We erected our tent on a patch of reedy grass just a few feet above the river, tied the boats to a tree and hoped the water wouldn't rise too much.

The next day, we continued past Vukovar, Croatia's largest river port. We passed several docked barges, and a handful of hefty cranes reached over the water, plucking cargo off the ships. The riverfront boasted a few small factories, a hotel, several apartment blocks and houses and a number of brand-new structures. While not exactly pretty, it certainly wasn't bad for a city that had been destroyed just seventeen years earlier. If it hadn't been for a few skeletal buildings that had been bombed and burned, one would not have guessed its recent tragic history.

The devastation in Vukovar has been called Europe's worst conflict since World War II. In 2001, the town came under siege from the Serbian paramilitary forces and the Yugoslav People's Army. By then, Croatia had lost control of about a third of its country, including most of the regions around Vukovar. For three months, heavy artillery and daily attacks bombarded the city. The eighteen hundred defenders of the city were poorly equipped and seriously outnumbered by the attacking armies, which were estimated to include as many as fifty thousand soldiers. Yet they held on to the city for eighty-seven days before surrendering. The loss of life was tragic, as were the war crimes committed and eventually brought to trial. Over two thousand soldiers and civilians died defending Vukovar and more are still missing. People were sent to concentration camps, executed in large numbers and buried in mass graves. Although it was a devastating defeat for Croatia, the attacking armies also suffered major losses. As a result, Croatia garnered international support for its bid for independence. The battle became a turning point in the war.

On a sandy cliff in the outskirts of Vukovar stood a symbol of the town's suffering: a bullet-riddled, bombed-out water tower, a soaring cone of crumbling brick that proudly flew the Croatian flag. We slipped past it, imagining the bombs and mortars fired at it from the Serbian side of the Danube and the Yugoslav gunships that patrolled the very waters we now rowed on.

A stork flew across the river, and a gentle breeze rustled the leaves. The river's roiling current pushed us beyond the town and back into poplar forests. I quietly rowed out of Croatia for the last time and into Serbia; only the smallest of signs signalled that we had entered a new nation.

9

NEW FAVOURITE COUNTRY

SERBIA *(Colin)*

F OR THE PAST TWO AND A HALF DAYS, we had been flirting with
Serbia, entering and exiting the nation untold times as the
Danube flowed between Serbia and Croatia. The border
between the nations followed the old meandering S-curves of
the Danube, but the river had been straightened and now it
pierced the squiggly border like an arrow. There weren't any
visual clues hinting at which country we were in, and most of
the time we had no idea at all. For the first 130 kilometres, our
arrival into Serbia had been like an old TV set flickering
between two channels, but now the border veered away from
the river and we continued into the interior of Serbia.

Before embarking on our expedition, my knowledge of
Serbia had been delivered mainly through newspapers and
television as one of Europe's most recent wars played out. In
1999, escalating conflicts between Serbs and ethnic Albanians
in Kosovo, an autonomous province in Serbia, prompted UN
intervention. That spring, in an effort to subdue the violence,
UN forces heavily bombed military installations, bridges and
other infrastructure. The conflict resulted in a tremendous loss
of life, although the exact number is still disputed. It was estimated that more than six thousand ethnic Albanians of Kosovo
were murdered in an attempt to quash Kosovo's ambitions of
independence. Yugoslav President Slobodan Milosevic, who
then governed the Republic of Serbia, was accused of ethnic

cleansing in the Kosovo region and was brought to trial for war crimes. He died of a heart attack before the trial concluded. The ethnic tensions still exist, and Kosovo's independence is still disputed; Serbia does not recognize it, although fifty-five UN member states and the Republic of China do.

Then there were the earlier conflicts between Croatia and Serbia. When we rowed between those countries, it felt as though we were passing not only through a vast wildlife preserve of forested wetlands but also through a no man's land between two disparate nations. As ducks and herons flapped peacefully, I couldn't help but wonder how many mines lurked in the thick vegetation.

Most news from this region has been tied to violence, war and strife, and for this very reason, we were looking forward to visiting Serbia and getting a feel for the nation beyond what had been conveyed through the international media.

The Danube was now busier with commercial fishermen, usually perched in small wooden or aluminum boats with antique motors on the back, but we saw no one using the river for recreation as we had in Hungary. The wildlife preserve eventually slipped behind us, replaced by a thin strip of trees fronting endless tracts of farmland. We were now in the centre of the fertile Pannonian Plain, which was created when the Pannonian Sea dried up 600,000 years ago. It is a rich agricultural area and a boon to Serbia's farmers, who make up one-sixth of the population. Much of Serbia, 70 percent, is farmland, with agriculture split evenly between livestock production and crops, primarily wheat, maize, sunflowers and sugar beets.

As we neared the large city of Novi Sad, more villages and towns appeared, and we began searching for a place to take a break.

"This spot coming up looks promising," Julie said. She was studying a map as I towed her boat downstream. "There's a little icon with a hotel and a swimming pool. Maybe it's a cheap spa like the one back in Slovakia."

The village was about 11 kilometres upstream from Novi Sad on the right bank. I rowed around the tip of a large island and followed a ferry towards the shore.

"Hmm, doesn't look like there's much here," Julie said as we neared a handful of derelict buildings near the concrete ferry ramp.

I'd been pulling hard on the oars to get us across the river and wasn't yet ready to give up.

"Let's just go for a wander and see if we can find anything," I said.

We pulled up to a sandy beach and wandered over to the only commercial building. A sign advertised a restaurant. Inside, I queried the wait staff with a singular universal word: "Hotel?"

A woman nodded vigorously and led us to a well-dressed man in his mid-fifties.

"*Sprechen Sie Deutsch?*" he asked.

Julie nodded, and the two began conversing.

"This place is a hotel, apparently," Julie translated. "They have a couple of rooms upstairs."

"What about the therapeutic spa?"

"Uh-uh. This is the only hotel around and the only swimming is in the Danube."

"Internet?"

"No. He says it should be pretty easy to get online, though . . ." Julie paused and waited for the man to explain further. "You just take the ferry across the river, and then it's a half-hour bus ride to Novi Sad. They have Internet there."

It was far from ideal, but the place was clean, the staff pleasant and a threatening squall was moving our way. We moved our boats and bags up as the rain began pouring down.

Our room was clean and simple with pine furniture, a view of the river and a small bathroom. It was time to celebrate finishing another week's hard rowing in the restaurant below.

A collection of expensive European cars were in the parking lot, and the restaurant was already filling with well-dressed clientele. It was a somewhat pretentious establishment, but between the gaudy decor, circling flies and cigarette-holed linen, it fell short. The food, however, was spectacular. Serbians are very fond of meats and spices and do an excellent job combining the two. We ordered a meat platter of barbecued beef, lamb, pork and sausages, which were tender heavily spiced morsels that surpassed even the German bratwurst. We would find, as we continued through Serbia, that the cuisine remained outstanding, especially the cured meats, which were some of the best I'd sampled.

After dinner, Julie and I went for a stroll to the adjacent town of Beocin, two kilometres inland. The economy of this small town used to be dominated by the grape industry. The low limestone hills, ideal for growing vines, were eyed greedily by a growing nation hungry for concrete. In 1952, the government set up a giant cement-production facility that gnawed steadily into the limestone hills. In 2001, the factory was privatized and purchased by Lafarge. Today it is one of the largest cement producers in Europe, and a canal leads to the Danube, allowing for economical water transport.

Oddly, despite the high number of jobs provided by Lafarge, we felt as if we were entering a Third World community. Garbage was piled thick along the side of the road, and people lived in squalor. The row houses were cracked and sagging, with graffiti-stained walls, a patchwork of corrugated metal for roofs, and vegetation growing from the eavestroughs. Dirty children played on the road while TVs blared from open windows. But as we neared the entrance of the Lafarge facility, the setting

transformed. Homes that would have been condemned elsewhere were replaced by offices in brightly painted heritage
buildings with pleasantly landscaped borders.

As the sun slipped behind the hills, tough-looking
youths began gathering in groups, and we decided to return
to our hotel.

We departed early the following morning, catching the
ferry across the river. It was a rusty barge pushed by a small tug
and capable of carrying about nine cars. Passengers were
expected to help crank the manual winch that lifted the entry
ramp. On the far side of the river, a half-hour bus ride brought
us into the city of Novi Sad.

Novi Sad is Serbia's second-largest city, with a population
of about 300,000. Its economy has traditionally been resource
based, and it is placed in the centre of Serbia's main agricultural region. Today its economy is more diversified, and it is
quickly becoming a major financial and cultural hub. Despite
its increasing prosperity, our view of the city from the bus as we
emerged from the countryside was mainly of squalid slums.
Garbage, decrepit homes and cars belching black smoke were
suddenly replaced by a sophisticated and clean district as we
neared the city centre. Here, beautifully maintained nineteenth-century buildings graced clean cobbled roads. Tourists
milled about, drifting through gift shops and Western franchises. There were frequent sidewalk cafés and restaurants
where one could sit and admire the surrounding churches,
clock towers and ornate flower-draped balconies.

We raced through our chores—withdrawing money, updating our website and purchasing groceries—then spent the rest
of the afternoon exploring Serbia's cultural hub. The city
pulsed with a youthful rhythm, which intensified as dusk
approached and the cafés became busier and the music louder.
I wondered if it was always like this or if it was because we

had just missed Novi Sad's EXIT festival, a nine-day music event with an unbelievable roster: U2, Coldplay, Santana, Billy Idol, INXS, Manu Chao and Gloria Estefan. Everyone we talked to assumed we were there for the concert like everyone else. While we were having dinner our young waitress learned otherwise, and she asked in a quiet voice, "Have you had problems in Serbia?"

"No," I said, surprised by her question. "People here are very friendly."

But the kindness and pleasantries we had encountered so far were just the beginning, and soon Serbia would go on to become one of our favourite countries, far surpassing our expectations.

The following day we saw Novi Sad from a very different perspective as we drifted past in our boats. A spate of expensive-looking homes, some adorned with float planes and speedboats, preceded the city, but that was where the wealth ended. The city straddled both sides of the river, and most of what we saw were nondescript apartment blocks, grey and ugly, with a few pocket-sized beaches tucked here and there. The huge fort of Petrovaradin, nicknamed the Gibraltar of the Danube, sat on the right bank. The Celts originally had a stronghold on this hillside location, which was rebuilt by the Romans in the first century. The Huns destroyed the Roman fort in the fifth century, and it was rebuilt shortly after by the Byzantines. It peered down on the river, guarded by a cliff and thick fortified walls, looking austere and imposing. However, a few days earlier it would have pulsed with the massive crowds of EXIT festival as the biggest names in music performed on these grounds.

The theme of wartime destruction followed by rebuilding is evident right to modern times. We passed under the sleek modern form of the Liberty Bridge, a structure rebuilt in 2005 after its predecessor was destroyed by NATO forces in 1999.

In total, six bridges crossed the Danube in Novi Sad, including a railway bridge that is the lowest structure along the Danube's length. This bridge determines the maximum height to which Danube transport vessels can be built. During high water, larger boats sometimes are unable to pass.

~~~

THINGS WERE UNEVENTFUL for the next 150 kilometres to Belgrade. The relentless heat continued, and our two days of travel were a blur of rowing past endless flatlands and villages. Serbia's capital is located at the confluence of the Sava River and the Danube, and the city fronts both flows. The city has been destroyed and rebuilt so many times in the countless wars that have ravaged this region that it is as much a symbol of the resilience and fortitude of the inhabitants as it is a community. Unfortunately, the final rebuilding appeared to have been done at the hands of the Soviets, and most of the structures are the blank, communist-style concrete apartment blocks.

We had no plans to stop in Belgrade and instead relaxed in our cockpits, allowing the Danube's currents to take us on an interactive tour. Barges rumbled past, loaded with coal, cement, sand and gravel, and fishermen, cigarettes hanging out of their mouths, cast lines from the bases of bridge supports and nodded as we passed.

The current was moving a sluggish two kilometres an hour and would continue to slow for the next 400 kilometres as we approached the massive Iron Gates Dam. We were finally nearing the end of the Pannonia Plain. The Carpathian Mountains fringed the lower end of the plain, and the Danube had carved a spectacular route through the limestone mountains, creating the Iron Gates Gorge.

This narrow gorge was once the most difficult section to navigate between the Black Sea and Austria. The river gushed through it with currents exceeding 20 kilometres an hour in a maelstrom of whitewater and submerged rocks. Several attempts had been made to make these waters more navigable, including the use of explosives to clear the channel. However, the currents were still so strong that a railway track and a locomotive had to be installed along the river to haul barges against the current. A side channel was also built, with limited success. It wasn't until the completion of the massive Iron Gates hydroelectric project, in 1971, that the river's spirit was truly broken. The dam raised the water levels by 16 metres, and the gorge was turned into a reservoir—a manmade lake surrounded by spectacular natural beauty.

Fifty kilometres before entering the gorge, the river runs up against the Romanian border of Transylvania. We rowed down the broad, slow river with Serbia to our right and Romania to the left. We felt a little uneasy looking across to the forested homeland of Dracula.

The current had slowed to almost a standstill as we neared the gorge, and the skeletal remains of trees protruded from the water like ghoulish hands reaching for our boats. We passed the decrepit industrial town of Moldova Veche on the Romanian bank before the river veered towards the looming mountains.

The entrance to the gorge is marked by the fourteenth-century Golubac Castle perched on a limestone pinnacle. The outbuildings of this magnificent structure seem to defy the laws of physics as they sprawl down the precipice to the water's edge.

We were about to enter the world's most spectacular outdoor museum, and apart from a few passing barges, it felt as if we were the only occupants. Limestone cliffs rose straight from the water's edge, some over 600 metres tall. The soluble limestone was riddled with caves, many of which provided shelter to the first humans to inhabit this area. Interestingly, one of Europe's most impressive archaeological finds was discovered in the Iron Gates Gorge: Lepenski Vir—an eight-thousand-year-old mesolithic village, built on a flat riverbank flanked by steep mountains.

An archaeological dig appeared among the trees, a partially excavated terraced slope. Since nobody was around, we stopped and wandered through the area, imagining what life must have been like eight thousand years ago. Here, they discovered some of the oldest mesolithic sculptures ever found, stylized humanoids crafted with incredible skill. The geometric structure of the village spoke of a society that was incredibly complex socially. It is believed the intricacies of this advanced culture laid the groundwork for the agricultural period that followed.

Occasional tight valleys snaked down from the mountains, creating coves among the cliffs with room for a few farmhouses with tidy haystacks out back. After weeks of travelling through bland open landscapes, we felt as though we had entered the set of *Lord of the Rings*. The river snaked between vast precipices, mirrored above by a ribbon of sky. At one point, the river was squeezed to a width of less than 150 metres. The depths here were the greatest on the Danube, going down as far as 80 metres, and the river bottom was 20 metres below sea level. On the Romanian shore, we came across the remarkable sight of a bust carved into a pillar of rock over 100 metres tall. The sculpture was of Decebalus, king of the Dacians, who fought and won three battles against the Romans. The sculpture was as impressive as the heads on Mount Rushmore and had been carved in a setting of dramatic beauty.

Shortly after admiring the bust of Decebalus, we encountered a Roman tablet set at the base of a cliff in Serbia. The remarkably well-preserved monument celebrated Trajan's achievement of completing a road through this canyon, started in 14 AD. The road was an impressive feat of engineering, and large parts of it were constructed by drilling holes into the cliff face above the water. Logs were inserted into these holes and surfaced with planks. The wood had long rotted, but the two-thousand-year-old holes remained. Unfortunately, we couldn't see them, as they are submerged by the raised waters. Julie and I examined the tablet, accessible only by boat, and marvelled at the fact that we were alone in a rugged canyon next to such an incredible monument. The tablet was about three metres high with a carved header labelled *"Tabula Traiana."* Decorative fish, flowers and angels were carved around text inscribed neatly in (hardly surprisingly) Roman font.

We spent two delightful days travelling through the Iron Gates Gorge and were almost disappointed when we saw a large dam in the distance marking the end of our passage through the Carpathian Mountains. Two locks bypassed the dam, one on the Serbian side and the other in Romania. We had been advised to go through the Serbian side.

Julie hailed the lockkeepers on the VHF radio and asked in German (the language spoken by all lockkeepers along the Danube) for permission to pass. The Serbian lockkeeper replied immediately and advised us to go through with an approaching barge.

This was the biggest hydroelectric project along the length of the Danube, and approaching the lock was somewhat daunting. The control tower was about eight storeys high, all concrete, steel and glass, and the rest of the complex was enormous. Our tiny rowboats were dwarfed by the magnitude of such industry, and we drifted into the expansive lock chamber like flotsam in the waves. We took a position behind the tidy Dutch barge, and a wall rose silently from the depths, closing the chamber.

We were travelling through a double-lock system that reduced water consumption by 50 percent. At hydroelectric dams, any water lost through the locks amounts to decreased electrical production, so it is advantageous to reduce water usage in any way possible. Basically, the locks were formed as two steps, and usage is timed so that boats coming from below are lifted at the same time as boats in an adjacent lock descend from above. The water released from the dropping lock is used to fill the rising lock. When the water levels between the locks are equal, a door separating the two open, and the boats trade positions and continue the remainder of their ascent or descent.

Curious, I did a calculation to see how much potential energy was lost through water released in the locks of the Iron Gates Dam and came up with an impressive figure. The inner compound is 310 by 34 metres and contains about 84.3 million litres. With a 16-metre difference in water levels and 60 percent turbine efficiency, this amount of water would produce 3,676 kilowatt-hours, or one-third of the annual consumption of an average American home. The dual-lock system cuts this figure in half, so two sets of boats could transit—one up and one down—at a cost of 3,676 kilowatt-hours (about $300 at 8.5 cents per kilowatt-hour).

These figures gave me a new appreciation of the hidden costs tied to using the locks. At hydroelectric plants, we always shared the locks with commercial vessels, so we weren't a burden, but it was interesting to learn the direct value of the potential energy stored in the water. I wondered if technology could be developed to use a waterless system to transport boats past the dams—a funicular railway type of system where the weight of a descending boat assisted in lifting the downstream vessel.

~~~

WHEN WE WERE RELEASED into the swirling waters below the dam, I felt as if I had stepped out of an IMAX theatre into an industrial neighbourhood. Gone were the panoramic mountains, lime-stone cliffs, endless forests and small subsistence farms. The land on both sides of the river was now flat and criss-crossed with roads and industry. We rowed for about half an hour before pulling into the town of Kladovo and tying up in the first marina we had seen in Serbia.

Kladovo was a moderate-sized town that houses most of the workforce from the Serbian side of the Iron Gates Dam. The community has expanded rapidly during the construction of the dam in the 1960s, and most of the town was crafted to the functional but aesthetically lacking design of the Soviets. Despite a dearth of charm, it was perfect for our weekly break. The town possessed an inexpensive multi-storey Soviet-style hotel and abundant facilities at reasonable prices. The com-munity was a stark contrast to the Third World squalor we had experienced near the Lafarge factory upstream. Here the economy was thriving, and open-air restaurants and cafés were filled to capacity. We wheeled our boats down clean streets and past smiling inhabitants to our new home.

Everybody needs to stay in a Soviet-style hotel at least once in their lifetime. Whether in the depths of Siberia, in the middle of Moscow or in a small Baltic town, they are all popped from the same ice cube tray. The building itself is usually four to eight storeys high, made with concrete and punctuated by small windows. The foyer is large, draped with thick curtains and reeks of cigarette smoke. The real fun is in the bedroom. Often there will be a radio (of a sort that never existed in the Western world) that doesn't work, a rotary phone and two single beds. Double beds simply do not exist in hotels designed by the communists (and they wonder why the birth rate is declining so quickly in Russia).

Nonetheless, these hotels were designed to be economical and functional, exactly what two weary river travellers needed. The girl working behind the desk asked for our passports.

"I will need to register them with the police," she said in surprisingly good English.

Julie and I looked at each other. I had forgotten about this—another formality I'd encountered in Russia and many Eastern Bloc countries to keep track of all travellers.

The girl flipped through our passports. "Where is your entry stamp?"

The problem was we hadn't cleared into Serbia and therefore had no entry stamps in our passports.

"I'm not sure," Julie said.

The girl smiled. "Don't worry. I am sure there will be no problems."

She pulled out a map of Serbia and asked where we entered. We pointed to the correct location.

"Geez, I hope the police don't bust us," Julie said when we entered our room.

"Shh—this place is probably bugged," I said, pointing to a radio that looked like it had come straight from the 1940s.

Julie's eyes opened wide, and I burst out laughing.

"I'm only kidding. I'm sure everything will be fine."

Nonetheless, we couldn't help but be a little nervous for the rest of our stay in Kladovo.

After settling into our hotel, we went in search of dinner. The main street had no fewer than a dozen outdoor restaurants, and we ended up opting for a pizzeria serving delicious thin-crusted pies. After two days of eating, exploring, cleaning laundry in the tub and doing the rest of our errands, we were ready to hit the road.

We packed our gear back into the boats and returned to the front desk to check out and retrieve our passports.

As the clerk handed over the passports, she looked me in the eye. "We have a problem," she said.

My stomach tightened. "And what might that be?" I asked.

"The boats." My stomach tightened even more. "We had hoped to open the back door so you could remove them more easily, but I'm afraid the door is stuck. You will have to take them out the front."

"Not a problem," I said with relief.

Half an hour later, we were drifting down the river on the final leg to Bulgaria. The town quickly disappeared, and we passed a watchtower protruding from a thick swath of trees. Two figures stood on the lofty platform and watched our progress.

"Don't look at them," I said. "Maybe we can slip on by."

I noticed one of the men waving his arms. We paused momentarily, debating what to do next.

Suddenly, a series of explosive retorts sounded over the water. They were shooting into the air! We had no choice but to oblige, and I turned my boat towards shore. Now we would definitely be caught for not clearing into Serbia.

Julie burst out laughing. "They're just kids!"

I turned and stared at the tower. Sure enough, two young boys were playing on the abandoned military installation and tossing firecrackers over the side. I felt relieved and embarrassed.

Julie chuckled. "Who's my rough, tough adventurer who can't tell the difference between soldiers with guns and children with firecrackers?"

The following day we reached another dam. This structure was much smaller than the Iron Gates barrage and was used to even out any water fluctuation the larger upstream dam caused in order to meet varying electrical demands. Julie called the lockkeeper, and he advised us to wait for a cruise ship.

As we relaxed in the shallows, the 60-metre-long luxury cruising vessel nosed into the pier. Its decks were crowded with passengers, and a large French flag fluttered in the breeze.

The radio crackled to life, and the lockkeeper instructed Julie in German to enter ahead of the cruise ship, which was still tied to the pier. We slipped in front of its bow and moved towards the lock chamber.

A long blast of the horn sounded, and the ship's captain emerged from the bridge shaking his fist at us.

"What's his problem?" I said.

"He probably doesn't understand German and doesn't realize they told us to come through first."

We took our positions in the lock, and the French ship moved in behind us. As it drew near, the horn blasted again. Several of the officers came onto the deck and shouted at us in French.

So far on the river we had experienced nothing but friendly, laid-back behaviour from the working ships. Captains and crew from barges and tugs would wave merrily across the water, often shouting encouragement our way. Even when we were in the wrong, daydreaming and veering alarmingly close to the path of a loaded barge, they'd give a few warning toots and wave good-naturedly as we passed.

When the doors to the lock opened, we moved to the side of the narrow, high-sided chamber to allow the irate cruise captain to depart first. As soon as the stern had passed, the captain momentarily accelerated the engine. The diesels thundered and black smoke billowed from the stack. After about four seconds, he throttled back, but it was enough to send a surging wall of water into our boats, all but capsizing us.

"He did that on purpose!" I yelled in disbelief. I was aghast. How could someone entrusted with the responsibility of running a cruise ship commit such a dangerous and reckless act?

"Don't worry," Julie said. "He's gone, we're fine, and pretty soon we'll be in Bulgaria."

She was right. The river had a magical way of soothing away any stresses, and it wasn't long before the ship was forgotten. A rusty Romanian barge pulled alongside and a pot-bellied crew member leaned out the door.

"Go Canada!" he yelled.

10

BACK IN THE EU

BULGARIA (*Julie*)

I T WAS LATE AFTERNOON BY THE TIME WE ROWED across the boundary between Serbia and Bulgaria on the Timok. On the northern side of the river, it was still Romania, as it had been for the last 230 kilometres, but now Bulgaria replaced Serbia to our south. The Danube would border these two nations for 470 kilometres, and then it would flow fully in Romania. As so often seemed to be the case, there wasn't really much to define the border: a bit of marshland, a thin river, not even a sign in this instance.

"Well, that's it," Colin said. "We've made it back into the European Union. We don't have to worry about getting busted for not having our passports stamped."

Both Romania and Bulgaria had been in the European Union since 2007, which we assumed meant that border bureaucracies would be a non-issue until we reached Turkey. This was good news because Bulgaria has a reputation for wrapping tourists in red tape and making travel quite difficult. In one of the books we'd packed for this trip, the author shared a story of a German who arrived in Bulgaria by yacht only to find he had to pay for a two-week hotel stay in order to enter the country. The author, Rod Heikell, had it easier: he was merely waved over by a gunboat and instructed on protocol, which entailed considerable paperwork at several offices.

We were in a jovial mood, practising our Bulgarian and looking forward to our first night in Bulgaria. Our plan was to stop in the small town of Novo Selo, 10 kilometres past the border, fill our water containers and then find a quiet beach on which to pitch our tent. What we failed to realize was that although Bulgaria was part of the European Union, it, along with Romania, had not yet joined the Schengen Area, the European zone that had abolished internal border checks.

We were rowing along the shore fronting Novo Selo, looking for a place to land, when a police boat approached. An officer waved us to shore. We obliged, conveniently stopping metres away from the police dock. We took our passports out of their waterproof bag and whispered nervously between ourselves, pondering what we should say and what they would do. Their boat docked and four officers sauntered over. They were laughing and joking with one another, which we took as a positive sign.

"Where are you going?" asked one of the younger officers.

We explained our trip and pulled out Colin's book *Beyond the Horizon*, which we'd been carrying for just such an occasion.

They were as amicable as they seemed, chuckling over Colin's bearded photographs and showing genuine interest in our trip. Three of them spoke excellent English and translated for the fourth, who wore a different uniform and looked like the more senior officer. But eventually they asked the inevitable, and I handed over our passports. They flipped the pages searching for our entry stamp.

"We don't have one yet," Colin explained.

Then they asked about our Serbian stamps, which we, of course, didn't have either. Instead I pulled out our hotel receipt from Kladovo. By now there was a lot of discussion, and several cellphone calls had been placed. They seemed genuinely uncertain about what should be done with us.

Finally, the senior officer hung up his mobile and said something in Bulgarian.

"You will need to get an entry stamp, which you can obtain in Vidin," one of the younger officers told us.

"Great, thank you," Colin said. "We will do that." Problem solved. Vidin was 45 kilometres downstream and we'd stop there tomorrow.

"Thank you," I added, eager to get our passports back and leave.

"You will not reach Vidin tonight," the officer continued, "and without paperwork you cannot stop elsewhere."

We had less than two hours of daylight, and I doubted we'd be able to convince him that we could row at 25 kilometres an hour, so I nodded obligingly.

"You will have to stay here tonight. A controller from Vidin will come here and he will complete your paperwork. Tomorrow you can continue."

They left us to set up our tent. An hour later, one of the officers returned with a border official. He took down the names and measurements of our boats, asked for registration papers— which we didn't have—and stamped our passports. It was surprisingly straightforward and jovial. We thanked him for making the lengthy drive just on our behalf and gave him a *Beyond the Horizon* DVD as a gift.

Sleeping next to a police station has some benefits, including an armed guard, but being in town has drawbacks, which we discovered shortly after the sun set. It started with a sporadic bark and a few howls, and soon the entire town was alive with the banter of stray dogs. Their voices filled the night like the daytime chirps of birds, but without any of the charm or appeal. A small pack perched themselves near our tent and sang the saddest notes I have ever heard; it was half howl, half whine, and full of hunger and deprivation. Our tent seemed to have a knack for attracting creatures of the night, and we each gripped a heavy metal pole from our trailer, but thankfully they didn't come too close.

We reached Vidin by noon the next day, but as we already had our passports stamped, we continued past without stopping. It was a medium-sized city and the province's capital, containing the requisite number of cranes expected of a port city and standard Soviet-style architecture. The city would have been unremarkable if it hadn't been for the enormous fortress that preceded it. Constructed of grey stone with several towers topped by red roofs, it looked wholly intact and was indeed Bulgaria's best-preserved castle. Built in the tenth century, it had witnessed a profusion of attacks including, legend has it, one from Vlad the Impaler (a.k.a. Dracula) when in 1462 he killed some 24,000 people between Vidin and Nikopol, a Bulgarian city 200 kilometres downstream.

The river was full of islands lined with sandy beaches. There were a few towns on the Bulgarian side and, adjacent to one scenic beach, a collection of weekend tents and trailers. Romania, on the other hand, was generally deserted, and except for a father and son out for a jaunt with their horse and buggy, we saw only one other Romanian that day.

We were rowing between an island and Romania, farther from Bulgaria than we usually strayed because the accumulated sand made the other side of the island impassable. It wasn't only because of permissions that we stayed closer to Bulgaria, but because of stories we'd heard about this region. When A. J. Mackinnon was travelling this stretch in his dinghy *Jack de Crow*, he was kidnapped by two river pirates brandishing a large knife. Eventually, a border policeman discovered them and Mackinnon was released unharmed, but it was a frightening experience. We had been trying to determine the exact spot of his kidnapping and deduced it was farther down-stream, when a maniacal scream erupted.

"Holy shit!" I yelled, pointing to the Romanian shore.

The tree swayed, and I could see a dark figure running through the forest towards us. He was screaming with blood-curdling ferocity.

"He might have a boat," Colin said. "Keep rowing. I'm going to get the dog basher."

I had already intensified my speed to a full sprint, towing Colin's boat behind me at a pace we had never before travelled while princessing. As I rowed, Colin pulled out a heavy metal pipe belonging to the trailer, one of two that we had used for protection the previous night against prowling dogs, earning it the nickname dog basher. We rowed away from the island and into a more open region of the river. The screaming had stopped, and I couldn't see our pursuer any more, but I kept rowing at full force.

And then my oarlock broke. The oar pin snapped and my oar hung limp, useless for rowing, and we came to a full stop.

"Where's the tool kit?" Colin said.

"In the bow hatch of my boat," I said. "But it's buried beneath the food bags." Replacing an oar pin is easy on dry land—we had done it several times already—but on the water it would take longer and we might drop an essential tool overboard.

"Let's just switch boats," I said.

We converted Colin's boat into the tower by exchanging the cockpit contents and retying the boats. Soon we were a considerable distance away, once again surrounded by deserted shores and empty islands.

"Da, na, na na na na," Colin sang, performing his well-honed imitation of the duelling banjos from *Deliverance*.

"That was pretty creepy," I agreed.

"I think we should be careful where we camp tonight and stay only in places the TID recommends."

The TID was short for Tour International Danubien, a German organization that had been coordinating an annual paddling trip down the Danube since 1955. We had passed their group of a dozen or so boats in Austria, and in a few weeks they would also be travelling this stretch. Their journey began in Ingolstadt, Germany, near the source of the Danube, in late June and would end 2,082 kilometres later in Silistra, Bulgaria, just before the Danube veers entirely into Romania. One of our guidebooks was written for the TID and contained all the details the paddlers need to know, including camping spots to use. In Western Europe, these were often established campgrounds or rowing clubs, but here they were mostly beaches with sufficient high ground to accommodate a number of tents. That night, we slept on one of those beaches, just past the small town of Lom. It felt safe and would have been peaceful, except for the continuous canine chorus of barking, howling and whining emanating from the town.

Our TID guidebook also covered restaurants, and we spent the morning eagerly anticipating our first Bulgarian meal. When we reached the restaurant shortly after noon, we were surprised to find that it was actually more of a derelict recreation centre, with a swimming pool and collection of aging paddle boats and only the barest of kitchens.

I glanced at the menu written in Cyrillic characters and worried about which of these items might be the "delicacies" described in our guidebook—fried cow intestines, assorted organs and abundant fish from the polluted Danube. I looked at what our fellow patrons were eating and by way of a combination of pointing and charades managed to order three sausages, one piece of chicken, a tomato and cucumber salad, two pops, two espressos and a loaf of bread (for making sandwiches). The food was simple but good, the coffee above average, and the price, 8 leva (about $6), unbelievably cheap. We had read that the costs in Bulgaria had risen steeply and that tourists shouldn't expect rock-bottom prices any more, but this advice clearly didn't apply to obscure, off-the-beaten-track places.

The current galloped through this part of the river, averaging four kilometres an hour, and as a result we achieved record daily distances. The day before, we had travelled 93 kilometres, and that day we would, for the first time, reach triple digits. By the end of our third full day in Bulgaria, we had travelled 290 kilometres and to celebrate we decided to forgo a campside dinner and instead eat in the Danube-side village of Svishtov.

"Do you speak English?" Colin asked the waitress.

The young woman nodded vigorously. English-speakers were rare in this region, and the last tourist was probably a fat man climbing down the chimneys in December.

The menu was indecipherable, but at least our waitress would be able to offer some assistance.

"What would you recommend?" I asked her.

She stood mutely nodding her head.

"Do you have chicken or beef dishes?" Colin queried.

More silence and head nodding.

"Mooooo?" Colin said. "Cock-a-doodle-doo?"

The girl's eyes opened wide and she took two steps back.

I pointed to two random items on the menu and hoped for the best.

The girl shook her head.

Okay. I guess those items weren't recommended. I pointed to two other items. Head shake.

Finally I found two items that elicited head nodding, and we placed our order.

"Oh my god!" Colin suddenly said, laughing. "Remember? People here shake their heads to say yes and nod their heads for no."

Bulgaria is the only country in the world where head nodding and shaking are reversed, a fact we'd read in our guidebook and managed to forget. I wondered what we had just ordered. Ten minutes later it arrived: a plate of greasy Danube fish, bony and mushy, and a mound of shredded cabbage with a dollop of mayonnaise.

"Bon appétit," said Colin with a shake of his head. Or was it a nod?

Still hungry, we returned to our boats and discovered they had acquired two armed guards. The policemen asked for our passports and shook their heads approvingly at the stamps. They did not, however, agree with our plans to camp farther downstream and suggested we stay exactly where we were. We nodded obligingly and then quickly corrected ourselves.

"*Da, da*," we said, shaking our heads.

The men returned to their jeep and watched over us throughout the night.

Rousse is Bulgaria's largest river port and fifth most populous city. It is also thought to be the nicest Bulgarian city on the Danube, so we decided it was a perfect place for a day off. We were pleased to find a small marina in which to moor our boats, and even happier to discover it housed two other pleasure boats. Both sailboats were from Germany, one from Cologne and the other from Stuttgart, and soon after docking we met the owners. Klaus was sailing to the Mediterranean, a trip he had been planning for almost a decade; once there he intended to spend his retirement exploring its islands and coastline. On the other boat were his friend Helmut and his wife, Anne, who were spending a few months in Rousse repairing their vessel. It was our good fortune to meet them, especially

Klaus, who had an encyclopedic knowledge of the route ahead, which we mined. After a quick chat and a glass of juice, we stored our valuables on Helmut's boat and went into town to search out a hotel.

The city centre was a short and not particularly pleasant stroll away from the water. Rousse was not a city that embraced waterfront aesthetics. Instead, the river was lined with rangy trees, crumbling paths, dilapidated rail lines and, farther downstream, all the trappings of industry. But the regal neo-baroque architecture that filled its core atoned for this oversight. Elegant houses, pastel coloured and with cream trim, lined the streets. We walked past an expansive square of formal gardens and elaborate fountains with a commanding statue at its centre, and a profusion of ice cream stands, restaurants, hotels and museums. It was vastly different from any of the tiny Bulgarian villages we'd seen so far.

We settled into the Splendid Hotel, partly because of its name but mostly because it was big and Soviet and full of non-Westerners. It was the kind of place where the elevator doesn't have an interior door and you watch the floors rush by, trailing your fingers along moving glass and metal. The floors were carpeted in deep, rich colours, and dozens of plants in small pots were crowded near the windows.

We wandered around town happily, shopping at the local supermarket for the upcoming week's supplies and buying ice cream from the street-side vendors. The ice cream was priced by weight, not scoop, and, although fairly decadent, was not quite as good as Slovakia's. The food, however, more than made up for it, and that night our dinner was exceptional.

The restaurant was upscale compared to our previous choices, with cloth napkins, heavy wooden furniture and leather-bound menus in German, English and Cyrillic. Just as in Serbia, food here was a carnivore's dream, and the menu was replete with sausages and skewers and roasted meats, but it also had a hefty selection of salads and other vegetarian dishes. Bulgarian food is served à la carte, and we found ourselves ordering a profusion of dishes. The salads came out first. There was the quintessential shopska salad—chopped tomato, cucumber and onions covered in grated sheep's cheese—which was served everywhere and was synonymous with "side dish," and a smaller plate of peeled, roasted red peppers drizzled in oil. Next appeared kebabche, thin spicy sausages wound in a tight spiral and skewered to look like fairground lollipops, followed by dolmades and a sizzling iron skillet holding layers of roasted tomatoes and cheese. Even before dessert arrived—crème caramel and espresso—I had decided this was the best meal of the expedition so far.

From Rousse to Silistra, the most downstream Bulgarian town on the Danube, was 120 kilometres. In Silistra we would cease straddling the border of Bulgaria and Romania and fully enter Romania, which meant another border checkpoint. According to our guidebook, it would take two or three days to get our paperwork sorted. We would need to stop at the Bulgarian border port for an exit stamp, which was not necessarily a straightforward affair, row across the border, find the equivalent office in Romania and repeat the procedure for the required entrance stamp. This all seemed odd to me, as both Bulgaria and Romania are in the European Union, which I thought meant open borders. But that was clearly not the case. On the contrary, the last stretch of river was more heavily patrolled by police boats from both nations than any other, and we were stopped repeatedly to have our paperwork examined. It seemed that the rigmarole was focused on water traffic, and if you travelled across the border by land, things were much simpler.

When we reached Silistra, we pulled our boats out of the

water onto a gradual bank populated with fishing boats, gnarled fishermen and stray cats. We assembled our trailers, loaded our boats onto them and pedalled along a dusty, thin strip of asphalt into the centre of town. Colin stopped beside an old woman carrying a watermelon and asked directions.

"*Granitsa?*" he said, using the Russian word for border.

She understood and gestured that we turn left at the upcoming roundabout. We pedalled past brick and concrete apartment blocks and soon reached a line of about four cars waiting at the border. The guards chuckled as we wheeled our bikes and boats through the pedestrian zone. We handed our passports to the officer, who barely glanced at our boats before disappearing inside. Within a few minutes he returned with our passports, marked with both exit and entry stamps. We pushed past the booths and entered Romania.

11

CANAL OF DEATH

ROMANIA *(Colin)*

THE TOWN OF SILISTRA ABRUPTLY ENDED at the border, and we wheeled our bikes along a dirt road through a forest back to the Danube River. Here, a ferry crossed to the other side, and its ramp made a convenient spot to launch our boats.

From the river nothing looked different, but we were apprehensive. The next 76 kilometres on the Danube was reputed to be a hot spot for Romanian pirates. Foreign cargo ships from Germany, Austria, Bulgaria and other places were being looted and attacked while anchored. Aquamedia.at, an international water website, "urgently" recommended that all ships flying foreign flags not stop in this region.

A common strategy for the pirates was to pose as friendly fishermen (most of the pirates were, indeed, moonlighting fishermen) offering fresh fish. While the ship's crew were distracted, the fishermen's cohorts boarded from the other side and started looting. Violence often ensued.

We wondered what the pirates and opportunistic fishermen would make of small, vulnerable rowboats coming down the river. We knew of only one other small boater who had voyaged these waters—A. J. Mackinnon, who had been kidnapped by knife-wielding Romanian pirates and was lucky to escape alive.

Our experience upstream with the lunatic chasing us through the woods along the Romanian shore had left us shaken.

His demonic screams and unfettered hatred made the boys from *Deliverance* seem like chess buddies. It was a lawless region here, a land of forests, islands and small subsistence villages. Romania is home to some of the worst poverty in Europe, and commercial ships plying these waters provide the locals with an opportunity to gain some wealth.

To reduce our risk, we kept a vigilant watch during the day, eyeing fishing boats with suspicion and scanning the thick forests for movement. But nighttime was when we felt most vulnerable. It was easy to attribute malevolent meaning to the noises in the forest and on the river. Was that cracking branch an animal or a villain? Did that splashing sound like an approaching boat? Our strategy was to camp unseen, pulling our boats ashore when no one was watching and finding hidden places that were difficult to access. The braiding river often formed three or four islands between the shores, and mostly we camped on these remote, thickly forested islets.

On our second day in Romania, we came to a region where the river passed over exposed bedrock. A fairly developed camp with several portable buildings and a generator suggested some sort of research was going on—perhaps a mining company doing mineral analysis. Nearby, a young woman and a man wearing the fashionable clothing of non-locals strolled along the rocks. As we passed, the man pointed a camera with a large zoom lens in our direction.

Several weeks later, we received an email from this man by way of our website: "Hello, I have taken a few pictures with the team and their boats somewhere on the Danube in Romania, around the 360 km mark. Please reply to this message and include an email address so I can send you the pictures."

The man, who was from Bucharest, forwarded two photos. The first showed Julie in front of a thick canopy of trees, muscles bulging and soaked in sweat, as she hauled on the oars. The second featured my boat being towed; me slouched in the cockpit, my cheeks bulging as I ate a large sandwich. I was doing my bit as an ambassador for women around the world, showing the citizens of Eastern Europe that the tides of equality were lapping at their borders.

Sixty kilometres after passing the photographer, we neared the town of Cernavoda and had a decision to make. From here, it was 300 kilometres on the river to the Black Sea, a slow, convoluted route through a maze of islands and a very buggy delta. Alternatively, the 60-kilometre Danube–Black Sea Canal cut directly through to the coast from here. We knew very little about the canal apart from the fact that our German canoeing book stated that paddling in it was not advised.

"It would be a lot shorter through the canal," Julie said, studying the map.

"Yeah," I agreed. "We've got the current in our favour on the river, but we'd also end up much farther up the Black Sea coast and would have to row back down."

After weighing the pros and cons, we finally decided to travel through the canal. There were only two sets of locks, one at each end, so even if they didn't let us through, we could simply portage the locks and re-enter the canal out of the lock-keeper's sight.

We turned right into the side channel leading through Cernavoda and the mouth of the canal, bidding farewell to the wide, amicable Danube River. Then we entered a completely different world. Up until now, we had been relatively isolated on the river. Our main interaction with people had been with jolly barge captains. Our speed and the protection provided by the surrounding water allowed us to keep our distance from any people we felt might be threatening. Things would soon change.

We pulled ashore just before Cernavoda, and I strolled alone down a dusty track looking for the lock entrance and to inquire about travelling through the canal. It was surprisingly desolate, with only a few homeless people living among the scrub and trees. Feeling nervous, I turned and headed back to the boats, but a pack of about ten snarling stray dogs blocked my path. I cursed myself for not carrying our dog basher with me and instead picked up two grapefruit-sized rocks. The dogs snarled and snapped, but didn't attack. My two-shot ammo would have done little to stop them.

Cernavoda is a wretched place and a dichotomy of worlds. A large nuclear power plant was recently built, bringing an influx of engineers, technicians and managers to the city. A Canadian company, Atomic Energy of Canada, was in charge of constructing and running the facility, and a large number of Canadian staff live in a compound protected by guards and encircled by razor wire, an island of safety in a city scarred by persistent poverty.

We stopped in the city centre at a concrete ramp sloping into the water, and Julie clambered ashore to look for a grocery store. Several children swam in the water nearby. Another group of kids arrived in a horse-drawn cart; the largest boy jumped out of the cart and pulled the horse's reins, forcing its head down to make it stop. He then flogged the horse with a large leather strap.

I returned my attention to the boats. The other kids had stopped swimming and were clambering over our boats.

"No," I said sternly, walking up to them.

The five boys ignored me completely. Some used the boats as diving boards while others examined our equipment. I was unable to watch them all at once and suspected that this was what they were hoping.

"No!" I said and lifted one boy out of Julie's cockpit.

They continued to ignore me. These were the types of youngsters that every guidebook on Romania warns you about:

"gypsy" kids who swarm tourists intent on robbing them. I knew they would continue ignoring my calm requests, so I tried another approach.

"*Get off the boats!*" I screamed, shaking my fist above my head. "*Move or I'll rip your godamned heads off!*"

They moved.

Julie returned from the supermarket flustered.

"They totally overcharged me," she fumed. "They added another zero to the cost of this cheese. I said something but she refused to give me back any money."

I nodded knowingly.

"It's more the principle of it," Julie continued. "I was determined to make a point and I wasn't going anywhere. Finally the manager came out. At first she refused to fix the error, but eventually she did. It took forever and she needed my passport to do it."

"Let's get out of here," I said.

We hastily pulled away from the shore and the growing collection of kids.

Within ten minutes, we reached the gates of the enormous lock structure. The lock was completely quiet. There were no other boats around; we didn't see a lockkeeper, and Julie's VHF radio calls went unanswered. Our only option was to portage.

We pulled our boats onto a gravel slope next to the outfall pipe from the nuclear power plant. Trash fluttered on the shore and a cat-sized rat scurried between boulders. The plant was a sprawling rectangular structure, protected by guards and razor wire, and it disgorged a considerable volume of water into the river. I wondered about safety standards. A lone fisherman cast his rod into the water, obviously not sharing those concerns.

Construction of this canal began in 1949 with the use of slave labour made up of minor criminals and political prisoners—artisans, intellectuals, priests and farmers opposed to collectivization. With little more than shovels and pickaxes, they chiselled through rock and excavated 300 million cubic metres of soil, more than that excavated for the Panama and Suez canals combined. Some 100,000 people are thought to have died during the first four years of construction (estimates range as high as 200,000 and as low as 10,000), and by the time the massive project was completed in 1984, almost two people had died for every metre built. This is why the canal is unofficially called the Death Canal, Canalul Mortii in Romanian.

Despite the massive efforts that went into building this canal, it was all but disused. Very few foreign boats uses it because of the high costs, the required pilot boat and the complex bureaucracy. It is easier simply to travel the extra distance on the river.

A bumpy service track paralleled the canal, and on it we made our way past the lock. On our other side lay a scraggly field with a railway track and, in the distance, a road with the occasional settlement. Whenever we neared one of these habitations, stray dogs would appear, growling and chasing us down the path. The only other visitors to the canal were fishermen who sat next to the water, dangling homemade rods into water laced with a fluorescent green slime.

A train whizzed past, its open cars filled with scrap metal. Hanging off the back of each of the cars, affixed by harnesses, were security guards toting AK-47s. It was the kind of set-up one might imagine for a train carrying a load of bullion, but these men were protecting rusted chunks of steel.

We had read that this area is one of the most desperate in Romania, and as the sun transformed into a red ball touching the low horizon, we felt very vulnerable. Gone were the cloaking veils of the forest and mid-river islands of the Danube. We were completely exposed and quickly running out of time.

"Where are we going to camp?" I said.

"We don't really have much choice. We'll just have to set the tent up by the tracks," Julie said.

After the sun set, we slipped down the bank to the railway tracks and silently set up the tent.

"Do you think anyone saw us?" Julie whispered.

"No," I said, hoping that was true.

It was not a restful night. Once an hour or more, our tent was bathed in the headlamps of a passing locomotive. The trains thundered past, a mere two metres from our tent. They permeated our dreams and woke us in a panic.

In the morning, we packed early and continued down the track.

"Only fifty kilometres more, and we'll be on the Black Sea," I said, trying to console Julie but not convincing myself.

The canal began in a broad valley with scattered farms and a few villages, but soon flat land gave way to scrubby rolling hills that must have been torturous to excavate. Yet the canal lost none of its preposterous width, 120 metres, nor had any locks been created. Massive trenches, up to 90 metres deep, had been dug through the rocky terrain by doomed labourers. The waterway cut through the landscape unimpeded, as if God had taken a knife to the earth and pulled out a slice.

We looked for a spot to launch the boats, but the steep earthen dike gave way to a concrete wall lining the canal's edge. After a few kilometres, we realized that it would be impossible to launch. The sheer wall rose nearly three metres out of the water and was devoid of ladders or handholds. It was a death trap. Someone tumbling over the side would not be able to escape the waters unless rescued from above. Even then, offering assistance would be impossible without ropes or ladders. I could only imagine how many children and drunks had toppled into these waters never to emerge again.

They could swim for tens of kilometres without finding a place to exit the deep waters.

For this very reason, rowing in the canal was out of the question. If we were unable to voyage the full length in one day, it would be a disaster. What if stiff headwinds and choppy water stopped us? We would have no means of escape. Our only option was to continue along the disintegrating service track beside the canal.

We had relinquished our initial plan of navigating the canal in a day. It was now too rough to ride, and we pushed our bikes through deep potholes and over large stones. Our surroundings were desolate and arid. There were few trees, and a dry wind rustled long stalks of brown grass.

After two hours without seeing another soul, we spotted a group of men loitering on the far side of the canal. I waved across to them. One of the men started screaming, indecipherable shrieks and yells. He shook his fist at us, reminiscent of the crazed man on the banks of the Danube. His tirade continued unabated until we were out of earshot. I thanked providence that 120 metres of water and two three-metres walls separated them from us.

Shortly after, I was jolted by an explosion. I looked behind me in dismay at the remains of the poor-quality trailer tire I had purchased in France. The sidewall was shredded, and the inner tube had blown outward through a palm-sized hole. We had no spare.

"Oh my god," Julie said, staring at the mess.

There wasn't a worse place to have a mechanical failure. I was feeling increasingly paranoid about this region. My normally pragmatic outlook was overwhelmed by the increasingly uneasy feeling that we were being watched.

The only practical option right now was for us to split up, one to guard the equipment while the other went on a long journey to find another BMX tire. I felt trapped. We couldn't do that—the risk was far too high—but it seemed there was no other choice. The longer we remained in this area, the higher the chance that something would happen. What would have happened if those men had been on our side of the river? Who knows, maybe right now they were crossing the canal and planning to ambush us in the night.

I stared at the blown tire.

"Maybe we can fix it," Julie said.

We had no choice but to perform the impossible. I found a discarded plastic bottle and got out my multi-tool. While Julie removed the tire and inner tube, I cut a long rectangular strip from the plastic. We wrapped a new inner tube with a layer of duct tape (for additional abrasion protection), rolled the plastic around it, then inserted the tube and plastic into the tire and mounted it on the rim. When we inflated the tube, the rolled plastic prevented the tube from blowing out the gaping gash.

"We've done it!" Julie said optimistically.

I wasn't so sure. The terrain was now worse than ever, and the ground was covered in jagged rocks. With every revolution I expected the tire to blow again.

Across the water, in the middle of nowhere, stood a massive monument commemorating the efforts that had gone into creating the canal. It was a steel sculpture atop a concrete base that rose perhaps 60 metres into the air. The black shape was meant to be abstract, but it had an uncanny resemblance to a decapitated angel.

We reached a section of the canal where a concrete flood sluice angled down the adjacent steep slope and into the water. A bridge spanned the sluice, but most of the structure had collapsed. Only a thin line of concrete, less than a metre wide, still crossed the gap. Below was deep water and rubble dangling from lengths of rebar. To the left, a thicket of reeds flourished at the base of the 12-metre-wide sluice channel where water accumulated.

It was too narrow for our trailers, so we disconnected the bikes and carried the boats individually across the gap. I prayed that the crumbling remains wouldn't give way as we hauled the heavy boats across.

In all, it took over an hour to get everything across the gap, and the sun was getting low. We spotted a spring burbling from the limestone cliffs, and we decided this would be an ideal spot to set up camp. Things suddenly seemed more pleasant as we drank fresh water, made dinner and relaxed by the reeds.

When it was completely dark, we had the uneasy feeling we weren't completely alone. A dog began barking nearby and then suddenly yelped, as though someone had forcibly silenced it.

There were no homes in this region. (A later search on Google satellite imagery revealed that the nearest building was six kilometres away.) Was someone planning a stealth attack? I jumped out of the tent, brandishing a steel pipe.

Nothing.

The thicket of four-metre-high reeds behind the tent, so benign in the daylight, now seemed the perfect hiding spot. I stood quietly, waiting, sure someone was out there. I threw a rock into the reeds. The plants rustled and crackled, belying the movement of something: human or animal?

There was no point taking chances and leaving ourselves vulnerable. For the rest of the night, we took turns standing guard outside the tent, armed with heavy pipes from our boat trailers. Julie dropped the pitch of her voice an octave and I called her Fred; if people were listening, it was better they thought we were two men. For the rest of the night, we heard peculiar noises—movements within the reeds, small rocks dislodged from the steep slopes above our tent—but nothing happened.

By morning, we were exhausted and wanted to be anywhere in the world other than the Death Canal. We still had 20 kilometres to travel, and success depended on the tire not exploding and the track remaining passable.

We pushed our bikes through knee-deep water, dragged them over small boulders and through overgrown shrubbery. Miraculously, the tire held, and eventually a bridge loomed in the distance.

"We've made it!" I yelled.

Within half an hour, we passed under a busy highway and arrived in the industrial section of Costanta, Romania's largest port. Tired and dirty, we spent two hours cycling along potholed roads congested with burdened semi trucks while we looked for a place to launch our boats. Finally we realized the entire port was a secure compound protected by fences topped with razor wire, accessible only by well-guarded private roads. The security guards shook their heads firmly when we gestured towards the harbour.

It was getting late, and we were trapped in the squalid industrial zone with no way to get to the water. Julie studied the map.

"If we can't go on the water," she said, "there's only one way out of here—the freeway. We'll have to follow it down the coast to the town of Eforie Nord."

I groaned. To make matters worse, we had three consecutive flat tires on our way to the freeway (fortunately my heavily damaged trailer tire continued to hold). Finally, we pedalled up the onramp and into honking chaos. The four-lane highway was bumper to bumper with trucks and cars and had no shoulder. We pedalled furiously as cars blasted their horns and inched around our boats. We slowly made our way up a steep incline as the freeway arched over the canal we had just travelled. I prayed we wouldn't get another flat while on the bridge with hundreds of cars backed up behind us.

Our equipment held, and we made it over the bridge. We continued pedalling vigorously, hearts in our mouths, as impatient drivers squeezed past within inches of our boats.

After seven kilometres we reached Eforie Nord. It was the most packed beach town I've ever seen. The beach culture in Romania is strong, but since the country has only about 60 kilometres of gorgeous beaches along the Black Sea and a population of 22 million, the coast is synonymous with crowds. Traffic was gridlocked on all the streets, and we were stuck, too, unable to pass with our bulky boats. Sidewalks seethed with people. If the Danube River and the Death Canal are where Romania's most impoverished resided, we had now discovered where the other half lived and vacationed. The vehicles here were all late-model European (Western European, that is) and the people dressed in the latest fashions. For now, though, we weren't interested in the street life—we wanted a hotel and a bed to collapse on.

There were row upon row of Soviet-built high-rise hotels along with the complete range of motels, modern hotels and rooms for rent. But they were all full. We went to twenty-nine hotels without success and had almost resigned ourselves to a night on the street when we found a lone overpriced vacancy. It was a modern facility, and when the staff learned we had a couple of dirty boats parked in their lot among the shiny Mercedes-Benzes, Audis and Volvos, they were less than impressed. The next morning they informed us they would have to cancel our two-day booking (because of a clerical error, they insisted) and we would have to move on.

Respect in this part of the world is earned through blatant displays of wealth, and people work hard to project an air of affluence. Unlike any other country we'd been in, in Romania we felt as though we were a source of embarrassment for the establishments we frequented. Our soiled clothes, battered rowboats and weary manner generated not curiosity or conversation but looks of disdain and dismissal.

We strolled down a steep hill to the beach and for the first time laid eyes on the Black Sea. It looked like the open ocean, with a large, rolling swell crashing onto a sandy beach. The waters offshore were a deep blue, and Jet Skis and power boats hummed like mosquitoes. Most striking was the beach. Tens of thousands of people carpeted the soft beige sand, sunbathing, playing in the surf or just milling around. As far as I could see in both directions was a sea of bodies. The beaches were lined with carnival-style amusement and food stalls, and a long walkway fronted the beach.

It would be extremely difficult to push our boats through all the people, so we wandered over to a marina to see about launching from there. The security guard led us past gleaming, heavily powered boats to the manager. Through gestures, we inquired if it would be possible to launch our boats off their docks. We showed him a picture of our rowboats, hoping their diminutive size would convey what a simple task it would be.

The man looked at the pictures and laughed before ushering us away with a dismissive wave and resolute no.

At the end of the beach, we found a less crowded area and returned to fetch our boats. Launching was a challenge, and it was important to time our departure between the large breaking waves. With the scorching heat, the surrounding crowds and glorious sandy beach, we felt as if we were pushing a couple of rental boats out for an afternoon of fun rather than continuing with a 7,000-kilometre expedition.

Once we were beyond the breaking surf, we paused to relax in the rolling swell.

"Congratulations, honey!" Julie said.

It did feel pretty good. We'd made it down the Danube, along the Death Canal and through the coastal chaos. Finally, we were relaxing on the deep blue waters of the Black Sea.

~~~

ON A MAP, the Black Sea appears like a giant lake, but it is considered part of the world's ocean system thanks to its connection to the Mediterranean via the narrow Bosporus. The Black Sea is 436,400 square kilometres, almost twice the area of the United Kingdom. The far shore was over a thousand kilometres from our present position, meaning there was sufficient room for waves to grow into large, ocean-like swells. The water was salty, but only about half as saline as the ocean, owing to dilution from inflowing rivers.

The weather on the Black Sea is more volatile than on the nearby Mediterranean, and storms are more frequent. Rough seas combined with numerous rocky headlands mean shipwrecks are common. The sandy beaches we were currently enjoying alternated with jagged, rocky shorelines and precipitous capes.

Unlike in regular oceans, here there is almost no exchange through currents between the surface and the deeper waters. The consequent lack of oxygen means the lower waters are nearly devoid of life. Apart from a few extremophile bacteria, most life in the Black Sea is found within 80 metres of the surface. Organic debris that settles on the bottom does not decompose, because of the absence of bacteria. This phenomenon is a boon to archaeologists; some of the best-preserved ancient shipwrecks are found in the Black Sea.

The Bosporus, the strait that connects the Black Sea to the Atlantic Ocean via several seas (the Mediterranean, Aegean and Marmara), lies in Turkey. The channel is 30 kilometres long; its depth ranges from 36 to 124 metres and at its narrowest it is 700 metres wide. Although more water flows out of the Black Sea than into it (because river inflow exceeds the rate of evaporation), water simultaneously flows in both directions. The saltier, denser water of the Mediterranean flows north along the bottom of the strait, while the less heavy water of the Black Sea exits along the surface at about three or four knots.

We rowed a few hundred metres beyond the shore, past the swimmers and air mattresses, and suddenly things were peaceful again. Off our starboard side, thousands of people frolicked on the beach and in the near-shore waters, but we were once again alone, moving easily through the swells.

Before leaving Eforie Nord, we had purchased a large beach umbrella. We weren't worried about sun protection; instead, we were concerned about how we would camp at night. Between here and Bulgaria, there was a series of beach towns similar to Eforie Nord, and we expected the shores to remain busy. Large signs on the beach clearly indicated camping was not allowed, and the rules were likely to be enforced by the numerous security guards.

We realized the only way we could sleep near those crowded beaches was to catamaran our boats and camp on the water. Unfortunately, a vital component for assembling our catamaran had disappeared with the stolen trailer in France. Two two-metre poles, part of our trailer system, sleeved into holes in the sides of *Tantalum* and *Niobium* to create the catamaran. Since France, we had only had one of the poles.

I had spotted the umbrella in a tourist shop and noticed that the long metal shaft was the perfect size. We detached the fabric and packed the shaft inside my boat. That night we would catamaran the boats and keep our fingers crossed that the shaft would be strong enough.

We had had a late start, and after rowing for two hours past endless beaches, crowds and concrete hotels, we reached a tiny sheltered bay in Eforie Sud. We relaxed near our boats in the sand, cooked dinner, assembled the catamaran, pumped up the air mattress and waited for darkness. We inserted a turkey-sized rock into a dry bag and tied it to a rope for use as an anchor, then rowed away from the beach. Even after the sun set, the beaches were still busy, but we were invisible from the shore. Julie dropped the anchor, and we settled into our sleeping bags.

Compared to our previous camping spot along the Death Canal, this was luxurious. The waves gently rocked our bed, and we felt safe surrounded by a moat of water. I quickly fell asleep and slept solidly through the night.

At first light, when we woke up, the shore was already busy with strollers out to view the sunrise. I yawned, stretched and crawled out of my sleeping bag to the amusement of people walking past. We quickly breakfasted, disassembled the catamaran and began rowing the final leg to Bulgaria.

Later in the afternoon, we pulled in to a beach just before the Bulgarian border. As we drew near, it was apparent that we had discovered a third facet of Romania's society. So far, we had encountered the desperately impoverished and the pretentious middle class. Here, finally, were the eccentrics, artists and students. Old VW vans, clapped-out Volvos and motorcycles were parked along the shore. The beach itself was clothing-optional, and young and old paraded along the sand with all exposed. There were no concrete hotels here. Instead, a string of hundreds, perhaps thousands, of tents lined the shore. We pulled in at the very end of the beach, timing our entry carefully to avoid being swamped by breaking waves.

"Dudes!" A Romanian man in his twenties approached us. "Welcome to our beach."

He spoke excellent English and invited us to join his friends once we had set up camp.

"Who are those guys?" I asked, pointing to some uniformed men standing above the beach.

"Oh, just the border guards." Our new friend turned and blew them a kiss. "You don't need to worry about them. Just don't row any farther that way." He pointed towards the Bulgarian border.

"Great," Julie said. "We're actually going to Bulgaria. Do you know how the border works?"

"Border, schmorder," the man said. "You don't want to go to Bulgaria. Stay here with us. We can drink and be merry. There is nowhere better than here. Trust me, my friends."

With that he pulled out a flask and passed it to us. I took a sip. It burned.

After setting up the tent, Julie went up and spoke to the border guards, one of whom spoke some English. We would not be allowed to enter Bulgaria on the water; however, a road nearby traversed the border, and we could simply cycle around and relaunch in Bulgaria.

The next morning, we unpacked our bikes and trailers to the astonishment of our new friends, waved goodbye and pedalled the final two kilometres to Bulgaria.

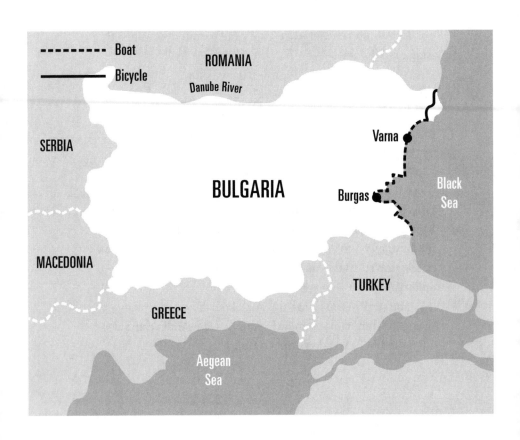

12

WEDDING ANNIVERSARY

BULGARIA AGAIN (*Julie*)

ONCE AGAIN, CROSSING THE LINE between Romania and Bulgaria was easier by land than by water. We had pondered slipping across the border—rowing out to sea and returning into Bulgarian waters—but after chatting with border police at the nude beach, we decided it was out of the question. They had high-powered binoculars and little else to do but watch our every move. When I asked how we could legally cross the border in our boats, they relayed from their supervisor the information that we would need to row seven kilometres back to Mangalia, clear with customs and immigration, and then row non-stop to Varna, a distant city, to clear into Bulgaria. The combined paperwork would take days. We decided to go the simpler route on asphalt.

At the border, the guard stamped our passports with only a cursory glance and waved us through. The road was immediately much better—wider, smoother and without the prolific litter that covered the roads in Romania. Still, nice roads didn't make up for the fact that we hadn't planned on cycling here and therefore hadn't replaced Colin's shredded trailer tire, which was patched with a pop bottle and duct tape.

The pop bottle was chafing through the inner tube, and within five kilometres we had to repair three flats.

"That's it," Colin said, prying the tire off the rim. "This tire is beyond hope."

"Maybe a little more duct tape will stop it chafing and bulging out so much," I suggested.

"There's already more tape than rubber on it. We need a replacement."

"Or a route to the sea."

But neither seemed likely. The nearest road leading to the water was still a long way off. The next reasonably sized town was closer—only 20 kilometres away—but it probably wouldn't have a bike shop, and even if it did, it would be closed because this was Sunday.

We wrapped the rest of the duct tape around the freshly patched tube and limped onwards. Colin's tire bulged so much that the wheel bounced into the air with each revolution if he exceeded eight kilometres an hour.

"I have a theory," I said, pulling alongside Colin.

"Uh-huh?"

"It's called the big bang theory. I predict that within an hour there's going to be a very big bang, and you will have no more tire."

"Harrumph," Colin said. "At least it's pleasant here and safe."

It was a quiet rural region, and the few farmers we had passed waved merrily to us.

"Hey, what's this coming towards us?" Colin said excitedly. "It looks like people on bikes."

"So?"

"They might have a tire we could use."

"So what are we going to do—club them over the head and take their tires?" I grumbled.

"Oh my god," Colin said, "one of them has twenty-inch tires on their bike. Perfect."

A couple and their teenaged daughter were out for a leisurely ride. Colin held his hand up as they neared.

"Excuse me, do you speak English?"

"Mmm, only little," the man said. "She speak Deutsche."
He gestured to his daughter.

In German, I explained our problem and asked if there
was a bike store in the next town. After conversing with her
parents, she explained that there was, but it would probably
be closed until the next day.

The man walked over to Colin's trailer and examined the
damaged wheel. He then looked over at his daughter's bike
thoughtfully. The family chatted quickly among themselves.

"Come to our house," the girl said. "We have a tire for you."

And that is how we met Boris, his wife, Maria, and their
daughter, Petia. They lived in Vaklino, a tiny village not far
away, in a rustic and homey abode made of stone and wood
and surrounded by grapevines and a jungle of native and cultivated trees. This was their summer retreat, and they spent
the rest of the year in Sofia, Bulgaria's capital.

Boris spoke a few words of English but we mostly con-
versed in German, which Petia spoke so fluently it was hard to
believe she had never been there. She planned to study and
work in Germany when she graduated from high school in two
years. It was common for students to leave Bulgaria when they
graduated, she told me.

"You make four hundred leva"—about €200—"a month
here, and to rent an apartment in Sofia costs a thousand leva,"
she said. "People here love their homeland, but it is hard to
make ends meet."

We ate sliced salami and drank beer while hearing about
their favourite coastal haunts. Tsarevo was everyone's darling,
while Burgas and Varna were too crowded and expensive.
Balchik was nice but packed with vacationing Russians, and
Kavarna the preferred nearby choice.

The cured meats were followed by steaming bowls of rich
lentil soup and bread. A large watermelon from the garden was

cut up for dessert. After we had finished our lunch, Boris dis-appeared into the garage and emerged with a spare 20-inch tire. Colin produced his wallet, but the entire family protested vig-orously. I felt bad that they were doing so much for us while refusing to take anything in return. Finally, we persuaded them to accept a copy of Colin's book *Beyond the Horizon*. I explained that this book, which was about a long human-powered journey, had itself been transported thousands of kilometres by human power. It was a little tattered, and in a language they barely understood, but they appreciated the gesture.

"This give reason for learn more English," Boris said, holding the book with a smile as we waved goodbye.

Local advice is often best, which is why we decided to celebrate our first wedding anniversary in the highly recom-mended city of Kavarna. With our new bike tire, cycling the 60 kilometres there was hassle free, and we arrived the fol-lowing day. As a beach-side getaway, Kavarna is definitely more Bulgarian than international, with no English-speaking tourists and rather bland architecture (unless you're a fan of Soviet-style concrete apartment blocks and sombre statues). For us, though, it was perfect. The surrounding landscape with its craggy coastline was beautiful, and the prices were low. We checked into a hulking resort that was probably one of the most affordable four-star hotels in Europe. Not only did it have a spa, a pool and a gym but our room offered a splendid view of a gigantic Billy Idol mural painted on the side of an eight-storey apartment block.

This obscure town of just over twelve thousand inhabi-tants is, understandably, proud of a 2006 performance by Idol in their community. While it might seem odd that such a rock legend had played in this town, what was even odder was that so had Deep Purple, Whitesnake, the Scorpions, Alice Cooper and Robert Plant, just to name a few.

We spent most of our anniversary indoors, at the restaurant, in the pool and at the spa. I'd never had a Bulgarian massage, and Colin had never had a professional massage period, so we were a little unsure of what to expect. We each went into our separate rooms and emerged an hour later. I felt relaxed and rejuvenated, but Colin looked a little flustered.

"How was it?" I asked.

"Great," he said. "Except for the beginning."

"What happened?"

"The woman handed me a small folded package and told me to put it on, which I did. I thought it was an eye mask to block out the light and so I slipped it over my head."

"I didn't get one of those."

"Well, it didn't fit very well. I slipped the elastic behind my ears, but another string caught on the top of my head. It seemed to be designed for a different sort of head."

"Maybe Bulgarian?"

"No, not quite. I figured I had done something wrong when the masseuse returned to the room. She looked embarrassed and was struggling to find the right words in English. She finally pointed to her hips and said, 'It is for here.'"

I laughed and Colin looked sheepish.

"How was I supposed to know it was a disposable G-string?" he said.

We had a romantic dinner in the upscale hotel restaurant and reminisced about our years together. Colin and I had met five years earlier at a bus stop in Vancouver; we were both en route to the Vancouver Sun Run, a 10-kilometre race, and we struck up a conversation. I was completely taken by him from the start, and for the first time in my life, I wondered if there was anything to the idea of love at first sight. The feelings were mutual, and before long we were eating most of our dinners together and spending our weekends on the water or in the mountains. Two and a half years later, we were rowing across the Atlantic Ocean, a monumental challenge not just physically but emotionally and a true test of our bond. Afterwards, he wrote *Beyond the Horizon* and I wrote *Rowboat in a Hurricane*, we produced a film, paid off a mountainous expedition debt through a self-organized film tour, got married and began a new expedition.

Since meeting Colin, my life had changed dramatically, with the relationship being only part of it. I had gone from being a molecular biologist working a nine-to-five job at a pharmaceutical company to something less stable but more exciting. It had been hard to relinquish the security of a regular paycheque and aspirations of ascending the corporate ladder, and replace them with a much more amorphous vocation. Now my career is a hodgepodge of titles—author, adventurer, motivational speaker, filmmaker, sponsored athlete, scientist-gone-awry. It was hard to explain, especially to my parents, who still hoped I'd come to my senses.

But I *had* come to my senses. I had learned a lot about myself, my priorities in life, my strengths and weaknesses and what made me happy. I wanted a career that always challenged me and offered opportunities to learn. I liked setting my own goals and milestones, and the entrepreneurial nature of our pursuits catered to this. I loved exploring new countries and wild places. And I relished doing all those things with Colin.

This expedition was, in a way, about our relationship. We had built the boats as we prepared for our wedding, and for their maiden voyage, we took them to the Broken Group Islands off Vancouver Island on our honeymoon. And now we were rowing *Tantalum* and *Niobium* thousands of kilometres on an extended meet-the-family trip.

Before beginning this journey, I thought spending five months in a rowboat on the Atlantic had taught me everything about Colin (and myself), but now I realized this wasn't true. Getting to meet his family and to view him within the context of my own relatives had exposed new facets. Family is a great illuminator, all the more when the clan tapestry is presented intact with the old and young framed within their homelands. Family revealed things about Colin that he would rather were forgotten—stories about hand-me-down underwear from his sister and atomic wedgies from his brother (this entails grabbing the victim's underwear at the small of his back and pulling the band over his head in one deft and painful strike).

Then there are more flattering tales, such as how he never cried as a kid, even when he broke his arm at the age of eight when he was bucked off a horse, or his determination to learn to ride after his arm healed. I discovered that Colin has always been dedicated and driven, a trait shared by his family, who are all super-achievers. When we travelled through the gales of northern Scotland, where most of Colin's family originated, I almost understood Colin's nonchalance towards cold weather and physical hardships. But the more I learned about my husband, the more I realized that we can never really know one another, and that this continual learning process is essential to keeping our relationship strong.

~~~

ON OUR 366th DAY OF MARRIAGE, we coasted down a long, steep slope to the sea to continue our voyage. A green sludge thickened the shallows, and the area smelled of rotting seaweed and other less natural things. As we packed our boats, we chatted with a middle-aged man in bathing trunks.

"It never used to be like this," he said, pointing to the putrefying mass. "When I was young, these waters were crystal clear. I don't know where this stuff comes from. Maybe the Danube."

"Definitely, some of it," I said, recalling the many noxious factories and outfalls we had rowed past.

Each year, the Danube supplies the Black Sea with 200 cubic kilometres of water, more than all the other rivers in the Black Sea basin combined, and it is one of the biggest polluters. Half of Europe drains into the Danube, which means any improperly disposed pollutants ultimately wash into the Black Sea. For decades, untreated sewage flowed from riverside towns and cities. Under communist regimes, during the so-called green revolution, state-owned farms dumped subsidized chemical fertilizers onto their fields that leached into adjacent streams and rivers. In addition, major inadvertent chemical spills and wartime bombings have released a gamut of toxic wastes. Vast wetlands, essential for filtering the Danube's waters, have been destroyed through agriculture and hydroelectric projects. Romania drained the Danube delta in an attempt to turn Europe's greatest wetland into a giant rice paddy.

The Black Sea has been called the dirtiest sea in the world, but the Danube (or more accurately, citizens of the Danube delta) is not solely responsible. The sea is bordered by six countries—Romania, Bulgaria, Turkey, Georgia, Ukraine and Russia; 160 million people live in its drainage basin and 16 million along its coastline. It is racked with rampant overdevelopment on its western shores and threats of violent conflict on the east. Sewage, industrial waste and agricultural runoff gush into it. Barges and tankers speed across it, leaving behind oil slicks and spills and discharging foreign species with their ballast water. Oil and gas pipelines penetrate these waters, and the Black Sea boasts the world's deepest undersea pipeline, carrying gas from resource-rich Russia to Turkey at depths of up to two kilometres.

Moreover, the Black Sea is exceptionally sensitive to pollutants because of its geography. It is one of the most isolated seas in the world, connected to the ocean only by the narrow Bosporus, which severely limits water exchange and circulation.

In the early 1990s, these combined factors, along with unregulated fishing, caused the Black Sea to finally collapse. Fish catches plummeted to one-seventh of their previous levels, and anchovy populations fell by 95 percent. Green malodorous slime coated the beaches, and some swimmers even died of cholera.

Eutrophication, the excessive enrichment of the water through fertilizers and sewage runoff, caused massive phytoplankton blooms. They starved the water of oxygen, blocked sunlight from reaching plants below and smothered bottom life. Colossal quantities of bottom-dwelling animals and plants died, perpetuating a cycle of decomposition that further depleted the sea of oxygen. Meanwhile, a voracious introduced species of jellyfish and overfished populations of top predators conspired to worsen the situation. There has been a slight improvement in the last fifteen years as a result of new sewage treatment plants, a reduction in fertilizer usage and extensive factory closures (because of the fall of communism), but the Black Sea still has a long way to go.

Our new Bulgarian friend obviously agreed and wrinkled his nose in disgust as he watched us squelch through the slime, offering a final goodbye wave as we slipped into cleaner waters.

The open sea was more pleasant. A slight wind kept the heat bearable, and waves lapped at our hulls as we paralleled a shore of limestone cliffs and steep slopes solidified by the tangled roots of scrub vegetation and grass. Occasionally, tall poles affixed to shallow reefs protruded above the water's surface, with fishing nets strung between and cormorants perched on top. This coastline was rugged and empty, a stark contrast to Romania's crowded commercial beaches.

Jellyfish pulsed beside our boats, translucent bodies tinged with purple, decorating the sea like polka dots on an *I Love Lucy* dress. These were comb jellies, invasive creatures introduced to the Black Sea in the discarded ballast water of a ship in 1983. Within six years, the population exploded from a handful to a cumulative biomass of one billion tonnes—ten times the weight of all fish caught in a single year in the world's oceans, rivers and lakes. Since then, another comb jelly, which feeds on the first invasive species, has been introduced (supposedly by accident), but the numbers are still very high.

We camped on a tiny beach at the base of a cliff, a perfect location to watch the setting sun. We were protected from the northerly swell here by the nearby Kaliakra Cape, and half-metre-high waves washed soothingly onto the beach.

The next day, we saw a pod of dolphins, sleek grey bodies arcing through waves, squeaking and trilling in high-pitched notes. These were bottlenose dolphins, similar to their Mediterranean counterparts but smaller and with a slightly different skull shape. Common porpoises also inhabit the Black Sea, preferring to stay near shore, while short-beaked common dolphins remain farther offshore. There is no accurate count of Black Sea cetaceans today, but everyone agrees the numbers are greatly diminished. Five million dolphins and porpoises were killed in the twentieth century through commercial hunts, which have been banned since 1966 by all bordering nations expect for Turkey, which kept hunting until 1983. Despite the ban, the porpoises' recovery has been hampered by poaching, pollution, shipping and limited food supply.

As we continued, we watched the landscape morph from steep, rugged bluffs to vast beaches and occasional headlands. We approached Varna, Bulgaria's largest seaside city with an official population of 350,000 (some say it's closer to a million). It was a mega tourist destination, and the beaches to the north were lined with casinos, glitzy resorts and amusement parks. Bronzed bodies covered the sandy shores, and the water was crowded with rented Sea-Doos and motorboats. People hoping to return home without tan lines lounged on air mattresses, enjoying the privacy offered farther out to sea. Bulgarian tourists were a minority here; most came from places like Britain on package holidays.

South of Varna, the crowds vanished, while the natural beauty only intensified. We wondered why this region had escaped development, and only later learned we were passing the vast Kamchia reserve. This 40-kilometre-long stretch of forest, swamps and dunes fronting the sea host forty species of trees and twenty-three types of fish in the Kamchia River. I was heartened that the Bulgarian government had the foresight to preserve this rare ecosystem. In a region where the coast seemed to be one non-stop development, this sudden stretch of wilderness was a balm for nerves frayed from too many near collisions with Jet Skis. By evening, we had rowed 56 kilometres and landed on a solitary stretch of beach.

It was a gorgeous spot. We went for a swim in clear water, set up camp and watched the sun set, a crimson orb swallowed by the jungle of trees. Dinner was also exceptional. I made what I called Bulgarian risotto. The key ingredient was Bulgarian lukanka, a widely available dry-cured salami. I sliced it thinly and sautéed it in olive oil alongside onions, then added water, rice and spices. The whole mixture was boiled gently until the rice was tender. Finally, cheese and powdered milk were added. Not bad for a one-pot meal!

Farther south, the coastline temporarily lost its beaches as the Balkan Mountains angled into the sea and jutted out in a formidable headland called Cape Emine. Fishermen had warned us that this was Bulgaria's stormiest and most dangerous cape. We passed the promontory on our sixth day in

Bulgaria. The rock was dark and menacing, cut with distinct diagonal striations like pinstripes on a suit. A lighthouse and abandoned monastery peered down from sheer cliffs while waves thundered against their flanks. The water was turbulent and confused as we struggled past. Beyond this promontory, the waves and wind immediately subsided, and we found a sheltered bay to spend the night.

"Listen to the sand," Colin said as we walked on the beach. As our feet slid through it, there were high-pitched whispers, like the hum of a violin string.

"Singing sands," I said. "I wonder why it does that."

The geology here was different from that of the other beaches we had stopped at. We were still at the butt of the Balkan Mountains, and the hillside was ribboned with distinct layers of stratified rock instead of continuous sandstone or limestone. The beach was composed of not only fine sand but also sharp-edged, somewhat crystalline rocks.

"Maybe the sand grains are a different shape, square instead of round," Colin hypothesized, "and when they rub there's more friction."

Whatever was causing it, it was a beautiful sound. We enjoyed another peaceful evening reading on the sand as we watched the sun set.

~~~

OUR STRING OF PEACEFUL CAMPING SPOTS was about to end. The following day, the shores were again crowded with modern resorts and casinos. We stopped in Nesebar—an ancient city that began as a Thracian settlement in the second millennium BC and was crowded with thirteenth- and fourteenth-century churches—and dragged our boats onto the beach. We explored the nearby Church of St. John Aliturgetos, a stunning stone and brick structure erected in the fourteenth century, and wandered through streets rich with ancient architecture, ornate mosaics formed from brick and grand religious edifices. The city is a UNESCO World Heritage Site and bustled with tourists. We ate kebabs and ice cream, perused tables of wooden statues and plastic trinkets, and bypassed storefront displays of tourist wares.

A series of large bays followed Nesebar, and we opted to cut a direct line across to the town of Pomorie instead of following the convoluted coast. It was rough, but we made the 13-kilometre crossing without any problems. The next bay was even deeper, veering some 19 kilometres inland to the port city of Burgas, Bulgaria's second-largest coastal city. But it was too late to attempt that 15-kilometre crossing. Instead, we stayed in Pomorie at the northern corner of the bay, but it was a busy community with nowhere to camp. There was no park, no secluded beach and no green space, only a concrete harbour wall and a waterfront of discos and restaurants.

"I guess we have to camp on the water tonight," I said without enthusiasm.

It was getting late and I was tired. It would take more than an hour to set up our catamaran, but we had no choice. There were a few sailboats and fishing boats anchored in this bay, and we planned to overnight with them.

We waited until dusk to set up our catamaran system. A small crowd gathered around to watch. The seawall provided them with ample seating, and the stone pier where we assembled our equipment was a perfect stage. We connected the boats, inflated and secured the air mattress, positioned our tent on top and then, to the dismay of our fans, rowed the contraption to a more secluded area a short distance away. We dropped our anchor, a dry bag containing a hefty rock, and settled in for the night.

"This is nice," Colin said as waves gently caressed our boat.

"Like a baby being rocked to sleep," I agreed. "Plus 360-degree waterfront."

I was awakened about midnight. The boat jerked uncomfortably and I opened the door to investigate. The wind had shifted and was blowing from the only direction not sheltered by land or the breakwater. I could already feel the rising waves licking the bottom of our air mattress.

"As long as it doesn't blow too long, we'll be okay," Colin said.

We waited anxiously in the darkness, hoping the wind would stop. The basin we were in was surrounded by concrete and stone walls, extremely dangerous in big waves. It was pitch black, and I couldn't see the shore.

The wind grew stronger, and the waves were about a metre high. Now they occasionally washed over the air mattress, and water was soaking through the tent. I curled into a ball, trying to keep my sleeping bag from the Black Sea's reach.

"Maybe the wind will shift direction and we'll be protected again," I said hopefully.

An hour later, the waves had grown larger, and the catamaran was pitching violently. Our air mattress was saturated, and water was soaking into our sleeping bags.

"We should go to shore," Colin said.

"You mean when the sun rises?"

"The catamaran might break by morning. I don't know how long that beach-umbrella pole can take this strain."

"If we go now," I said, "we won't be able to see anything, and we're more likely to lose things and smash into the rocks. Besides, how are we going to get everything onto the stone pier?"

Neither option was appealing. The catamaran couldn't be disassembled in deep water, so we'd have to paddle it towards shore, take it apart in chest-deep waters and then carry everything over the boulders to the pier, which was being pounded with waves. It would be hard enough to do this in the day. At night, with howling winds and big waves, it would be next to impossible. But sunrise was still three hours away. It was very likely that before then we would drag anchor and be shipwrecked or the umbrella would break, pitching our tent into the sea.

After considerable discussion and procrastination, we decided to stay put. We spent the rest of the night lying stiffly in sodden sleeping bags, expecting to be plunged into inky waters at any moment.

Finally, at 5:30 a.m., a glow began to fill the sky, and we prepared to extricate ourselves from our Maytag mayhem. We flattened the tent and pulled anchor. We each paddled from opposite sides of the craft, steering the vessel by varying our paddle power. Waves slammed the boat, and suddenly, as we neared the beach, the umbrella pole finally snapped. The other pole was now under tremendous strain, and I jumped into the water to remove it before it snapped or was bent irreparably.

Our vessel was a sad mess, with bits and pieces hanging off everywhere while the wind shuttled us towards the rocks. Eventually, we were able to get it under control and to position it in an area of shallow water near the pier. We freed the boats from one another by untying the ropes. Then we carried the oars, air mattress, sodden tent, sleeping bags and other miscellaneous gear onto the shore. With careful, well-timed thrusts, we were able to use the waves washing over the pier to assist us in getting the boats out of the water. We were wet and exhausted from our sleepless night, but luckily no major damage was done.

"I need a coffee," I said, slumping against the wall. "That was the second-worst night of the expedition."

By eleven the wind had abated somewhat, and we continued, rowing 15 kilometres across the bay to the fishing village of Chernomorets. Here, we found a popular local beach surrounded by serrated rocks, and we stopped at a café in a wooden hut for a lunch of hamburgers and shopska salad. Then we did our best to recover from our previous sleepless night with a short nap on the warm sand.

The wind was picking up again as we continued around the headland and past the ancient city of Sozopol, which sits on a stony promontory jutting into the sea. Sozopol is even older than Nesebar, where we had stopped the day before. It dated back to the Bronze Age. It was fetching from the water, a jumble of red-roofed homes perched atop a high precipice. Although a popular tourist destination (it's dubbed the Bulgarian St. Tropez and has been visited by superstars like Brad Pitt and Angelina Jolie), it has the rustic charm of a community that has preserved its architecture and culture. By now, a one-metre swell was exploding off the cliffs, and the sun was close to setting. The rocky shoreline seemed never-ending, and I worried that after dark it would be impossible to find a safe place to land.

Fortunately, a crack in the rocks appeared just as the sun dipped behind the cliffs. We pulled our boats ashore on the five-metre-long beach of shells and pebbles and set up camp. By now we had travelled most of Bulgaria's 378-kilometre coastline and were a day or two from the Turkish border. We were apprehensive about crossing this border, which delineated not only two countries but also the edge of Europe. Travelling between EU countries on the water had been difficult enough, but now we required a visa, and there was no coastal road connecting Bulgaria and Turkey. No longer did we have the simple option of unpacking our bikes and pedalling overland.

The German sailor we had met in Rousse, Bulgaria, explained the protocol he had followed in his yacht: check out of Bulgaria in Burgas (which has customs and immigration facilities) and clear into Turkey in Istanbul. But some 250 kilometres separated those cities, and it would be impossible for us to row that stretch non-stop.

"You might be able to sneak ashore at night," he offered consolingly, "but I'd be careful. The border guards are all armed."

Another option he suggested was to go ashore at a Turkish marina. He had once stopped in a Turkish marina before entering in Istanbul, and they allowed him to stay, although he wasn't allowed off his boat and an armed guard made sure he abided.

On our last day off, we made a number of futile phone calls to embassies and consulates to inquire about proper protocol. The problem, though, was that no one fully understood what we were asking. It seemed that rowing across this border was an incomprehensible concept.

"Just fly home to Canada, get your visa and fly to Istanbul," the daft girl at the Turkish embassy in Canada said.

"You can get your visa in Burgas," a woman from the Turkish consulate in Bulgaria explained.

"And then can we cross into Turkey by boat?"

"Yes, you can enter Turkey at Malko Tarnovo."

"But that's inland. We're travelling by boat."

"You can get your visa at the border too, but I think it is better you come to Burgas."

We didn't know what the solution was. Journeying through the land border would involve travelling 300 kilometres inland over narrow mountain roads, some being little more than tracks in the forest, just to get a few hundred metres down the coast—a journey that would take ten minutes in our rowboats. There had to be a way to travel by water. We hoped to solve our problem in Tsarevo, the last city before the border.

In Tsarevo, we checked into a small place called Family Hotel, which was decorated with photos of groping sultry couples and glistening bikini-clad girls straddling motorcycles.

"When they say family establishment, it's the procreation side of things they have in mind," Colin mused as he examined the artwork.

We spent the day searching for solutions, reading blog postings online and making additional calls. The Canadian embassy in Turkey was the most helpful. The man I spoke with was the first official who fully comprehended my question, although his answer wasn't what we'd hoped for. He explained that we would have to follow the same protocol as a sailboat, which would involve clearing from a port city in Bulgaria and voyaging non-stop to Istanbul. And if that wasn't bad enough, he left us with a warning about heightened tensions on the Black Sea due to the armed conflict between Russia and Georgia that had erupted the previous week.

~~~

THE NEXT DAY, we continued rowing towards Turkey without knowing how we would enter. By late afternoon, we could see the tantalizing hills of Turkey just down the coast. Twenty minutes of rowing would take us into a new country.

"Maybe we should just head way out to sea, out of sight of land, and come in farther along the coast," Colin said.

It was tempting. "I wonder what they'd do if they caught us," I said.

"I dunno. They might confiscate the boats and deport us."

"Or maybe it would be like when we entered Bulgaria from Serbia without clearing," I said optimistically. "Maybe they'll truck in a couple of immigration officials who can stamp our passports for us."

"And bring us visas? I somehow doubt it."

A small cove opened in the rocky shoreline, and we decided to pull in for the night.

The bay was split into two beaches divided by a rocky outcrop. One beach was crowded and the other deserted apart from a single beach house and a couple lounging on deck chairs. We pulled ashore onto the private beach.

Colin strolled over to the pair to ask if it was okay to camp. The woman spoke English, and they cheerfully gestured over the beach. "Wherever you want."

We set up our tent and considered the possibilities.

"Perhaps we could walk over to the border and talk to the guards," I said. "Perhaps they might be able to get us through somehow."

"Maybe," Colin said doubtfully.

I thought back to the Romanian border guards who had been unable to assist. Most likely it would be the same here.

The man brought us two icy cold beers. He spoke little English but was able to extend a dinner invitation. We strolled over to the comfortable cabin, and I immediately warmed to the couple. The man introduced himself as Vladi and his partner as Dessi. Vladi was about forty, stout and dark haired with a warm smile and easy laugh. Dessi was a little younger, blonde and attractive, with the glamorous air of someone from a big city. She was fluent in four languages, including English, and easily interpreted for us and Vladi.

Vladi had the rounded belly of a man who likes his food. And as we discovered, he was a dab hand at cooking it, too. Dinner started with herring wrapped around olives and small conch, both pickled and from the Black Sea. The main course was a small, firm-fleshed, white fish, soaked in salt and grilled over an open flame, and accompanied by shop-ska salad. We drank Vladi's favourite wine, an expensive

Bulgarian red that he'd been saving for a special occasion. Then came Havana cigars and rakia, a clear brandy made from grapes.

It was a dinner for a king, but even better, Vladi thought he could make our border problems go away with a few phone calls. While he was talking animatedly on his iPhone, Colin turned to me.

"Did you catch what he does for a living?"

"No, but he sure seems to know a lot of people," I said.

Vladi put the phone down with a smile, and Dessi relayed to us that the problem was solved.

"Just like that?" I asked, incredulous.

"Yes, you just need to go to Tsarevo tomorrow, and they will give you a permit to cross the border."

The food, wine and rakia were kicking in. It seemed too good to be true, but who knows, maybe we'd be able to row out of there after all.

Close to midnight, three policemen scrambled down the steep embankment and asked to see our paperwork. The conversation was in Bulgarian, and we were bewildered. Had Vladi called these guys to help us or were we under surveillance? It turned out to be the latter, and we wondered if we had been watched all the way down the coast. It seemed we were sufficiently unusual to garner attention from those guarding the coastline.

Dessi took us to Tsarevo, where Vladi assured us we would get our permit. She sped along narrow, potholed roads and grumbled about any car travelling at the speed limit. With the effects of the wine long gone, I was having doubts that our permit would materialize. Five officials were waiting for us, sitting in an outside gazebo, four men and one woman. She spoke fluent English and did most of the talking.

"The problem," she said, "is we can give you clearance

to depart Bulgaria, but we can't do anything for your arrival into Turkey."

I groaned inwardly. It was our arrival into Turkey we were primarily concerned about.

"So, you'll give us permission to leave, stamp our passports, and we can row away from Bulgaria?" Colin said, trying to clarify.

"Yes," the woman said.

"And what do you think will happen when we cross the border into Turkey?"

"I don't know," she said.

"You are brave," one of the men added.

I assumed he was referring to the Black Sea's reputation for nasty weather, and I was about to assure them of our boats' seaworthiness.

"The Turkish are not like us," he continued. "They are fully armed and with big guns."

"But you guys carry guns, too," I said, thinking back to the rifles I'd seen the border guards carrying.

"Yes, but we just have little guns."

The officials went inside, and we discussed our options.

"They probably didn't want to scare you," Dessi said, "but there was a border accident a few months ago."

"An accident?" I repeated, suddenly curious.

"Yes. A Turkish fisherman accidentally crossed the border, and the Bulgarian guards shot him."

"Shot him . . . dead?" Colin said.

"Yes."

I couldn't believe it. "They shot him for a mistake in navigation? Wow!"

"So the Turks are probably a little annoyed at the moment," Colin hypothesized. "They're likely just waiting for someone to come from the other direction so they can get retribution."

"And that just happens to be us," I said glumly.

The officials came back out and we told them that we would prefer to take the inland border crossing.

"Can we tow our boats along the roads?" Colin asked.

The woman looked doubtful. "They are narrow, windy roads. I don't think you'd be allowed."

One of the men offered to arrange to have our boats trucked to the coast on the other side of the border. It seemed the only option, but we were a little disappointed. From Scotland to here, we had hauled our boats every inch of the way using only our muscles. Realistically, though, we weren't out to break any records, and it certainly wasn't worth getting shot over.

Dessi took us back to the beach, and we celebrated our final night in Bulgaria.

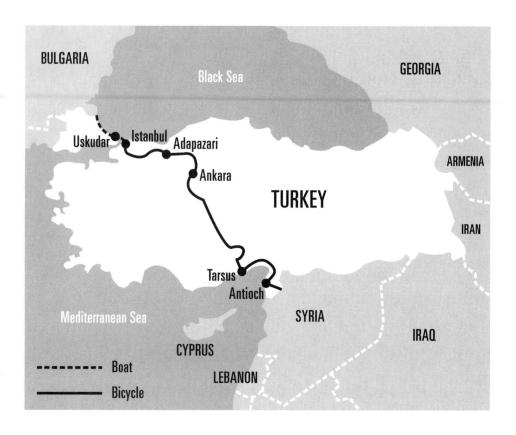

13

DANGEROUS BEAUTY

TURKEY (Colin)

THE TURKISH STRETCH OF THE BLACK SEA was nothing like what we first experienced in Romania or even in neighbouring Bulgaria. In Romania, it was crowded and heavily developed, and the shores were predominantly sandy beaches. Bulgaria had more unadulterated beauty, but it was nothing compared to the isolation and ruggedness of Turkey's coastline. A few fishing villages dotted the water's edge, but much of it was treacherous, lined with long basalt cliffs pounded by exploding waves. Occasional sandy beaches fringed small bays, but there was more rock than sand. It was a dramatic and beautiful seascape, but also more dangerous as far as we were concerned, especially now that strong winds seemed to be more frequent. Perhaps we were in a gustier region, but more likely it was because summer was waning. June and July are the calmest months on the Black Sea; the weather starts degrading in September. It was already late August.

After clearing through the inland Turkish border, we travelled to the walled medieval village of Kiyikoy, just down the coast from where we had been stopped at the Bulgarian border. Adverse weather prevented us from departing immediately, and we spent an extra day exploring in this bluff-top fishing community. This region was Muslim and markedly different from the primarily Christian nations we had just left behind. Churches were replaced with mosques, and for the first time since leaving Scotland, we no longer heard pealing bells; instead, a rhythmic call to prayer reminded inhabitants of their religious duties. In the centre of the village, chairs and tables were filled with men drinking tea from petite glasses. There were few tourists, but we were welcomed warmly in the small shops.

The architecture was a mix of old and new, mostly stone with ceramic roofs. The Byzantine wall surrounding the village had been built in the sixth century and was in partial ruins, but the arch over the main entrance still stood. In the northeast corner of the village, a tunnel led to the base of the cliffs, allowing the villagers to escape to the sea in times of siege. Julie and I strolled to the bottom of the cliffs to explore the ancient Monastery of St. Nicholas, an impressive structure carved into a cliff. The entire building—with its colonnaded aisles, vaulted ceilings and a semicircular apse of tiered seats— had been chiselled out of stone. There was once a labyrinth of tunnels beneath, with underground rooms and escape routes. It had long since caved in.

When the winds partially abated, we departed from the small, sheltered boat basin below the village. Fishermen mended nets and nursed old motors as we slipped quietly into the large rolling swell. After a short stretch of beach, the coast gave way to a serrated line of wave-carved basalt. Rocky headlands occasionally projected out from long expanses of sheer cliff. Above the crags, thick forests of oak stretched up the hillsides.

It was both invigorating and nerve-racking being in the midst of such splendour. The wind and waves were driving hard onshore. A mechanical failure or sudden increase in the winds could quickly spell disaster. Earlier, we had carefully run through various worst-case scenarios and formulated emergency plans. If both of our boats were about to be shipwrecked onto the rocks, we would abandon our vessels and swim parallel to shore until reaching a safe point to go ashore. If one boat faltered, the other would try to tow it to safety. I made a point of noting any pockets of sand we passed that could provide an emergency landing in case of trouble.

We made good time despite the large swell and crosswinds. By the end of the day, we had travelled about halfway to the Bosporus, the channel that leads south to Istanbul. A long stretch of beach appeared, and we angled towards shore.

A large shipwreck sat in the shallows near the terminus of the beach. The freighter had snapped in half, and its bow angled out of the water at 45 degrees. It was heavily rusted and looked as if it had been there for some time, but as we neared, I realized that wasn't the case. A pungent smell of fuel oil filled the air and a black slick coated the sea's surface, belying the recentness of the accident. It was no wonder that this is one of the world's most polluted seas when nobody could be bothered to remove the fuel from a shipwreck, instead allowing it to leak into the surrounding waters. I could still make out the name of the boat, *Blue Way*, and beneath those white letters were the faded markings of its original name, *Lord*. But contrary to what those handles implied, the ship's disposal wasn't very divine or concerned with blue waters. (Later research revealed the ship's details: 110 metres long, built in 1973 and capable of carrying 8,228 tonnes. It had changed names five times, most recently in 2002 when it acquired the name *Blue Way* and switched its flag from Georgia to Panama. We could, however, find nothing saying it had sunk; on the contrary, the Miramar Ship Index listed it as still in service as of 2005.)

We gingerly pulled up to the beach, steering between submerged rocks marked by occasional plumes of spray. Once through the surf break, we dragged our vessels to the safety of high ground. The shore was littered with remnants from the shipwreck—emergency rations of drinking water (aluminum packets labelled in Russian and made in St. Petersburg), shoes, a large Turkish flag (the courtesy flag) and other odds and ends.

In the night the wind increased, and by morning a full gale blasted across the water. Waves swallowed the shipwreck in a fury of foam and thundered against offshore reefs. There was no chance of rowing past the shore break, and we resigned ourselves to a day off. Our drinking water was low, but we topped up our supply with packets of Russian emergency reserves. Even then, we had only enough water for one more day. If the storm continued, we'd have to hike out in search of water, but we weren't sure how far the nearest settlement or road would be. Above our campsite, there were only windswept forests of pine and oak.

We whiled away the hours exploring our surroundings, writing in our journals and building a patio for our tent using beautiful flat sedimentary stones.

In the afternoon, three men appeared from the forest. They had the weathered look of fishermen and were combing the beach for usable timber that had washed ashore. When they passed our tents, they waved cheerfully, and we tried our best to converse.

"Canada," Julie said, pointing between us.

"Ahh, Canada," a man of about sixty replied.

He pointed to himself and his colleagues and said something unintelligible. The men disappeared into the forest with logs over their shoulders. About fifteen minutes later, the older man reappeared, smiling and holding a bag of peanuts for us.

Several hours later, the old man along with two others returned. The youngest of the group, dark haired and in his mid-forties, was trying to communicate something to us.

He pointed to the waves and issued the sole word, "Problem."

Through gestures and pictures drawn in the sand, he made it clear that the storm was expected to intensify, and soon the waves would wash completely over the beach right up to the cliff behind our tent.

Communication was extraordinarily difficult. We tried to convey the fact that this was all right; if the waves did increase we'd move our gear and boats onto the cliff, up the same steep embankment the men had come down. I pointed at our camp-site and the top of the cliff.

The men shook their heads and indicated this was not allowed. The words "gendarme" and "problem" were used frequently.

"Maybe we're camped in a military zone," Julie surmised. "Obviously they're saying we're not allowed to be here."

I cursed the weather. The easiest solution would be to head out to sea, but the weather was too rough. The men became more and more insistent we had to leave otherwise we would be in trouble with the gendarme. They would help us move the boats to a public beach eight kilometres back.

Confusion reigned. Were these guys from the local gen-darmerie or the military?

"Geez," Julie said. "Not only will this be a royal pain, but we're going to lose eight precious kilometres."

We struck camp, carried our gear up the embankment and continued through a trail in the woods to a track about 200 metres inland. A beat-up station wagon was waiting, and we strapped one of the boats onto the roof. The other would be shuttled in a second trip.

We crawled along a rutted track for half an hour before emerging from the woods. A security guard opened a gate and we came out onto a public road. We were unable to deter-mine what it was we had emerged from, apart from the fact it was heavily guarded. We continued to a familiar-looking beach. I recalled that we had passed it the day before.

We still had no idea exactly what was going on and weren't pleased to have backtracked eight kilometres and lost the privacy of our remote beach. Nonetheless, it was obvious the men were well intentioned, and we made the best of our situation.

Although there was no settlement nearby, there was a ram-shackle bar on the beach with a few men nursing beers.

"Don't worry," I tried to placate Julie. "Once the wind stops, we'll be back in the water and rounding the Bosporus into Istanbul."

The gales didn't stop; instead, they intensified and were forecast to continue for the next week. As the crow flies we were only 30 kilometres from Istanbul, and so we finally decided to head overland with our bikes.

~~~

IN THE MORNING WE PACKED OUR GEAR and began pedalling down a quiet, well-maintained road through the countryside. Away from the coast, the forests disappeared and we entered an agricultural landscape. It wasn't long before we could make out the tall buildings of Turkey's largest city shimmering beyond fields of wheat.

Quiet country lanes quickly transformed into eight lanes of chaos as we neared this city of 12.6 million inhabitants. The traffic was beyond anything we'd yet experienced (even topping our cycle through Mexico City), and after we'd endured hours of near misses with semi-trailers and terrifying dashes across lanes of relentless traffic, our frayed nerves were on the verge of snapping. Eight kilometres from the city centre, we discovered a wide pedestrian boulevard on the waterfront, which we gratefully followed into Istanbul's oldest and most historic region, Sultanahmet. We veered away from the seawall, bumped up cobbled roads and before long settled into an inexpensive but comfortable hotel.

Istanbul is the cultural and financial capital of Turkey and has lost its status as political capital only because of its vulnerability to seafaring invaders. It is the fourth largest city in the world and one of the most beautiful. Incredibly well-preserved architecture dates back through the ages, and the city is a living museum, displaying construction from the Roman, Byzantine and Ottoman periods, just to name a few. We spent three days admiring the sights, happily wandering narrow cobbled streets.

We visited the Ayasofya—built in 537 and the largest cathedral for nearly a thousand years afterwards, even though it was converted to a mosque in 1453—and, down the street, the Blue Mosque, a stunning cascade of domes encircled by minarets. We explored an ancient cistern of marble columns and great arches deep beneath the city's surface created during the Byzantine reign to store water. We ate at streetside vendors and in small restaurants: simits (baseball-sized rings of bread coated in sesame seeds), donor kebabs, kofte (hamburger-meatball hybrids), lahmajun (wafer-thin pizzas topped with minced tomatoes, onions and parsley) and for dessert sutlac, a creamy rice pudding caramelized like crème brûlée.

We had now been on the road for six months and were 1,000 kilometres from our final destination of Aleppo. Initially, we had planned to row all the way to Syria from here via the Mediterranean, but now we were having second thoughts. It was important to us that we could ship our boats back to Canada, and our research indicated this would be next to impossible from Syria.

Losing rowboats thanks to bureaucratic quagmires was something we were much too familiar with. The rowboat we used to cross the Atlantic Ocean (which we paid more than $30,000 for) was still in Costa Rica, where we completed the voyage. We had spent two years wrangling with Costa Rican authorities and ultimately had no choice but to write the boat off as a loss. Since we were determined not to let that happen again, we decided to ship the boats from Istanbul and cover the final distance on our bicycles.

Sending *Niobium* and *Tantalum* home from Turkey wasn't exactly easy. The actual shipping was straightforward—a sophisticated supply line connects Istanbul to the rest of the world, and we easily found a shipping agent. The challenge, as usual, was government bureaucracy. Before we could ship the boats, we had to give power of attorney to our agent, the shipping company and customs brokers working on our behalf, a pricey process that required documents to be drafted, translated (to English so that we could understand them) and notarized. A few days later, we had our first snag.

"Customs requires the boats' import papers," said our shipping agent, Sinan.

"But we don't have any," Julie said. "We just pulled them through the road crossing behind our bikes. They gave us visas, stamped our passports, and that was it. Nothing for the boats."

"I am afraid they won't let the boats go unless you have the required paperwork."

By this time, we had spent almost a thousand dollars on legal fees, translation and an array of miscellaneous charges. Why was it so hard to ship out a couple of beat-up homemade rowboats? If they had been small enough to be transported as personal baggage, customs wouldn't bat an eye. Why was shipping by freighter such a customs quagmire?

After three days of stalemate, the problem was finally resolved with an additional $400 fee. Then, we were told that the United States no longer accepted shipments of personal goods and a different shipping company had to be sourced, one that didn't stop stateside. By now, administrative costs, which don't yet include transportation and shipping, had exceeded $1,300, we had devoted a solid week to the process, and we still weren't sure if our boats would leave. We delivered our boats to an industrial compound on the east side of the city and wrapped them in 100 metres of tablecloth-width bubble wrap we bought at the Grand Bazaar. We left *Tantalum* and *Niobium* on a pallet at a shipping warehouse, uncertain whether we would ever see our faithful companions again. (After a week, we got word that they were loaded onto a ship, and two months later, we cleared them with Canadian customs, which took all of two minutes and was completely free, and picked them up at a Vancouver warehouse.)

~~~

CYCLING OUT OF THE WORLD'S FOURTH-LARGEST CITY wasn't any more enjoyable than coming in. We travelled along a non-stop sea of fumy asphalt. There was a shoulder at the edge, but we shared it with clapped-out buses belching clouds of black smoke. They pulled over often and without checking for traffic. Twice we tried passing, narrowly avoiding being hit when they accelerated. By the end of our first day, we were still within the industrial outskirts of Istanbul, pedalling past vast factories, parking lots and rundown satellite sub-divisions. We searched for a camping spot, but all vacant lots were protected by security guards or dogs, and it was only when the sun had set that we found a highway hotel to check into.

The following day we emerged from the outskirts of Istanbul. Dry, hilly landscapes separated the large industrial cities of Gebze, Körfez and Adapazari, which were the antithesis of desert oases: unlovely collections of factories, rundown housing, gas stations and roadside restaurants.

It was now September, and while still hot, it was significantly cooler than the blazing months of July and August, and we found the dry 30-to-35-degree temperatures more bearable than some of the blistering humid days we had encountered on the Danube. And as we ascended through a series of passes, the temperatures dropped even further.

While it was a good time for cycling with regards to weather, it was less agreeable from a culinary standpoint. Ramadan, the Muslim holy month, coincided with almost our entire stay in the Middle East—that year it began on September 1 and lasted until September 30—which meant most Muslims abstained from food and drink between dawn and dusk. This made finding meals a challenge, as many (but not all) roadside restaurants were closed during daylight hours.

Although they themselves didn't eat or drink, the Turks had no hesitation about offering Julie and me food and drink. They were the most hospitable people we had yet encountered. Half the passing vehicles tooted their horns in greeting, gas station attendants waved, and people beckoned us into their homes or businesses for a tea and food. We regularly took up these invitations, sipping strong Turkish tea under a patio umbrella or tree canopy while chatting (usually with difficulty) to our gracious hosts.

Even the dogs in Turkey were amicable, a stark contrast to Bulgaria and especially Romania. There were fewer strays, and those we saw were markedly different from their destitute Eastern European counterparts. They were all enormous, muscle-bound creatures that belonged to a breed called kangal, which is ubiquitous in Turkey but does not exist in neighbouring countries. It is thought that this dog originated from central Asia and accompanied Oghuz Turks when they fled Genghis Khan's armies in the eleventh century. While they looked fierce and averaged 50 kilograms, they had a docile demeanour that is attributed to their vocation. Kangal dogs were bred to guard (not herd) sheep from predators and are known to be gentle and protective around children, small animals and anything considered part of their flock, but very aggressive to perceived threats. So as long as we weren't suspected of sheep snatching, we should be safe.

We were headed for Ankara, Turkey's inland capital. Two parallel roads covered this route, a high-quality toll freeway and a reasonable state road. We travelled on the public highway, and about 150 kilometres from Istanbul, the traffic diminished to a tolerable level. We followed a broad agricultural valley laced with towns and villages. Abundant service stations dotted the highway, and it was within these establishments we discovered the eighth wonder of the world: Turkey's washrooms.

One might expect that since Turkey has been developing rapidly over the past few years, it might be a little like France with scant resources allocated for toilet facilities. To be honest, I expected the toilets in gas stations to be little more than overflowing, fly-infested messes out back. I was quite shocked when I walked into the first spacious washroom. Gleaming marble and granite covered every surface. The facilities were sparklingly clean, capacious enough to relieve an Ottoman army, and, unlike in Britain, always free of charge.

We could be in the middle of a dust bowl with three houses and a gas station and could count on a luxurious restroom. We'd retreat from the blazing heat to rinse our faces within the cool marble confines. The gas station attendants were always friendly, and more than once we camped on their premises, setting up our tent in small green gardens tucked along the side and making frequent trips to the luxury loos.

On our second day on the road, we left the broad agricultural valley and ascended the interior highlands via a series of steep mountain passes. We traversed a succession of steppe-like plateaus covered in farms and ringed with high mountains. Eventually, beyond the city of Gerede, the plateaus disappeared, and the terrain buckled and folded in an endless chain of mountain ranges. Arid forests cloaked the mountains' flanks, and peaks stared down like dry, withered faces. The road climbed pass after pass through winding switchbacks. It took hours to pedal up each mountain, sweat trickling and muscles aching. Then we sped down the far side only to repeat the process.

On September 10, we reached Ankara and the broad, arid valley it sits within. The terrain rolled gently despite the high elevation, and distant rugged mountains created a natural barrier. It was the very inaccessibility of Ankara that helped it become Turkey's capital in 1923. Istanbul had been attacked and occupied so many times that it made sense to move the capital to a less vulnerable position. As the national capital, Ankara has seen rapid development over the past ninety years, and after piercing the industrial exterior, we passed many modern and luxurious developments on the city's periphery. We emerged on the south side of the city on a relatively quiet highway that cut through a vast plateau at an elevation of about 900 metres.

The following day we reached the northern tip of Lake Tuz, 115 kilometres south of Ankara. It looked more like a moonscape than a body of water, a vast expanse of salt that is Turkey's second largest lake. In the winter, the water rises to a height of one to two metres, but in later summer, it almost completely dries out, leaving a 30-centimetre-deep layer of salt. It is fed by ground and surface water, but has no outflow. There is an island in it on which most of Turkey's flamingos breed. Several mines extract enough salt from the lake to supply much of Turkey. We took a cycling detour onto the salt flats.

Bumping over the rough surface was like riding on a gravel road. A big, friendly kangal dog from a nearby building joined us and cantered by our side.

We spent the next three days riding across a plateau. The landscape was uninspiring, vast fields of dirt and scrub and a few struggling crops, but the terrain was flat and the temperatures cool. That all ended when we reached the Taurus Mountains, the same range where the Tigris and Euphrates rivers are born. The road snaked up a high pass, then came down an eternal descent along a long, narrow canyon leading to the Cilician plain. We lost some 1,200 metres in that descent, plummeting to nearly sea level.

The arid scrublands of the high plateau were replaced with rich groves of orange trees, cotton, corn and an array of other crops. The Mediterranean was only 30 kilometres away, and this was one of the most agriculturally productive regions in the world. It was also hot and humid. As we entered the province of Adana, which, for Turks, is synonymous with sweltering heat, the mercury soared to a muggy 38 degrees Celsius.

In the provincial capital, also called Adana, we found ourselves a hotel and escaped into air-conditioned comfort. Adana is Turkey's fifth largest city, a growth driven by the prosperous agricultural industry. It had a slew of hotels and restaurants, a thriving downtown market and an impressive mosque. All the shops catered to locals, and we seemed to be the sole tourists, which in some ways made it nicer than Istanbul, where ripping off visitors is an accepted business practice. We ate Adana kebabs, which as the name implies originated here, and tried a drink that everyone seemed to be enjoying.

The first clue that it might be an acquired taste came when we ordered it and the woman asked, "Are you sure?" She ladled a deep red fluid into a glass, added a splash of something pink and decorated it with a slice of pickled carrot. It tasted like vinegar, and I guessed it to be some sort of pickled juice, maybe beet. It was, I later discovered, şalgam suyu, a fermented blend of pickled carrots and turnips that also originated in Adana but hasn't quite acquired the fame of the Adana kebab.

From Adana, it was 200 kilometres to the Syrian border. We ascended another lofty mountain range and dropped into a final valley. We spent our last night in Turkey in the town of Kirikhan. Its name means broken inn in Turkish and is a reference to the abundant inns that were once here. But when we asked at a gas station if there was someplace to stay, the young man laughed.

"There are no hotels here," he said, "but you can sleep at my gas station."

He introduced himself as Ozit and showed us to a grassy meadow next to a barn with sheep. Ozit told us he was twenty-two and taking a break from university to help in his father's gas station. That night he brought us dinner, which his mom made, and drove us to a restaurant he said served the best baklava in Turkey. His car was a mix of testosterone meets money—black leather interior, powerful stereo blasting Turkish pop music—and he drove at reckless speeds, which he assured us was of no concern because he had befriended all the police in town, and besides he had already lost his licence. The baklava was indeed the best we'd ever had, especially the kunefe, a mouth-watering mix of melted cheese, baklava pastry and rich syrup.

It was a fitting last night in Turkey, one that was representative of the kindness and generosity we had experienced here. We had spent almost a month in Turkey, travelling some 1,200 kilometres within its borders, but I could easily have stayed and continued exploring. It was a beautiful country, both geographically and culturally, and leaving was bittersweet. But ahead, in a mere 40 kilometres, lay Syria. It was Julie's chance to understand a culture she was only tenuously connected to and to meet family she had never or rarely seen. I was also curious to learn about this part of her heritage and excited to celebrate the completion of the journey with the newest members of my family.

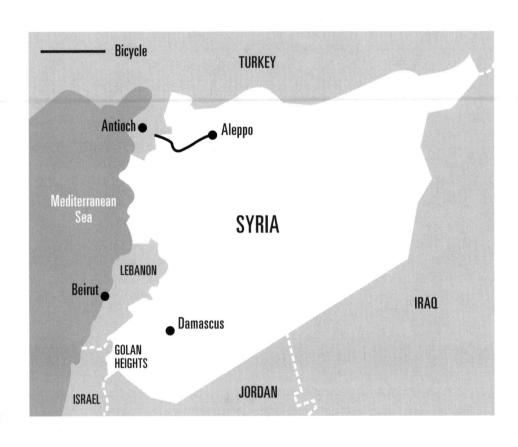

14

JUST LIKE OUR FAMILY

SYRIA *(Julie)*

I HANDED THE SYRIAN BORDER GUARD MY PASSPORT, nervous he would discover my lie. We had obtained our visas three weeks earlier at the Syrian embassy in Istanbul. At first, we weren't sure if we'd be able to get them. The rules are such that if your home country has Syrian consular representation, you have to procure your visa there. Canada has a Syrian embassy, and we had tried to get our visas at home, but then we discovered they were valid for only three months—not long enough for this trip. Nor could we send our passports to Canada while travelling through Europe. Our only option had been to try at the Turkish Syrian embassy.

At the Syrian embassy, the German couple in line in front of us, also hoping to procure Syrian visas, was flatly told they had to go back to Germany to apply. We were armed with a letter from the Canadian consulate in Turkey that we had obtained a few hours earlier. Really it was nothing, a "letter of recommendation" that offered a few ambiguous words and a fancy stamp, but at least it looked official. We gave the young woman our paperwork, and she scrutinized it silently for about twenty seconds.

"These are incomplete," she finally said and pointed to the empty blank on the application: *Religion—Muslim, Christian or other.* "You have to answer all the questions."

"I'm not really religious," I said.

"Then you are Christian." She amended our applications.

I am as much Muslim as Christian: I grew up with a Christian mother and a Muslim father. But I didn't say anything for fear of exposing the lie on my application.

I knew that as a woman under thirty-five, I could be refused entry for a few reasons. I had to travel with a father, husband or brother, which I was, and because my father was Syrian, I also needed his permission and proof of it. My father approved of this trip and would have readily granted me permission, but he was in Toronto and I wasn't sure what obtaining permission meant. Did he have to complete an application? Would it need to be notarized or processed through a consulate? It seemed a procedure likely fraught with endless bureaucratic obstacles. So instead of listing my father's very Arabic name, which was archived in state records, I used the name of a friend and put his place of birth as Canada.

There was another issue with my heritage: it made me eligible for Syrian citizenship, which meant I would be subject to all rules and conditions reserved for Syrian nationals. This status could make a big difference in treatment, including limited help from Canada's consular services, potential difficulties entering and leaving the country, and, for men, compulsory military service. In short, I would be subject to a whole different set of rules and regulations than would apply to a regular tourist.

"Come back tomorrow between ten and noon," said the young woman as she added our documents to a large stack.

As promised, our Syrian visas were ready the next day. They took up a whole page in our passport; there was a small Syrian flag in the left-hand corner and a watermark of a ruin behind Roman and Arabic script.

Before entering Syria at the Turkish Cilvegözü border crossing, we stopped at a modern complex that housed duty-free shops, a restaurant, café, washrooms and even showers. We ate our final Turkish meal in air-conditioned comfort, then rolled our bikes through a series of guarded posts, procuring our exit stamps and officially leaving Turkey.

A gravel road led three kilometres through a no man's land to the Syrian customs and immigration facilities. A line of parked trucks bordered the road for most of that distance, occupants sitting or lying in the shade of their trucks waiting to inch closer to Turkey. Most drivers smiled and shouted "*Marhaba*," a common Arabic greeting that means welcome. Some invited us to share tea with them, yelling "Chai, chai" and waving us over in typical Turkish fashion, their hands slapping the air as if dribbling a basketball.

We were travelling through a pass in a very low massif, and the dirt road snaked through a canyon. At the highest point, we reached a blue sign that heralded Syria in Arabic and Roman script. "Wellcome to Syria," it said. We stopped to take a picture of the misspelling and of the desert-like landscape of rock and dirt shimmering in the heat.

"Welcome home," Colin said.

We had the video and still cameras out and were snapping shots when a guard approached.

"Hide the cameras," I whispered, aware that it was illegal to photograph military and government property.

But he wasn't coming to give us a scolding; instead, he held up two icy cold bottles of water and warmly welcomed us to Syria.

~~~

WE REACHED A COLLECTION OF LARGE BUILDINGS and were directed into one to clear customs and immigration. A row of immigration officials sat behind glass-fronted desks. People milled about, mostly Arabs and Turks, forming loose lines in front of windows or sitting on benches. On the wall were signs offering direc-tions, including one, I was amused to see, that guaranteed courteous and speedy service and provided a contact number in case of complaints. Imagine if U.S. immigration and customs had the courage to make such an offer; they'd have to contract out a call centre in India to deal with demand.

We approached a lean man in his forties with thick, dark eyebrows and an equally robust moustache. I handed him our passports along with a small form we'd just completed and waited nervously.

"You are from Canada. Niagara Falls, ice hockey." He gave a slight smile.

"Yes," Colin said.

"Where are you going?"

"Aleppo," I said.

He punched our details into the computer and asked a few more questions: profession, purpose of visit, whether we ever visited Occupied Palestine. We answered appropriately, and after a lengthy pause he stamped our passports.

The Syrian landscape was very different from the lush agricultural landscape just ten kilometres back. The land we passed through was barren and arid, little more than rolling hills of dust and rocks, compared to bucolic Turkish fields of cotton and wheat and shepherds roaming with their livestock. The homes also differed; made of sandstone with decorative carvings, they blended into the beige landscape, looking like a bungalow version of the sandcastle.

We were cycling on a minor highway, the number 5, which led all the way to Aleppo. It was smooth and well maintained, although often devoid of lane markings, so traffic flowed with less demarcation than it had in Turkey. Motorcycles wove around trucks, red and white checkered headscarves flapping wildly, while horns blared and unmuffled engines growled. We reached a small village and bought a bottle of cold pop (unlike in Turkey, bottled water was not commonly available) from an open stall. We held off drinking the sweet liquid until reaching the outskirts so as not to be disrespectful of those fasting for Ramadan. As travellers, no one would expect us to fast, and even Muslim travellers are exempted from fasting, a fact demonstrated by the presence of small roadside stands selling espresso-style coffee to truck drivers.

"It seems we're returning to a land that appreciates coffee," I said happily.

We were surprised while travelling through Turkey that coffee was not common. Although Turkish coffee is famous around the world, it is like Canadian bacon or French toast in that the citizens consume very little of the product named after them. Turkey is a tea nation, and most of the coffee we did find there was Nescafé. Now in Syria, coffee was everywhere.

Coffee was first consumed in Ethiopia, but it was the Arabs who learned to roast and grind the beans and to create a beverage similar to what we drink today. It spread quickly through the Muslim world and wove its way into the social fabric as coffee houses appeared. Even the word "coffee" is Arabic and was adopted by the Italians, who were the first Europeans to start sipping this imported beverage, in the 1600s. So it made sense that coffee seemed to be a dominant part of the culture as we entered the Arab world.

Before long, we were in the outskirts of Aleppo, or Halab as it is called in Syria. Aleppo is Syria's biggest city, with four and a half million citizens, almost a quarter of the country's population. It is one of the world's oldest cities and has been continuously occupied for at least seven thousand years (although there is evidence of habitation thirteen thousand years ago). It has been a pivotal place throughout much of history as a key trading juncture positioned between the

Euphrates River and the Mediterranean Sea. Aleppo has been ruled by an astounding array of cultures, including the Amorite Dynasty, Hittites, Assyrians, the Persian Empire, Greeks, Romans, Arabs, Byzantines, the Ayyubid Dynasty, Mongols, the Ottoman Empire and the French. The city is filled with archaeological treasures above and below the ground; many remain undiscovered because the modern city sits on top of the old.

This ancient hub on the Silk Road has seen its share of travellers, invaders, migrants and displaced cultures. Located within the cradle of civilization, it is where humans first began adopting agriculture and a more complex social structure. For me, this city had more significance than just its rich history: it is where I come from. It is the city where my father was born, and it marked the end of our expedition. For more than 7,000 kilometres, my husband and I had travelled by human power to link our points of origin.

It was a world apart from Scotland. I thought back to the countries in between—the shifting landscapes and mosaic of cultures. Our slow, difficult mode of transportation had given me an appreciation for the distances and hurdles we don't notice when teleported by Airbus. In a world where we are losing touch with the earth and forests that have shaped our kind, the struggle had been strangely satisfying.

Several months before our expedition, I was curious about what science could reveal about my background through genetic analysis. Colin and I had both sent off DNA samples for testing, and I remember my disappointment when the vague results came back. We were told Colin's family came from Europe, and my paternal lineage was from the Middle East. That was it; $125 for something Colin's six-year-old niece could have told us.

But those results emphasized the fact that I will never fully know where I come from. Our journey was intended to provide a collection of experiences that wouldn't necessarily answer questions but would place our backgrounds and origins in a context far removed from a world of pixels, scientists and statisticians. The cornerstone of civilization has traditionally been the family unit. This, however, is changing as technology steers us further from the natural rhythms of the biological world, allowing us to operate independently, supported by our systems and machines.

As Colin and I travelled across Europe, the world revealed its natural cycle. We woke with the sun, were perpetually exposed to the elements, and feared creatures in the night. Sometimes we'd go hungry or thirsty, and often we were overwhelmed with the fatigue of hard physical labour. These were experiences my ancestors would have shared, whether on a subsistence farm in East Prussia or here in the Middle East. And somehow I found that reassuring.

~~~

I HAD BROUGHT MY PRECONCEPTIONS WITH ME, and our entry into Aleppo was dispelling the latest. I had envisioned a majestic metropolis, but instead the approach into the city was decrepit. Trash cluttered the roadside, and patches of thin olive trees, brushed brown with dust, acted as sieves, collecting plastic bags and wrappers in their branches. The density of housing increased until finally we crested a hill and the heart of Aleppo unfurled before us, an expanse of pale buildings in a valley of sand.

In Turkey, I had called my uncle for directions to his home. He had rattled off a complex set of instructions, and now I realized we would never be able to find it. The streets were a haphazard labyrinth of multidirectional lanes with signs in Arabic script. Instead, we decided to call when we reached the city centre, and he would come find us.

The traffic became increasingly frightening as we neared the centre. It seemed there were no rules, and cars squeezed and honked around each other at breakneck speeds. The roads were a free-for-all, and with no divided lanes, cars passed and veered with adept fluidity, filling empty spaces like flowing water. It reminded me of crowds I'd seen on TV rushing into a discount store on Boxing Day, only now it was cars instead of people. All the vehicles were covered in dents, as they suffered the inevitable damage. For us, without a protective surround of metal, it was outright dangerous, and we continually swerved or slammed on our brakes to avoid vehicles that moved into our paths.

We paused twice at traffic lights to check our map, and both times a pedestrian stopped to give us directions in good English, followed by an invitation to dinner. We had to decline, but it was a heartwarming display of kindness from complete strangers. Arabs are known for their generosity and hospitality to travellers, and during Ramadan, which is all about giving and sharing, this trait is even more prevalent.

We couldn't make head or tail of our map and instead followed the directions we'd been given. We were headed for the New City, which despite its name, wasn't particularly modern (it had been developed in the nineteenth century) until you compare it to the Old City, where buildings date back centuries and even millennia.

At last, as the city settled into darkness, we reached our destination. It seemed surreal that we had started the day in a sleepy Turkish village and now we were in this massive Syrian city. The streets were crowded with newspaper shops, baklava bakeries, restaurants and hotels. The restaurants were laying out feasts in preparation for Iftar, the evening meal ending a day of fasting. Given the late hour and our state of exhaustion, we decided to spend the night in a hotel and contact my relatives in the morning.

We checked into the Baron Hotel, a place with a roster of esteemed past guests including Charles Lindbergh, T. E. Lawrence, Theodore Roosevelt and Agatha Christie, who began writing *Murder on the Orient Express* in one of its rooms.

Stepping into the grand old hotel was like taking a time machine into the past. Steamer trunks as big as fridges adorned the hallways, and old posters advertised 1950s air travel on hulking planes from Pan Am, BOAC and KLM. We stayed in Charles Lindbergh's room, which was full of wooden furniture that had likely been there for the best part of a century.

In the morning, I called my uncle Bassam. I had not seen him for seventeen years, and I wondered if we would recognize each other when he arrived at the hotel to pick us up. The last time we saw each other was in Canada, where he briefly lived before returning to Syria to get married and start a family. While Colin and I waited for him on the patio, I was suddenly nervous. What would my Syrian family be like? Would they welcome me warmly or was our visit going to be an inconvenience for them— just distant relatives placing a strain on the family?

A thin man with a slight shuffle approached.

"Julie," he said without hesitation.

He clasped me in a bear hug, and I introduced him to Colin. Bassam's English is excellent, and he immediately began peppering me with questions about the trip and how my parents were doing.

When I looked into Bassam's intense eyes, I felt as if I was sitting in front of my father. They shared the same dark eyes, overgrown eyebrows, broad forehead and high cheekbones. Even their mannerisms were similar, and I watched in amazement as Bassam moved his hand while he talked or angled his head, mirroring movements I had associated only with my father. If I closed my eyes, I wouldn't be able to tell their voices apart.

Although the similarities were striking, there was one major difference: weight. My father was rotund whereas Bassam was gaunt, almost fragile.

"Let's go," Bassam finally said, leading us along the crowded sidewalk.

We reached his ground-level home in a tidy brick apartment building. His wife, Alia, and three children (aged three to twelve) rushed to the door to greet us. They proudly showed us around their home, and I felt bad that they had designated one of the two bedrooms for us to stay in. I insisted we sleep in the living room, but they flatly refused.

The apartment was functional and included a studio where Bassam created oil paintings he sold professionally. The living room was furnished with two floral couches, and white lace curtains covered the windows. The white plaster walls were bare apart from a portrait I immediately recognized as my late grandmother (painted by Bassam). The scent of jasmine filled the air, carried in on a light breeze from the garden.

Alia prepared dinner, and when the sun set, we crowded around the kitchen table and feasted on lentil soup, fattoush salad, kibbeh (patties made of ground beef and bulgar), rice pilaf and pita. Afterwards, I insisted on helping and made Arabic coffee, arabica, naturally following the steps my father had taught me. It is made in a similar fashion to Turkish coffee: finely ground beans with a touch of cardamom are mixed with water and boiled twice (that's the important part) in a small pot. The thick slurry is poured into tiny cups and served with sugar.

We sat in the living room sipping arabica and eating baklava.

"Do you still play the guitar?" I asked my uncle.

I have a photo from the first time I met Bassam. He's strumming a guitar and I'm a shy four-year-old smiling beside him. I can still remember him singing "Leaving on a Jet Plane."

He shook his head. "The only guitar I have is the one your

father gave me." He disappeared and returned holding a child's acoustic guitar with one string remaining.

"Your father gave me this as a parting gift before he left Syria. It's what I learned to play on."

I examined the battered wooden instrument. A small sticker revealed its country of origin, China. I imagined my father packing his worldly possessions, readying for the journey that would forever change his life and the generations ahead. He was probably excited and apprehensive, yet sensed the melancholy hanging over his thirteen-year-old brother.

My father, Mohammed Husam Wafaei, was nineteen when he immigrated to Canada. He longed to travel and was discontent with life in Syria, unhappy with the political situation and lack of opportunities. During the summers of his final two years in high school he worked in Beirut, Lebanon, at construction sites during the day and a bowling alley in the evening, to save money for his trip to Canada. He enrolled in the University of Aleppo, but spent only a few weeks studying architectural landscaping before leaving. Saying goodbye must have been tough, not only because he didn't know if he'd be allowed back again but because he defied his father's expectations. He compromised a family structure where proximity was paramount and for that, his father refused to communicate for the next eighteen months.

When my father arrived in Toronto, he was penniless and had a limited grasp of English. He quickly found work as a waiter, moonlighted as a security guard and studied English in night classes. In school he met Victor, an Italian whose wife was friends with my mother. Introductions were made and six months later my mother and father were married, and not too long after that they had their first and only child.

When I was born, my dad was twenty. Suddenly he was a father and a husband, immersed in a very different culture and saddled with serious responsibilities. He continued working dead-end jobs to pay the bills and began a four-year program to become an aircraft maintenance engineer. He joined the Canadian air force when I was four and moved up through the ranks to become a flight engineer. In his free time he completed a university degree in psychology followed by an MBA. When he was my age, thirty-three, he had a teenaged daughter and was on the cusp of his first divorce. He has since remarried and is now wedded to a lovely Syrian woman and has two young children. Along with his family life, his career has also evolved and he now manages flight training for Air Canada.

At my wedding, my father gave a touching speech. He said that he and I had grown up together. It was true. When I was young, my father had only recently departed from his own family, and he desperately missed his homeland. He wanted to eat Syrian foods, listen to Arabic music and make me a Muslim. Now, he has spent nearly two-thirds of his life in Canada and is more Canadian than Syrian. He prefers steak and doughnuts to kibbeh and foul (a fava bean breakfast dish) and talks about Canadian culture with the kind of adoration that he used to lavish on Syria. In a way it is as if we are going in opposite directions: as I grow older I am more eager to explore the cultural diversity of my roots while he finds comfort in all that is Canadian.

After we finished our coffees, we took a taxi to the Old City. It was already past midnight but the streets were packed with crowds, including families, infants and young children. It seemed during Ramadan no one slept at night; lethargy was saved for the day, when fasting took its toll. We wandered through the streets of the souk, a marketplace of narrow, cobbled lanes crowded with shops selling spices, pistachio nuts, gold jewellery, books, soap and a vast assortment of clothing and fabrics. The sellers flaunted their wares but without the aggressive sales tactics of the merchants in Istanbul's Grand Bazaar.

The next day we crossed the city to visit my aunt Noura and her husband, Nabeh. Noura is kind faced and portly; a headscarf covered her dark hair but a few strands slipped out. Nabeh is grey haired, bespectacled and dressed in a tan knee-length tunic. They are both English teachers.

"Your aunt has been cooking ever since we heard of your arrival," Nabeh said. "She stayed up until three in the morning preparing food."

The table was heavy with food, but untouchable until sunset. Bassam readied a cigarette, and Nabeh sat a glass of water nearby.

I cannot imagine the challenge of not drinking or eating all day. I tried fasting during Ramadan sporadically when I was younger. I think I once made it through half a day, but I never committed myself to it because I did not fully understand its significance.

It was an old man in Turkey who made things clear. "It is so that we don't forget what it is like for those who don't have food. It reminds us to share."

The melodic call to prayer sounded, drifting in through the window, and we began our feast. We ate a Syrian version of dolmades, elongated rolls of lentils and bulgar called lentil kofte, stuffed eggplants, pickled garlic, fresh peppers, fattoush salad and of course, kibbeh, which Aleppo is famed for. Noura poured us glasses of sous, an inky drink with an intense, earthy licorice flavour that is made by soaking licorice root in water. We ladled rice with golden vermicelli into bowls of flavourful tomato and beef stew. And just when I thought I couldn't eat another morsel, the main course materialized: lamb stewed in a rich tamarind broth and chicken in a thickened yogourt sauce. I had never eaten Middle Eastern food of this calibre, bursting with extraordinary complexities and subtleties. For dessert, we ate grapes that grew on my family's olive farm.

"I want to show you our olive trees," my cousin Farhad said.

Farhad is six years younger than me and covered in thick dark hair—on his head, above his eyebrows, sculpted into a goatee and bursting from his buttoned-down shirt. His wife, Anna, teases him about his swanky strut and white leather shoes and calls him Don Juan. She is a blond gynecologist. They met in her home country, Ukraine, where Farhad studied to be a pharmacist. They married eight years ago and now have a six-year-old boy.

On our final day in Syria, we hurtled towards the border with Farhad and Anna to see the olive farm that had been in my family for more than three hundred years.

"Julie!" Farhad yelled over the roar of the wind blasting through the open windows.

"Yes?"

"You are like a lost sister for me. All my life everybody in our family talked about your father and his daughter. You were a big mystery. Noura had a picture of you on the wall and told me to always pray for my sister in Canada. And I always thought about you."

I felt ashamed that I couldn't say the same thing. For me, they were always distant family, a collection of names in a faraway land, characters in stories I rarely heard and felt little connection with.

We reached the olive farm, only eight kilometres from the Turkish border. Row upon row of trees stretched up the slopes, their branches laden with small green fruit. Farhad gestured to the ancient trees and told us how the olives were grown and transformed into oil. I ran my hand over the withered trunk of a particularly large tree and marvelled that it was able to thrive in such thin, rocky soil.

It was the final day of our journey. The next day we would fly home to Canada. I felt I was only just getting to know my family and that we should be staying for another month, but our flights were booked and obligations back home were growing.

~~~

FARHAD PLUCKED AN OLIVE FROM A BRANCH and squeezed it until the skin burst and a small droplet of oil appeared.

"The olive tree grows best in difficult soil," he said.

Just like our family, I thought.

We had embarked on this trip hoping to learn more about our history, so that we would better understand our backgrounds and each other. Seven months later, we had a clearer comprehension of the forces that sculpted our family, the hardships that inspired monumental changes, and the strong bonds that kept kin close. We had discovered a living web of love and friendship that stretched from the remote Highlands of Scotland to the flatland of Germany to the olive fields of Syria. The magnitude of geographic distances separating our relations dwindled and our small family unit grew exponentially. We became connected to the generations before us and that had transformed our heritage from a vague concept to one with structure and permanence. Just like these olive trees, we were a part of something that had existed for many generations and would for countless more.

APPENDIX A

DATE	PLACE	TRAVEL	KM
	Duncansby	cycle	20
03-09-08	Castletown	cycle	27
03-10-08	Melvich (near)	cycle	42
03-11-08	Syre (near)	cycle	48
03-12-08	Altnakano	cycle	19
03-13-08	Barren Bridge (before)	cycle	48
03-14-08	Tain (past)	both	32
03-15-08	Beauly Firth (west end of)	both	48
03-16-08	Inverness	cycle	13
03-17-08	Inverness		0
03-18-08	Loch Ness	row	29
03-19-08	Fort Augustus (past)	row	27
03-20-08	Laggan Locks	row	19
03-21-08	Loch Lochy	row	8
03-22-08	Fort William	both	24
03-23-08	Port Appin	row	27
03-24-08	Port Appin		0
03-25-08	Taynuilt	row	27
03-26-08	Inveraray (before)	both	25
03-27-08	Lochgoilhead	both	31
03-28-08	Greenock (past)	both	30

03-29-08	Largs	cycle	20
03-30-08	Largs		0
03-31-08	Largs		0
04-01-08	Fenwick	cycle	33
04-02-08	Skares (past)	cycle	48
04-03-08	St. John's Town of Dalry (past)	cycle	53
04-04-08	Collin	cycle	54
TOTAL SCOTLAND			752
TOTAL JOURNEY (including Scotland)			752
04-05-08	Kirkbride (past)	both	42
04-06-08	Penrith	cycle	49
04-07-08	Penrith		0
04-08-08	Penrith		0
04-09-08	Orton (past)	cycle	48
04-10-08	Well (near)	cycle	55
04-11-08	Ripon (past)	cycle	45
04-12-08	Linton on Ouse (before)	both	42
04-13-08	Naburn (past)	row	29
04-14-08	Goole	row	43
04-15-08	Goole		0
04-16-08	Goole		0
04-17-08	Lughton Forest	cycle	40
04-18-08	Fenton (before)	cycle	62
04-19-08	Pickwell	cycle	56
04-20-08	Naseby	cycle	44
04-21-08	Culworth (near)	cycle	48
04-22-08	Brackley	cycle	26
04-23-08	by Brackley	cycle	7
04-24-08	Bunker's Hill (near)	row	22
04-25-08	Oxford	row	17
04-26-08	Oxford		0

04-27-08	Wallingford (past)	row	21
04-28-08	Reading (past)	row	32
04-29-08	Hurley	row	21
04-30-08	Windsor (past)	row	28
05-01-08	Suburbia	row	34
05-02-08	London		0
05-03-08	London		0
05-04-08	London		0
05-05-08	Hammersmith Bridge	row	7
05-06-08	Thamesmead (near)	row	37
05-07-08	Allhallows (past)	row	33
05-08-08	Conyer	row	37
05-09-08	Chartham (past)	row	36
05-10-08	Dover	both	29
05-11-08	Dover		0

TOTAL ENGLAND		990
TOTAL JOURNEY (including England)		1742

05-12-08	Calais	row	48
05-13-08	Calais		0
05-14-08	Audruicq (around)	row	28
05-15-08	Clairmarais	both	25
05-16-08	Wavrin	cycle	66
05-17-08	Bouchain (before)	cycle	60
05-18-08	Wassigny (near)	cycle	46
05-19-08	Hirson	cycle	45
05-20-08	Hirson		0
05-21-08	Charleville-Mezières (south of)	cycle	66
05-22-08	Sassey-sur-Meuse (past)	cycle	55
05-23-08	Verdun (past)	cycle	46
05-24-08	Koeur-la-Petite (near)	both	41
05-25-08	Troussey (near)	row	29

05-26-08	Pagny	row	9
05-27-08	Pagny		0
05-28-08	Pagny		0
05-29-08	Montenoy (past)	cycle	56
05-30-08	Lagarde (past)	cycle	58
05-31-08	Arzviller (past)	cycle	42
06-01-08	Offendorf (past)	cycle	68
TOTAL FRANCE			788
TOTAL JOURNEY (including France)			2530
06-02-08	Elchesheim (near)	row	39
06-03-08	Altrip (before)	row	66
06-04-08	Worms (past)	row	44
06-05-08	Mainz	row	48
06-06-08	Mainz		0
06-07-08	Meppen	side trip	0
06-08-08	Meppen	side trip	0
06-09-08	Meppen	side trip	0
06-10-08	Mainz		0
06-11-08	Mainz		0
06-12-08	Unterliederbach (near)	row	26
06-13-08	Frankfurt	row	9
06-14-08	Mühlheim am Main (before)	row	18
06-15-08	Mainaschaff (near)	row	32
06-16-08	Fechenbach	cycle	61
06-17-08	Fechenbach		0
06-18-08	Dittigheim (past)	cycle	54
06-19-08	Archshofen (past)	cycle	53
06-20-08	Hochstetten (past)	cycle	39
06-21-08	Treuchtlingen	cycle	77
06-22-08	Walting	cycle	57
06-23-08	Kratzmühle (past Kinding)	cycle	27

06-24-08	Kratzmühle Campground		0
06-25-08	Kapfelberg	cycle	63
06-26-08	Friesheim (before)	both	38
06-27-08	Pfelling (past)	row	54
06-28-08	Passau (past)	row	82

TOTAL GERMANY	887
TOTAL JOURNEY (including Germany)	3417

06-29-08	Unterlandshagg (near)	row	55
06-30-08	Enns	both	53
07-01-08	Enns		0
07-02-08	Au (near)	cycle	35
07-03-08	Melk (near)	cycle	45
07-04-08	Altenworth Dam (near)	both	50
07-05-08	Wien (past)	cycle	76

TOTAL AUSTRIA	314
TOTAL JOURNEY (including Austria)	3731

07-06-08	Bratislava (past)	cycle	67
07-07-08	Klizska Nema (past)	cycle	71
07-08-08	Komarno	cycle	26
07-09-08	Komarno		0

TOTAL SLOVAKIA	164
TOTAL JOURNEY (including Slovakia)	3895

07-10-08	Nagymaros (past)	row	75
07-11-08	Sinatelep (near)	row	87
07-12-08	Gerjen (near)	row	92

TOTAL HUNGARY	254
TOTAL JOURNEY (including Hungary)	4149

07-13-08	Batina (before)	row	88
07-14-08	Vukovar (before)	row	93
TOTAL CROATIA			181
TOTAL JOURNEY (including Croatia)			4330
07-15-08	Beocin	row	69
07-16-08	Beocin		0
07-17-08	Belegis (island across from)	row	69
07-18-08	Ritopek (near)	row	60
07-19-08	Veliko Gradište (before)	row	78
07-20-08	Donji Milanovac (past)	row	78
07-21-08	Kladovo	row	55
07-22-08	Kladovo		0
07-23-08	Ljubicevac (before)	row	40
TOTAL SERBIA			449
TOTAL JOURNEY (including Serbia)			4779
07-24-08	Novo Selo	row	61
07-25-08	Lom (past)	row	93
07-26-08	Baykal	row	100
07-27-08	Svishtov (past)	row	90
07-28-08	Rousse	row	55
07-29-08	Rousse		0
07-30-08	Ryakhovo (before)	row	24
07-31-08	Silistra (island before)	row	88
TOTAL BULGARIA			511
TOTAL JOURNEY (including Bulgaria)			5290
08-01-08	Balta Vederoasa (on island)	both	60
08-02-08	Faclia (near)	both	35

08-03-08	Death Canal	cycle	30
08-04-08	Eforie Nord	cycle	25
08-05-08	Eforie Nord		0
08-06-08	Eforie Nord		0
08-07-08	Eforie Sud	row	6
08-08-08	Vama Veche (near)	row	42

| TOTAL ROMANIA | 198 |
| TOTAL JOURNEY (including Romania) | 5488 |

08-09-08	Shabla (near)	cycle	43
08-10-08	Kavarna	cycle	28
08-11-08	Kavarna		0
08-12-08	Ikantaluka (before)	row	9
08-13-08	Bliznatsi (near)	row	53
08-14-08	Cape Emine (past)	row	46
08-15-08	Pomorie	row	39
08-16-08	Kavatsite (before)	row	29
08-17-08	Tsarevo	row	39
08-18-08	Tsarevo		0
08-19-08	Sinemoretz (past)	row	29
08-20-08	Sinemoretz (past)		0

| TOTAL BULGARIA | 315 |
| TOTAL JOURNEY (including Bulgaria) | 5803 |

08-21-08	Kiyikoi	cycle	20
08-22-08	Kiyikoi		0
08-23-08	Kiyikoi		0
08-24-08	Durusu (near)	row	48
08-25-08	Yalıköy sahil		0
08-26-08	Istanbul (outskirts)	cycle	70
08-27-08	Istanbul	cycle	25

08-28-08	Istanbul		0
08-29-08	Istanbul		0
08-30-08	Istanbul		0
08-31-08	Istanbul		0
09-01-08	Istanbul		0
09-02-08	Istanbul		0
09-03-08	Istanbul		0
09-04-08	Istanbul		0
09-05-08	Istanbul		0
09-06-08	Gebze (past)	cycle	55
09-07-08	Hendek	cycle	111
09-08-08	Bolu (past)	cycle	101
09-09-08	Kazan	cycle	110
09-10-08	Ankara (past)	cycle	72
09-11-08	Lake Tuz	cycle	105
09-12-08	Aksaray	cycle	97
09-13-08	Ulukışla (before)	cycle	101
09-14-08	Yenice	cycle	123
09-15-08	Adana	cycle	31
09-16-08	Dortyol (near)	cycle	99
09-17-08	Kirikhan	cycle	77

TOTAL TURKEY			1245
TOTAL JOURNEY (including Turkey)			7048

09-18-08	Aleppo		102

TOTAL SYRIA			102
TOTAL JOURNEY (including Syria)			7150

ROWING/PADDLING RESOURCES

IT WAS DIFFICULT OBTAINING advance information about more than a few of the waterways we travelled, especially regarding human-powered craft. Much of what we did receive was vague or incorrect. For those interested in voyaging these waterways, we have compiled some of the most relevant information.

CALEDONIAN CANAL

The Caledonian Canal is 100 kilometres in length and cuts diagonally across Scotland. It follows the Great Glen Way (a tectonic rift valley) with two-thirds of the waterway made up of natural lakes. It passes through stunning Highland scenery past farmland, mountains, moors and occasional villages. Loch Ness is part of this route, and waters can get very rough here. This waterway has an accompanying hiking trail, and British Waterways has done an excellent job of providing facilities shared by both trail walkers and canal users. These include clean toilet facilities, showers, coin-operated washing machines and complimentary camping spots near some of the locks. Pubs, bed and breakfasts and hotels can also be found along the length of the route.

The canal runs between Fort William and Inverness. It is said to be easier going west to east to take advantage of prevailing winds, but we found the going reasonable in the other direction. Outside of summer vacation and spring break, this is a quiet waterway.

Those in human-powered craft should plan on portaging the locks. British Waterways does allow such craft to use locks but only if the lockkeepers are willing. Lockkeepers along the Caledonian Canal generally are not obliging.

A canoeing permit (free) is required for any human-powered vessels using the canal. This can be obtained from the British Waterways office in Fort William or Inverness along with a key for the washroom facilities. British Waterways also has excellent maps and additional information for canoeing the Caledonian Canal.

More information at: www.scottishcanals.co.uk

WEST COAST OF SCOTLAND

Cold waters, frequent heavy winds, and powerful tides make boating off Scotland's coast treacherous. It is possible, with proper precautions and preparations, for experienced boaters to navigate these waters, and their efforts will be rewarded. Wave-sculpted rocks, sandy headlands, ruined castles and bird colonies on rocky islands make for a journey of endless diversity. Small, sandy bays provide ideal camping spots and there are towns and villages at which to resupply.

Owing to the large number of islands and inlets, various routes can be chosen taking advantage of the more sheltered waters. It is important to have good charts, tide tables and regular weather updates.

ENGLISH CANALS

The canals in England offer the quintessential old-waterways experience. They are beautifully restored, narrow and lined with mossy stonework, weeping willows, gardens, fields and quaint villages and towns. Commercial traffic is rare and has given way to brightly painted steel recreational river barges—designed on the same charming lines as the original working craft. The speed limit for powered craft is four miles an hour (no limit for paddlers), so the danger of a collision is low.

There are almost no human-powered long-distance travellers on the canals; however, these waterways present the perfect paddling experience, with diverse landscapes, sheltered waters, ample camping opportunities and frequent points to resupply or have a pint. There's nothing more pleasant than tying up to a pier in front of a three-hundred-year-old pub and relaxing on the waterfront patio watching swans and the odd river barge.

England is criss-crossed with canals and offers hundreds of long-distance routes. Wild camping is easy with pleasant spots found in adjacent forests or meadows. British Waterways provides washroom facilities in the larger centres, and there are also private marinas and pubs along the canal side offering services for boat traffic.

British Waterways does allow human-powered craft through the locks, but leaves the final decision to the lockkeepers. Lockkeepers can be unobliging so prepare for the possibility of portaging when travelling through manned locks.

Fortunately, most locks (especially along the more quiet routes) are self-operated, and it is a fun process moving your boats through the small locks. A metal crank handle, on sale at British Waterways offices, is required to open the sluice gates. A canoeing permit is required for human-powered craft and is available from British Waterways for a reasonable fee.

Operating the small locks is a simple affair. The lock doors are opened with giant wooden levers. The doors will only open when the water level is equal on both sides. Sluice gates are opened on the upstream side (by inserting crank handle and manually turning cogs) to raise the water level and the downstream side to drop the water. Be sure that only one gate is open at a time, otherwise water will simply flow through the lock chamber.

Summer is the busy period on the canals and we definitely recommend travelling in the spring or fall to avoid crowds and queues for locks. Our journey down the Oxford Canal in spring was very peaceful, and most of the time we had the canal to ourselves.

There are a few long tunnels and lengthy portages over hills, which should be avoided in route planning. British Waterways has detailed maps of the canals outlining locks, tunnels, etc.

More information at: www.waterscape.com

THAMES RIVER

A voyage down the Thames River is perhaps the ultimate way of taking a self-guided tour through some of England's top sights. This journey will provide views of some of Britain's most enchanting architecture including Windsor Castle, Oxford University, Big Ben and Tower Bridge. The wonders en route never cease as you pass through university towns, medieval villages, riverside castles, farms and riverfront mansions, not to mention estates owned by some of Britain's wealthiest.

The Thames River has been canalized, meaning that weirs and locks have been placed about every three to seven kilometres along its length to increase navigability. The river is under the jurisdiction of Thames Environmental Agency (not British Waterways) and the quality of service offered by the lockkeepers on the Thames is exceptional. The employees here are friendly, helpful and happy to allow human-powered craft through the locks. There are also some excellent campgrounds run by the Environmental Agency with nominal fees. One of our personal favourites is a campground at Hurley Lock (by the village of Hurley), situated on a small island. Wild camping spots can still be found along the Thames; however, they are not as plentiful as some of the more rural areas along the canals.

Despite being among the world's renowned rivers, the Thames is surprisingly only 346 kilometres in length. Its discharge is about 66 cubic metres per second, or one-three-thousandth that of the Amazon, and the source is located in the Cotswold Hills in west-central England. It is navigable by paddle craft starting in the small town of Cricklade, about 60 kilometres upstream from Oxford.

The non-tidal Thames (above London) is relatively safe for paddling, and the smaller nature of the river means waves are never too big. The current averages one to two kilometres an hour, but will increase during heavy rains. There is a strictly enforced speed limit of 4 miles an hour for powered boats.

The tidal section of the Thames occurs downstream of Teddington Lock in the western suburbs of London. Through London and further downstream, the tidal range is enormous (about seven metres at London Bridge) and can make navigation difficult, and currents are strong going both directions. Steep stone and concrete embankments run through the city centre and downstream through the industrial suburbs, meaning there are few places to pull ashore. Barges, ferries and other commercial traffic create a steep chop, while convection winds build powerful standing waves. Paddling beyond London into the industrial area is not recommended.

It is necessary to obtain a canoeing permit from the Environmental Agency. These can be purchased directly from the lockkeepers. A month-long permit is about $25. The lockkeepers also have maps available detailing the locations of campgrounds, locks and other facilities.

More information at: http://www.environment-agency.gov.uk/homeandleisure/recreation/boating/default.aspx

FRENCH CANALS

Our experience on the French canals near Calais was disenchanting. However, this is not representative of waterways in the rest of France. There are more scenic routes in other areas including those we later passed such as the Meuse River.

France has an extensive canal system. Some of the waterways are industrial, designed for accommodating larger transport vessels, while other smaller canals retain their historical charm and cater more to pleasure craft.

Higher walls (as compared to England) along the edges of the canals make it more difficult to enter or exit the water. Plan to portage all locks, so bring a cart and pack light. There are several long tunnels, which are best avoided.

Wild camping spots are easy to find in forests and pastures. Resupplying is straightforward with abundant services and fresh, tasty foods available.

RHINE

The Rhine flows 1,320 kilometres through Switzerland, France, Germany and the Netherlands. It passes through steep mountain valleys in Switzerland, rolling mountains and vineyards between Bavaria and France, and a fairy-tale landscape of castles, canyons and medieval villages along the "Romantic Rhine" below Mainz. In the Netherlands the current slows and the landscape flattens.

For most of the Rhine, the current is brisk, sometimes exceeding 12 kilometres an hour. There are a few hydro-electric dams between France and Germany, but these are easily bypassed through the locks or along bypass streams accessible via a short grassy portage.

More information at: http://www.loreley-info.com/eng/ rhein-rhine/sporty-activities/canoe-tour-trip.shtml (this website details the section along the Romantic Rhine).

GERMAN CANALS

Germans have done a good job of creating waterways for both commercial transport vessels and pleasure craft. Many of the dams and weirs have two lock systems—one for larger commercial boats and the other (using less water) for sport boats. Some dams also have portage paths and complimentary trailers for those who do not wish to use the locks. There are no fees to travel on the waterways.

We sometimes travelled through the large locks with commercial barges. Communication with the lockkeepers is done by VHF radio and the frequency is posted on signs before the lock. The small adjacent locks are self-operated, and the hydraulic controls are straightforward.

Of the countries we travelled through, Germany has the best infrastructure for human-powered travel. Lockkeepers were pleasant, the inhabitants inquisitive, and we shared the rivers and canals with other kayakers, canoeists and rowers.

It is usually possible to find spots for wild camping, but Germany also has excellent commercial camping grounds.

Many of the cycling routes parallel the waterways, so a good source of information for maps, campgrounds, etc., are the abundantly available cycling guidebooks.

DANUBE

The Danube is 2,860 kilometres in length and flows through twelve countries in eastern and western Europe. It originates in the Black Forest of Germany and spills into the Black Sea through the vast Danube delta.

The highlights of the Danube are its headwaters in Germany, the mountainous stretch where it traverses Austria, and the Iron Gates Gorge between Serbia and Romania. The political difficulties in crossing borders is much less of an issue now, as most countries along its banks are part of the European Union.

In Germany and Austria there are a number of dams making the river more navigable and producing hydroelectricity. These dams are easily bypassed through locks. Lockkeepers are obliging in letting human-powered craft through with commercial vessels. Communication is via VHF radio. It is also possible to portage the locks along adjacent paved bicycle paths.

In Austria and Germany the river flows up to 12 kilometres an hour, although it slows significantly as the dams are approached. Beyond Austria there are three major hydroelectric dams blocking the Danube. Slovakia has a large lake-like reservoir behind its dam, and farther downstream two dams follow the Iron Gates Gorge between Serbia and Romania.

Beyond Slovakia the river becomes wide, and wind-driven waves are an issue. The current averages two to four kilometres an hour from Budapest to the Black Sea.

Additional information: The German canoeing club has published an excellent handbook on canoeing the Danube. It is in German only, but the diagrams and maps are still of use to non-German speakers. The book recommends wild and public camping spots, points to resupply, and offers advice on such matters as how to get through the locks. This book, *DKV-Auslandsführer Band 9—Donau,* can be purchased from the club at www.kanu-verlag.de

DEATH CANAL

This canal is as delightful as it sounds. It is a 60-kilometre shortcut, through a desolate tract of Romania between the Black Sea and the Danube. It was made by slaves. There are just two locks on each end, and 2.5-metre concrete walls rise from both sides of the channel. The lockkeepers will not let you through and high walls make it next to impossible to exit the water.

Definitely not recommended.

BLACK SEA

If you're looking for a scenic region that nobody paddles, try the Black Sea. We didn't encountered a single long-distance paddler along the shores of Romania, Bulgaria or Turkey. Rough seas, rocky headlands and cliffs make this a destination for experts only.

An absence of tides makes it easier to pull boats above the high-water line at the end of the day. June and July are the calmest months. A slight current of about 0.1 to 0.5 kilometres an hour moves in a clockwise circuit around the Black Sea. There is a lot of development along the shores, but less where the geography becomes more rugged.

Crossing borders between countries is extremely difficult on the water, so it is best to plan your trip along the shore of one nation.

TRANSPORTING YOUR BOAT

One of the toughest logistical challenges when planning a paddling trip on another continent is transporting your boat. Most sea kayaks, canoes and rowboats are too long to be transported as excess baggage or even separately as air cargo. With our boats, the only option was to ship them by sea in wooden crates. It is a costly and difficult process.

The easiest solution is to use folding boats (such as Klepper kayaks) that can be transported as baggage.· Alternatively, renting or purchasing a secondhand boat on location can be a simple and inexpensive way to procure a boat. For those with time and easy-going friends or relatives to stay with, building a kit boat near the start of the voyage is also an option.

APPENDIX C

HOW TO BUILD A ROWBOAT IN YOUR BACKYARD

PEOPLE ARE OFTEN SURPRISED to hear we transformed a few scribbles on paper into proper, functioning boats. Is it really possible for non-experts to create something that performs well and doesn't look like a grade-seven woodworking project? Absolutely. There is a type of boatbuilding called "stitch and glue," which is within the capabilities of those with basic carpentry skills and results in strong, lightweight boats every bit as good as commercial carbon-fibre ones.

The boats are made from precisely shaped plywood panels. They are temporarily held together by drilling a series of holes in both sides of the joining edges, then looping sections of copper wire through and winding them tight (like twist ties). Bulkheads (hull partitions) are also added and secured with wire. Once the basic shape of the hull is formed, thickened epoxy resin and fibreglass is applied to the inside of the hull, solidifying the shape. The copper-wire fasteners are trimmed off the hull exterior, the corners sanded round and the entire surface covered with fibreglass cloth and epoxy resin.

The decks are created by nailing roughly cut sheets of plywood over the hull (the wood will follow the curved form of the bulkheads), trimming the excess overhang and then adding a layer of fibreglass and resin. Hatches are made by cutting holes in the decks and topping them with watertight lids and gaskets.

We created the dimensions for the hull panels using basic boatbuilding software. There were five main attributes we needed the boats to have:

1) **SEAWORTHINESS:** To make the boats seaworthy, they had to be fully decked, sealed and stable. To further enhance seaworthiness, we ensured air chambers ran along the edge of the cockpit so that in the event of a capsize, all water would drain from the cockpit when the boats were righted and would allow the vessels to be underway again within seconds of flipping. Additionally, the hull was shaped to be as stable as possible.

2) **ABILITY TO ACCOMMODATE FULL-SIZED BICYCLE AND BOAT TRAILER:** The vessels had to be quite beamy—wide—to allow the disassembled bicycles to fit inside. The hatch accessing the bicycle compartment needed to be near the centre of the vessel so it could be made large enough to fit the wheels and bicycle frame. The bicycle trailer was designed to disassemble and fit within the same compartment.

3) **TRAILERABILITY:** Weight is the most important issue when pulling an object behind a bicycle. The vessels were made as light as possible without sacrificing strength. The empty weight of each boat was 43 kilograms.

4) **SPEED:** Because of the extra width of the boat, it would be difficult to paddle like a sea kayak. We installed sliding-seat rowing systems, which enabled all major muscle groups to contribute to propulsion, allowing us to travel at a good pace.

5) **CATAMARANING CAPABILITIES:** Travelling with two boats offers the possibility of creating a catamaran. We affixed two aluminum pipes inside our hulls, with one end open. The two-metre trailer tubes could sleeve into these pipes, creating a quick and solid catamaran. A comfortable, secure

platform was created by laying oars over the cross supports and topping with an air mattress. The main purpose for the catamaran was for camping (setting the tent up on the platform and anchoring) in urban areas.

We've received a lot of inquiries on these boats and as a result we have created a more expansive online resource, as well as pans and kits for constructing the boats.

For more information, please visit www.angusrowboats.com

ACKNOWLEDGEMENTS

THERE ARE MANY INDIVIDUALS, organizations and even animals that have helped us with this journey, and we would like to thank every single one of them. We have done our best to acknowledge everyone involved, but don't feel hurt if you don't see your name below, as the cat ate the first page of our list—the one with the really important people on it.

The theme of our expedition was discovering our heritage, so a big thank you to all our family for just being. It would have been a rather dull journey without you. But of course, as kin tend to do, our family offered much more than their presence. From Scotland to Germany to Syria, we were loved, fed, housed and protected. A huge thanks goes to all of you, including (remember the hungry cat): Bassam Wafaei and family, Noura Wafaei and Nabeh El-Hajj, and Farhad El-Hajj and family, in Syria; Herbert Sadowski, Waltraud Sadowski, and Maria Sadowski, in Germany; and Avril and Tom Rae, Betti Angus, Helen Sinclair, Peter Sinclair and family, and George Spentzos and family, in Britain. And then there are our folks at home who are every bit as lovely, although slightly less exotic: Husam Wafaei and family, Valerie Spentzos, Helga Wafaei, Jane and Willy Spentzos, Patty Spentzos, and Frank and Irmgard Susztar.

We are also appreciative of help from our friends and the ones we made en route, including (damn that cat): Dan Audet, Shelley Russell, Dean Fenwick, Frank Carey, Jackie Bellerose,

Anthony Dalton, Marc St. Jules, Robert Clapperton, John Scott, the English couple who gave us *The Unlikely Voyage of Jack De Crow*, Louise and Jack, Jean-Jacques Biehler, Camping Maintal, Kratzmühle Campground, Margaret Avenue School Geography Club (for giving us great advice!), Boris Jakimow and family, Juri Tscharyiski, Vladi and Dessi, the crew of *Firefox*, Klaus Flach, Boyut Logistics, Adnan Mulayim, Zirve Mountaineering Club in Istanbul, and the many others who offered us food, drink and friendship during our travels.

We could never have made this journey without the help of our sponsors. A big thanks to Commerce Resources, our title sponsor and supporter throughout. Helly Hansen kept us warm and comfortable for the duration of the journey. Others who helped us realize our goal include Healthy Heart and Active Communities (two organizations that play an important role in motivating youth to make healthy choices), Wallace and Carey, Career Joy, Mountain Equipment Co-op, Tony's Trailers, Croker Oars, RidethisBike.com, Martina Cross Photography, Petzl, Camp n' Trail and Suunto.

The creation of this book has been a journey of its own. Big thanks to everyone at Doubleday Canada involved in bringing it to life. Our editor, Tim Rostron, who has an uncanny knowledge of Scotch whisky and a knack for words, did a marvellous job of guiding us through the process.

And a final big thank you goes to the readers. We are grateful for the opportunity to embark on adventures spawned from our wildest dreams, and to share these journeys with you.

ABOUT THE AUTHORS

COLIN ANGUS completed the first human-powered circumnavigation of the world when in 2006 he cycled into Vancouver after 43,000 km of travel. During the course of two years he rowed across the Pacific and Atlantic Oceans, trekked and cycled through 16 countries, endured winter in Siberia and searing heat in the tropics.

Colin has made a career exploring remote parts of the world and sharing his adventures through books, films and presentations. He has navigated the Amazon and Yenisey Rivers from source to sea, sailed the South Pacific Ocean, and rowed thousands of km in waterways around the world. He has co-produced four documentaries which collectively won ten awards at international festivals including the Dijon and Telluride Festivals of Adventure Films. He has written for numerous publications including the *Globe and Mail*, *Reader's Digest* and *Cruising World*.

Outside Magazine listed Colin as one of the top 25 "bold visionaries with world-changing dreams" for his work in promoting lifestyle changes to help the environment. Colin and Julie continue their efforts in promoting zero-emissions transportation as a healthy way to maintain a healthy world.